ROMANTIC LOCHABER

SCOTS PINE

[*Frontispiece*

ROMANTIC LOCHABER

BY

DONALD B. MacCULLOCH

Author of *The Wondrous Isle of Staffa* and *Prince Charlie's Country*

With twenty-seven illustrations from photographs by the author and two historic plates

THE MORAY PRESS
EDINBURGH

First published 1939
New and Revised Edition 1948

PUBLISHED BY THE MORAY PRESS, 57 GEORGE STREET, EDINBURGH
LONDON: FREDERICK MULLER LTD., 29 GT. JAMES STREET
PRINTED IN GREAT BRITAIN BY NEILL AND CO. LTD., EDINBURGH
BOUND BY HUNTER AND FOULIS LTD., EDINBURGH

TO

SIR DONALD WALTER CAMERON
OF LOCHIEL, K.T., C.M.G.,
XXV<small>TH</small> CHIEF OF CLAN CAMERON

IN APPRECIATION OF HIS INTEREST IN THIS BOOK,
AND HIS VALUABLE ASSISTANCE

CONTENTS

		PAGE
LIST OF ILLUSTRATIONS		9
PREFACE		11

CHAPTER

I.	THE APPROACH TO LOCHABER THROUGH GLEN COE	17
II.	NETHER LOCHABER	39
III.	FORT WILLIAM AND BEN NEVIS	52
IV.	GLEN NEVIS AND INVERLOCHY	77
V.	THROUGH THE HEART OF LOCHABER	104
VI.	BRAE LOCHABER	135
VII.	BY THE SHORES OF LOCH EIL	162
VIII.	WESTWARD FROM GLENFINNAN	196
	BIBLIOGRAPHY	223
	INDEX	225

LIST OF ILLUSTRATIONS

SCOTS PINE	*Frontispiece*	
BEN ACHALADAIR, FROM THE DOIRE DARACH	*Facing page*	16
LOCH TULLA	,,	17
KINGSHOUSE, STOB DEARG AND GLEN COE	,,	32
GLEN COE	,,	33
WESTWARD, FROM BALLACHULISH	,,	48
STRONCHREGGAN, ARDGOUR	,,	49
THE OLD FORT, FORT WILLIAM	,,	64
BEN NEVIS, SHOWING THE TRACK	,,	65
THE ROAD INTO GLEN NEVIS	,,	80
GLEN NEVIS	,,	81
INVERLOCHY CASTLE AND BEN NEVIS	,,	96
BEN NEVIS, FROM BANAVIE	,,	97
TOR CASTLE, SUGGESTED APPEARANCE	,,	112
BANQUO'S WALK, NEAR TOR CASTLE	,,	112
LOCH LOCHY, NEAR ACHNACARRY	,,	113
LOCH ARKAIG	,,	113
BEN NEVIS GROUP, FROM ABOVE SPEAN BRIDGE	,,	128
GENERAL WADE'S ROAD AND LOCH LOCHY	,,	128
THE GLAS DOIRE HILLS AND LOCH LOCHY	,,	129
BEN NEVIS, FROM CORPACH	,,	129
THE ANNAT BURN	,,	144
CUMMING'S LOCHABER AXE	,,	145
THE VILLAGE OF CORPACH AND LOCH EIL	,,	160
PRINCE CHARLIE'S MONUMENT, GLENFINNAN	,,	161

PRINCE CHARLIE'S MONUMENT—ORIGINAL
    APPEARANCE   *Facing page* 176
LOCH BEORAID   ,,   177
THE HILLS AROUND LOCH AILORT   ,,   192
EIGG AND RUM, FROM ARISAIG   ,,   193

PREFACE

THE revival in the spirit of Scotland which has become apparent during the past few years is expressing itself in many ways. One obvious sign is the large number of books published recently dealing with almost every aspect of our country. Scottish scenery and history having inspired many volumes, it is very surprising that no modern book has appeared devoted to the district of Lochaber. It is certainly not for lack of material, for no part of Scotland is richer in scenery or history. Naturally, most books on the Highlands mention the district, but lack of space necessitates such mention being brief.

The most comprehensive book on the subject is Drummond-Norie's *Loyal Lochaber*. There is also W. T. Kilgour's *Lochaber in War and Peace*, but both these books were published many years ago in a limited edition, and are long since out of print.

The present volume is a small contribution towards rectifying this neglect of Lochaber in modern literature. I have endeavoured to convey something of the scenic and historic appeal of the district, in the hope that it may form an introduction to those who have not yet visited it, and stir in those who know it a desire to learn still more about it. I also hope, sincerely, that, as a little link of friendship, this book may find its way to Lochaber exiles in lands across the sea and recall to them pleasant memories of their days in the Old Country.

In describing the district, I have advanced geographically, rather than chronologically, as the latter method results in haphazard and overlapped roving when exploring its haunts of historic interest. Excepting the approach to Lochaber, I have made Fort William the centre from which to radiate. In order to explore the district thoroughly, we must rove at leisure and, therefore, I have written from the tramper's point of view as, naturally, one can penetrate on foot to places inaccessible to the motorist or cyclist, who may learn to *know* the country but cannot learn to *understand* it in the intimate way of the tramper.

I have a special interest in Lochaber, as it was there I spent my boyhood days, roving its mountains, glens, lochs and rivers with my school chums as only boys can. Those of us who served in the Lochaber Boy Scouts had good opportunities for exploring many parts of the district intimately when scouting, trekking and camping. Alas! many of those boys now lie on the battlefields of the first World War. During the past few years I have retraversed on foot almost every mile of the routes described in these pages, in order to refresh my memory and note any changes in the district. In these recent rovings my constant companion has been my trusty camera, with which I have endeavoured to capture some aspects of the remarkable scenic attractions of Lochaber.

Finally, I wish to express my sincere thanks to Mrs. St. John Secker of Callart, Onich, and to my good friends Mr. and Mrs. Grant of Borrodale House, Arisaig, for their kind assistance in my search for information.

DONALD B. MacCULLOCH.

GLASGOW, 1938.

PREFACE TO SECOND EDITION

NATURALLY, it is very gratifying to an author to learn that his work has been appreciated sufficiently to necessitate a new edition. In acknowledgment of this confidence, I have endeavoured to make this edition more worthy of its subject than my original work by incorporating the results of a considerable amount of new research. It is a complete revisal, and contains many modifications and additions, especially regarding local traditions and the Jacobite Rising of 1745, with which Lochaber is so intimately associated. Where any statement in this edition differs from the corresponding statement in the previous edition, the present one is to be regarded as being more correct.

The desire to recall and discuss the lives and deeds of our forefathers is not reactionary, as many of their principles and ideals were of high merit though, naturally, their methods differed from ours. No sensible person wishes to set back the clock of time and revert to more primitive conditions, but we can learn from the past and hold fast to that which is good. As one writer has said, "We do not exist to restore a past, but to create a future which shall embody the greatness of that past."

The eight years which have elapsed since the previous edition of this book was published include six of the most momentous years in the history of the world, almost every nation having suffered in the havoc of war. During these years of strife Lochaber played its part worthily.

The sons of Lochaber responded readily, as they have always done in the past, when their king and country called them, and with no less response did the daughters of Lochaber answer this call in the recent war. The local regiment, the Queen's Own Cameron Highlanders, formed an integral part of the famous 51st (Highland) Division.

The district of Lochaber itself was utilized fully by the Service Authorities as a training area. Fort William was commissioned under the name of H.M.S. *St. Christopher* as a training centre for officers and men of Coastal Force craft (Motor Launches, Motor Torpedo Boats, etc.), and Loch Linnhe was busy with all kinds of naval light craft. As St. Christopher is the patron saint of ferrymen and travellers by sea, the name was chosen as being an appropriate one for this base as the majority of officers and men trained here served in naval ferrying duties on light craft.

A base for motor launches, consisting of a boat shed and slipway with ancillary buildings, was established to the west of Corpach as part of the *St. Christopher* organization. Later, a naval repair base was set up adjacent to the site at Corpach with workshop, pier and floating dock capable of dealing with much larger craft than that centred at *St. Christopher*. This repair base at Corpach functioned as a civilian establishment independent of *St. Christopher*. Ocean tramps and Naval Auxiliaries carried repair material to the base and it was a unique sight to see them lying at anchor, while awaiting return cargoes, in the quiet waters near the head of Loch Eil surrounded by beautiful secluded Highland scenery.

At Achnacarry, the ancestral home of Lochiel, Chief of Clan Cameron, was established in 1940 the first depot of Commandos in Britain, and it functioned continuously throughout the war. The isolated nature of this region, which in addition was under strict military protection from all unauthorized persons, and its very rugged scenery made it an ideal centre for the arduous training which all Commandos required to undergo. There were also training centres, naval and military, in the vicinity of Arisaig and Morar, and lesser military camps in other parts of Lochaber.

Enemy bombers visited Lochaber on several occasions. Their main targets were the Hydro Electric power-house and its adjacent aluminium and carbon factory at Inverlochy, but, fortunately, the damage done was negligible.

A great deal of timber-felling was carried out during the war in the rich woodlands of the district, which has altered to a great extent many of its features, unfortunately not to their scenic benefit.

As Hitler's war is such a recent event, and as the world is still rather war - weary, the above brief description of Lochaber in war-time is the only reference which I intend to make to the war in this edition, except for minor items regarding changes in the scenery caused by timber-felling.

Lochaber is likely to be affected by the new Hydro Electric and other schemes for the purpose of introducing industry into the Highlands, but it is to be hoped that its scenic grandeur will be disturbed as little as possible. While the introduction, or development, of some forms of industry seems necessary to prevent the Highlands becoming further depopulated, the spoliation of many of its finest scenic and historic attractions, as has been done elsewhere, seems a high price to pay.

Since the previous edition was published, I have learned with pleasure from several sources that this book has found its way to exiles from the district, now far from their native land. I hope sincerely that this new edition may reach many more of these old friends and help to warm their love for Lochaber.

To Miss Edith Macgregor, the energetic secretary of the West Highland Museum, Fort William, and a descendant of the Camerons of Glen Nevis, and also to her cousin, Mrs. Marion Comyn How, M.B.E., a direct descendant of the Cummings of Achdalieu, I owe a debt of gratitude for assistance in helping to locate and unravel a number of very interesting items included in this edition. I am also indebted to Mr. Hugh Macphee, Gaelic Producer in the B.B.C., Glasgow, for granting me access to his library of Highland literature which contains many interesting references to Lochaber.

DONALD B. MacCULLOCH.

"ARDALANISH,"
    KIRKLEE ROAD,
        GLASGOW, W. 2.
            1948.

BEN ACHALADAIR, FROM THE DOIRE DARACH

[To face page 16

LOCH TULLA

CHAPTER I

THE APPROACH TO LOCHABER
THROUGH GLEN COE

FOR the benefit of those who may not be acquainted
with Western Scotland, perhaps it should be explained
that Lochaber is a district and not a loch. The name,
however, is said to be derived from a loch which
existed at one time in the heart of this region but has
long since dried up.

Lochaber lies in the south of Inverness-shire and
around the western end of the Great Glen of Scotland,
which stretches from Loch Linnhe to the Moray Firth.
It is a region unexcelled in Britain for inspiring scenery
and romantic history. Every acre radiates historic
interest. Among its rugged mountains and glens were
enacted the first stirring scenes and the tragic finale of
the Jacobite Rising of 1745. It was here that Prince
Charles Edward Stuart — Bonnie Prince Charlie —
rallied the Highland clans before leading them in his
valiant, but unavailing, venture to win back the crown
of his fathers: the greatest campaign of the clans in
history. Consequently, Lochaber is often described
as "the land of Prince Charlie," but it is more than
this title suggests, for it has witnessed many stirring
events apart from the "Forty-five." No part of our
country merits more the Gaelic phrase, *tir nam beann nan
gleann's nan gaisgeach* ("Land of the bens, the glens and
the heroes").

The bounds of Lochaber have varied during the
course of history. When Banquo was Thane of
Lochaber, in the days of Macbeth, the district, or

province, is said to have included all the lands between
the River Spey and the Atlantic. On maps of the
sixteenth century it is shown extending from the
Sound of Mull northwards to Loch Duich and Fort
Augustus, and eastward to Loch Laidon. That was
in the days of the old divisions of Scotland, such
as Breadalbane, Badenoch, Mar, Strathnavern, etc.
Duncan Campbell, in his *Lairds of Glenlyon*, when
referring to a cattle *creach* of 1580, says, "they called
all beyond the Moss of Rannoch and the Blackmount,
Lochaber men in those days," and the Rev. John
MacLeod, in his *Lochaber and its Evangelical Traditions*,
when referring to the days of creachs, says, "In connection with those early days the name Lochaber was taken
in a wide sense, and the dwellers in the Rough Bounds
of Clanranald were spoken of as Lochaber men."
Since then, Lochaber has become more circumscribed.
On modern geographical publications it is often given
merely as the district lying between Glen Spean and
Loch Leven, that is, to the east of the River Lochy.
The district between Loch Arkaig and Loch Eil in
these publications is either unnamed or called the
district of Lochiel. The local conception of Lochaber
at the present time, however, and the one adopted in
this book, may be roughly defined as the area bounded
on the north by the northern hills of Loch Arkaig, on
the east by Loch Treig, on the south by Loch Leven
and on the west by Glen Finnan, excluding Ardgour.

The present-day inhabitants of the region lying
between Loch Arkaig and Loch Eil always regard
themselves as residing in Lochaber and never use the
term "Lochiel" to designate this district. The original
district known as the "thirty merklands of Lochiel"
extended from Upper Banavie to the head of Loch Eil,
but it did not include the "forty merklands of Glenlui
[Glen Loy] and Locharkaig." In 1492 Alexander
MacDonald of Lochalsh, who styled himself "Alexander

of the Isles, of Lochalsh and Lochiel," granted to
Ewan, thirteenth chief of Clan Cameron, the "thirty
merklands of Lochiel." Alexander was superior of
these lands under his uncle, the Lord of the Isles,
indeed, owing to the feebleness of his uncle, Alexander
really held the reins of power. In 1528 the king,
James V, gave a legal grant to Ewan of all the land
Ewan possessed, which included the "forty merklands
of Glenlui and Locharkaig," under the title of the
Barony of Lochiel. The legal grant was necessary
as the Lordship of the Isles had now been abolished.
This deed is the first one in which the chief of Clan
Cameron is designated "of Lochiel," the title previously
held by the MacDonalds of Lochalsh. The chief's
previous title was "Captain of the Clancamroun."
The title "of Lochiel" would, naturally, be transferred
along with the lands of that name from MacDonald to
Ewan Cameron. The Barony of Lochiel, however,
was only a part of the much more extensive domain of
the Lordship of Lochaber. In course of time, the title
Barony of Lochiel fell into disuse and these lands
became included in the wider term Lochaber. I have
been unable to find any satisfactory reason as to why
the territorial title should be spelled Lochiel and the
name of the loch spelled Loch Eil.

Originally, Lochaber was part of the territory of
the MacDougalls, Lords of Lorn, the most powerful
clan in the west of Scotland about the end of the
thirteenth century. Owing to their enmity with
Bruce, however, he, on his accession, confiscated the
MacDougall lands and bestowed Lochaber on the
MacDonalds for services rendered. It passed, later,
from the MacDonalds to the Camerons.

Naturally, the real spirit of a region like Lochaber
can only be appreciated fully by an acquaintance with
it in all its varying moods of spring, summer, autumn
and winter, as well as a knowledge of its history. Also,

many of its most interesting and beautiful parts lie off
the beaten track, and must be visited on foot and at
leisure in order to receive their true impression. But
even the transient visitor is bound to feel something
of the romantic appeal of this district, and the more
he learns of its scenery and history the more he will
wish to learn.

Lochaber is the land of the Clan Cameron, whose
chief, Lochiel, still resides at Achnacarry,* about
fourteen miles north of Fort William, though the north-
eastern part of the district, called Brae Lochaber, is
the original clan land of the MacDonnells of Keppoch.

The approach to Lochaber by road from the south
is a fitting one, as it leads through the grim gateway
of Glen Coe.

A good starting-point for our rovings is the village
of Bridge of Orchy, which lies in the north-east of
Argyllshire, where the only roads leading northwards
are the old and new roads to Glen Coe, and thence to
Lochaber. This small Highland village snuggles in
a hollow at the foot of the western slopes of Ben Dorain
(3,524 feet), the mountain made famous by the writings
of Duncan *Ban* MacIntyre, the celebrated Gaelic poet.

The new road, and main highway, to Glen Coe,
which was completed in 1935, sweeps northwards
through Bridge of Orchy, along the eastern bank of
the River Orchy, towards the Moor of Rannoch, and
then curves round to the west towards the glen. The
old road crosses the River Orchy at the village and
follows a westerly circuit in its approach. Though
the distance to the entrance of Glen Coe is about
sixteen miles by either road, the number of habitations
which appear can be counted on the fingers of one
hand, thus we realize that we are entering the real
Highlands.

* Achnacarry Castle was badly damaged by fire during the recent
war and Lochiel now resides temporarily in Inverness.

The new highway, with its smooth surface and easy gradients, is the only road for the motorist, as the old road was closed to traffic when the new road became available and is not being kept in repair. The tramper has the choice of either road, and there is no comparison between them from his point of view. The old road is by far the more picturesque, as it follows an elevated route, through woodlands, over moorland and by mountain tarns, while its disrepair and absence of traffic are additional attractions. By this road we are following in the footsteps of the early pilgrims to Glen Coe.

Though not a very poetic word, I use the term *tramper* in preference to *hiker*, as this latter word has a somewhat "fashionable" atmosphere about it (there were *trampers* long before there were *hikers*), though the hiking movement is a splendid one. The term *pedestrian* is now usually reserved for something that gets knocked down by a motor-car, while the term *tramp* smacks of the professional vagrant. The word *wayfarer* is a good one, but would seem to be more appropriate among the dales and uplands of the Lowlands and England. The term *tramper* suggests the ruggedness of the Scottish Highlands.

Taking the old road from Bridge of Orchy, we first cross the hog-back bridge over the River Orchy, and follow its western bank for about two miles to Loch Tulla. Thence round the head of the loch, passing through the picturesque grove of old Scots pine, called the Doire Darach, a remnant of the Old Caledonian Forest.

At the head of Loch Tulla we come to Inveroran, where the inn, the only building in the vicinity and a relic of the old coaching days, is the last dwelling, except a shooting lodge and gamekeeper's house, which we shall pass for about eleven miles. A coach service between Fort William and Glasgow, via Glen

Coe, was started in 1843, the Loch Lomond part of the journey being traversed by steamer. The coaching season was from the middle of June to the middle of October.

About half a mile beyond the inn a cart-track leads off from the road and climbs along the side of a little hill into Glen Euar, to Druimliart, or Druimlaighart, which is a place-name rather than a place, as there is now no habitation here. But there is an old ruin of special appeal to all Highlanders and those interested in Gaeldom. This ruin is all that remains of the humble home of Duncan *Ban* MacIntyre—*Donachadh Ban nan Oran* ("fair-haired Duncan of the songs")— the greatest of all the Gaelic bards, who was born here on 20th March 1724. It is a remarkable fact that he could neither read nor write, as schooling was practically non-existent in this lonely region in his day. Most of his songs were composed and committed to memory on the rough mountain-slopes of Ben Dorain, and the Buachaille Etive, when he was gamekeeper to the Earl of Breadalbane.

Having skirted the head of Loch Tulla, we turn northwards on a very rough road and stiff incline for about ten miles over the high moorland of Blackmount. As we near the summit the rippling waters of Loch Tulla gleam far below in their green setting, while stretching northwards, on the same level, to a far horizon is the bleak Moor of Rannoch, recalling the wanderings of Alan Breck in Stevenson's *Kidnapped* and Neil Munro's hero in *John Splendid*. To the west rise the high and lonely group of mountains known collectively as Blackmount, a famous deer forest. Here, in 1887, one of the finest stag's heads ever "grassed" in Scotland was brought down by the Marchioness of Breadalbane. It was an eighteen-pointer.

Mention of a deer forest suggests a region thickly clad with trees, but the great deer forests of Scotland

are almost barren of trees. They consist of high
moorland and bleak mountains and corries. The
reason for this paradox is that in the distant past
these regions were clad with dense forests up almost
to the two-thousand-feet level which formed sanctuary
for the red deer. Since then, however, various causes
have stripped these high lands of their trees—such as
change in climatic conditions, forest fires and indis-
criminate felling of trees—until now the deer roam
over treeless wastes, but still the term "deer forest" is
retained in connection with these areas.

From the summit of the moor, the road sweeps
down steeply for about two and a half miles to Kingshouse Inn, where it unites with the new road to Glen
Coe.

The new highway to Glen Coe follows a much lower
level and a more northerly circuit than the old road.
Beyond Bridge of Orchy it skirts the eastern shore of
Loch Tulla, and crosses the Tulla Water not far from
the farm of Achaladair, where stands the gaunt ruin
of Achaladair Castle, an ancient seat of the Fletchers,
and later of the Campbells of Breadalbane. On the
upper reaches of the Tulla Water appear the pines and
birches of Crannach Wood. These pines are gnarled
remnants of the ancient Caledonian Forest, which at
one time covered the greater part of Scotland and
harboured the wolf, wild boar and wild ox, when our
ancestors roamed from one hunting ground to another
clad in wild-beast skins. They are not the tall stately
pines which we usually find in Scotland, but are stout
and sturdy, many being twisted and bleached by the
storms of centuries. They cling precariously to a
shallow turf, and where it has been washed away by
floods they twist their strong roots around boulders and
into crevasses in their fight against the elements.

Beyond the Tulla Water the road winds up an
incline, and leads across the south-west corner of the

Moor of Rannoch, bridging lonely Loch Ba with its green islets, where the trout are lusty and plentiful. Onwards, over the moor for several miles, this new highway sweeps, and crosses the old road near to Kingshouse Inn, called, in the Gaelic, *Tigh an Righ*, a very isolated hostel which, to travellers in the olden days, must have been a veritable oasis in a moorland desert.

By whichever route we reach Kingshouse, we are bound to be impressed with the bleakness and solitude of the Moor of Rannoch. Not a tree breaks the monotony of the landscape, where black peat bogs and rushy pools are veritable traps for the unwary who venture to leave the road. In midwinter the scene here is an unforgettable one of desolation.

> "East and west, and northward sweeping,
>   Limitless the mountain plain,
>   Like a vast low-heaving ocean,
>   Girdled by its mountain chain.
>
>   Yea! a desert wide and wasted,
>   Washed by rain-floods to the bones;
>   League on league of heather blasted,
>   Storm-gashed moss, grey boulder stones." *

Autumn is the time to see the moor at its best, when it is clad with wide stretches of purple heather and waving expanses of white *cannach*, or bog-cotton. Then the busy bees put music in the air with their buzzing, and the grouse whir swiftly from knoll to knoll. In the peaty burns the speckled trout dart about, and on a calm evening clouds of midges help to liven things up.

A conspicuous feature of the moor is the numerous dead and bleached roots of ancient trees which appear in the peat cuttings. How long they have been buried no one knows, yet they retain to the full the resinous oils which the trees originally possessed. Until well

* Principal Shairp's *The Moor of Rannoch*.

on into last century this timber proved the principal means of illumination in the thatched sheilings of the district during the long winter evenings. Usually the roots or logs were dried and a splinter from them inserted in a plain split-iron bracket and lighted like a candle: the bracket could be driven into any convenient interstice in the wall. Another method was to cut up the resinous wood into small pieces a few inches long and place a few at a time on a small grating, like a barred girdle, that was hung over the fire. The heat of the fire beneath, without the flames touching them, caused the splinters to blaze up and illuminate the humble apartment. It was the duty of the *bodach* ("the old man") to keep replenishing the illuminant while the *calliach* ("the old woman") whirred her spinning-wheel, and the collie dozed on the earthen floor in the glow of the peat fire.

The peat and heather of the Moor of Rannoch overlie an extensive undulating surface of granite. Granite is a *plutonic* rock, that is, it solidified deep underground (its large crystals denote this fact), thus we know that at one time there must have been a vast accumulation of rocks overlying what is now the moorland. It was into those pre-existing rocks that the granite was intruded from below during the *Old Red Sandstone Period*. These superimposed rocks have been eroded away and even the irregularities of the present granite surface were formed by early river erosion and are not the intruded surface levels of the granite.

How long ago is it since the Old Red Sandstone Period? Well, according to the most modern estimate of science, it is between four hundred and five hundred million years ago. We cannot be so accurate as the guide who, when showing a party of tourists over some interesting scenery, pointed out an outcrop of rock and exclaimed: "These rocks are ninety million and two years old." One of the tourists said: "How can you be so accurate as to know the age of the rocks to within two years?" "Well," said the guide, "there was a geologist here two years ago and he said that these rocks were ninety million years old."

The moor forms a wide flat saucer, or basin-like hollow, about sixty square miles in area, which was filled with ice during the last great Ice Age. Through the gaps in its mountain-ring—Strath Ossian, Glen Coe, Glen Etive and Glen Orchy—the ice flowed away in glaciers. The scratching of the rock surface by the ice is still clearly visible in many parts of the moor and indicates the direction of the ice flow.

Standing sentinel on the southern side of the entrance to Glen Coe (usually called "The Pass" by the local inhabitants) is the shapely cone of Stob Dearg (3,345 feet), the northern peak of the *massif* called Buachaille Etive Mor ("the big herdsman of Etive"). It also guards the northern entrance to lonely and picturesque Glen Etive, which branches off to the south at right angles to Glen Coe, leading away into the land of Deirdre, the celebrated beauty of ancient Gaeldom. Rising steeply from the flat moorland, Stob Dearg seems to keep guard over its scenic treasures like a shepherd watching his flock. On the opposite (northern) side of the entrance to Glen Coe stands Beinn a' Crulaiste. A mile or so west of this gateway an old military road, or rather track, called the "Devil's Staircase," leads over the hills to the north, and ultimately descends to the head of Loch Leven.

The name Glen Coe—or Glen Cona, as it is sometimes called—has been given several derivations, but the best is, probably, "the glen of dogs, or hounds," from the Gaelic *cu*, meaning a dog, or the plural *coin*, dogs; referring perhaps to the hounds of Fingal and his warrior band, the Feinne, who are reputed to have roamed these mountains and passes in the chase, or perhaps it refers to the dogs kept by the MacDonalds for cattle *creachs* and as watchdogs. One of the clachans in the glen is called *Achnacon*, meaning "field of the dogs." Glen Coe is occasionally called "the Glen of Weeping," and this term is sometimes mistaken for a translation of the name, but though there is a note of sadness in the name, Glen Coe, it was applied to this glen long before the tragic massacre of 1692. The name "Glen of Weeping" was first given to it by Macaulay, the historian, thus: "In the Gaelic tongue, Glen Coe signifies the Glen of Weeping, and in truth that pass is the most dreary and melancholy of all the Scottish passes—the very Valley of the Shadow of Death." To the true lover of nature, however, Glen Coe appears wild and impressive, but not gloomy.

Passing Buachaille Etive Beag ("the little herdsman of Etive") on the left, a peculiar-shaped eminence appears ahead on the right, called the "Studdy." This name does not refer to the abode of a student but to the resemblance the shape of the rock bears to an anvil. *Studdy* is the broad Scots term for anvil, and the Gaelic name of the knoll is *Innean*, also meaning anvil.

As we descend through the gorge the mist-wreathed precipices and dark corries of Beinn Fada, Gearr Aonach and Aonach Dubh tower above us to the south. These huge buttresses are the northern spurs of the *massif* called Bidean nam Bian (3,766 feet), the highest peak in Argyll, and are known as "The Three Sisters" of Glen Coe, named by some modern wit—Faith, Hope and Charity: Beinn Fada must be "Charity," for it is "the greatest of these." Their features are well furrowed by the lines of age, which, if it does not give them the refined beauty of paint-and-powder maidens, gives them expressions of *distinction*. High up on the precipitous ramparts of Aonach Dubh, and often hidden in the mists and clouds that swirl around the mountain-top, appears the entrance to Ossian's Cave, a dark, vertically elongated aperture, where the mountain winds sigh and moan. Though situated in an apparently inaccessible situation, this cave is occasionally visited by mountaineers.

The northern side of Glen Coe is bounded by the long serrated ridge of Aonach Eagach, which always appears brighter than the shadowed southern side of the glen. On the eastern side of a cleft in this ridge there is a peculiar piece of natural sculpture, like the head of a legal dignitary wearing his wig, which has been named "The Chancellor."

Down its rocky bed through the glen the River Coe, or Cona, foams and hisses in its headlong course to the sea, pausing only where it expands into little Loch Triochatan, darkly shadowed by the high bastions towering over it. This lochan was reputed at one time to harbour a fearsome water-bull which was not averse to carrying off human victims to its lair beneath the dark waters. On its shores Ossian, the celebrated bard of the Gael, is said to have been born. Mention of the River Cona occurs frequently in his poems. On the site of the lonely little cottage which snuggles at the foot of Aonach Dubh, at Loch Triochatan, there was at one time a hut in which the wife of MacIain, chief of the MacDonalds of Glen Coe, died on the day after the massacre. Her death was caused partly by grief and partly by the ill-treatment to which she had been subjected by the soldiers who shot her husband.

The part of Glen Coe which we have, so far, traversed, from Buachaille Etive Mor to Aonach Dubh and across to Aonach Eagach, is composed of volcanic rocks—*rhyolite* and *andesite* lavas. It forms an oval-shaped area, about nine miles by five miles, which is really a solidified volcanic cauldron formed by sub-sidence into the molten reservoir of *magna* beneath, during the Old Red Sandstone Period. During the subsidence of this area the molten magma welled up around the sinking block, and solidified into a remarkable *ring dyke*, which is almost complete and can be traced among the other rocks.   The amazing feature of this process is that this area sunk for some thousands of feet into the then existing rocks, yet the erosive powers of nature have since that time stripped away the surrounding rocks to such an extent that the area of subsidence is now an area of projection, or elevation, above the surrounding district.   It includes about a dozen peaks over three thousand feet high.

At Loch Triochatan the new road and the old road diverge, the old road following the north side of the river and the new road following the south side.   They do not unite again until they reach the foot of the glen. By all means follow the old road, with its mossy banks and ferny nooks, as it winds through fresh woodlands of fir, oak, ash and hazel.

Soon we come to Clachaig Inn, which was one of the stage-houses of the five-in-hand coaches that linked Fort William with the Lowlands in the olden days. Beyond the inn the road skirts an ornamental lochan, surrounded by spruce and fir, and rising among the trees to the south of this lochan is a conspicuous high rock which recalls grim memories.   It is called the "Signal Rock," and from its summit, tradition says, the signal was issued to commence the massacre.   One version of the tradition says that the signal was a beacon-fire lighted on the summit of this rock, while another version states the signal to have been the firing of two shots from its summit.   Both statements are surprising, because if the signal were a beacon-fire it could not have been very effective owing to the thick screen of the snowstorm on the morning of the massacre. If the signal was two shots, why climb a small eminence, such as this rock, to fire them, as it would not increase, to any appreciable extent, the carrying power of the

sound? It may be that the original intention was to
light a signal beacon on the summit of this rock, but
owing to the snowstorm this signal was substituted by
the firing of two shots.

We are now in the fertile part of the glen where the
famous, or rather infamous, massacre of the Mac-
Donalds took place in 1692. There is an iron notice,
to the east of Clachaig Inn, purporting to be erected on
the site of the massacre, but this indicator now occupies
its *third* position since it was first erected at Invercoe
at the foot of the glen. It is not likely that the massacre
would be confined to any one clachan, as the homes of
the clansmen were spread throughout the glen and the
whole clan was intended to be exterminated. The
Government troops who carried out the cruel edict
numbered one hundred and twenty, and they are said
to have been billeted from three to five in each cottage
according to accommodation. Taking an average of
four soldiers to a house, this means that they occupied
at least thirty houses, and there may have been some
cottages too small to accommodate troops or over-
crowded with a large family. Therefore the massacre
would appear to have extended throughout the glen.

This gruesome deed was an act of vengeance by the
Government as dire punishment for the failure of the
Chief of Glen Coe to swear an oath of allegiance before
the stipulated date.

In 1691 the Government of William of Orange
determined to subdue the warring clans of the Highlands and ordered every clan chief to take an oath of
allegiance before the 1st of January 1692, or "be
prosecuted with the utmost severity of the law." As
this submission was, naturally, resented by the chiefs,
they delayed as long as possible, but ultimately they
submitted. Owing to lack of communications, it was
near the end of December 1691 before the chief of the
MacDonalds of Glen Coe (who was known by the

patronymic of MacIain—"Son of John") became aware that all the other chiefs had taken the oath and, when he went to Fort William on the second last day of 1691, to swear allegiance, he found that he must go to Inveraray, as the Governor of Fort William had no authority to administer the oath. On reaching Inveraray on the 2nd of January 1692, after being held up in a snowstorm, with a letter of explanation from the Governor of Fort William, MacIain found that the sheriff was away on a Hogmanay visit. On his return, on the 5th of January, the sheriff, after considering the matter, administered the oath and forwarded it, along with a letter explaining the circumstances, to Edinburgh. MacIain returned home thinking everything was in order. Unfortunately, his delay in taking the oath allowed his enemies in the Government to vent their wrath on him and his clan in a very treacherous manner. The two chief conspirators were the Earl of Stair and the Earl of Breadalbane, the latter of whom has been described as "wise as a serpent, cunning as a fox and slippery as an eel."

On the 1st of February 1692 a detachment of one hundred and twenty "redcoats," of Argyll's Regiment, under the command of Captain Robert Campbell of Glenlyon, marched into Glen Coe from the Loch Leven road. Glenlyon told the MacDonalds that he and his men had been up at Glen Garry on duty and on their return to Fort William found the accommodation of the fort fully taxed. The Governor there, he said, had packed them off to Glen Coe to seek bed and bite for a short time.

After receiving the hospitality of the MacDonalds and feigning friendship, for a fortnight, they treacherously slew their hosts during a raging snowstorm in the early morning of the 13th of February. Thirty-eight of the MacDonalds were killed by bayonet and bullet and seventy-five perished while trying to escape in the bleak snow-drifted mountain passes. There would also be a number of wounded. The total population of the glen at that time was about two hundred, but it is not so much the extent of the massacre as the method by which it was carried out that rankles in the Highland heart—

> "The hand that mingled in the meal,
> At midnight drew the felon steel."

Also, other massacres in the Highlands had been carried out by one clan upon another, whereas this one was carried out by order of King and Government.

Though the snowstorm made the conditions very severe for those who escaped the soldiers, it actually minimized the massacre by sheltering the fugitives in its thick mantle. It also delayed the detachment of troops, under Lieutenant-Colonel Hamilton, which was proceeding to the glen from Fort William; so much so, that the avenues of escape which these soldiers should have closed were left open.

The fact that only thirty-eight persons were slain, out of the two hundred MacDonalds in the glen, suggests that some of the soldiers were reluctant to carry out their brutal orders. Though the officers knew the real purpose of their visit to the glen, the soldiers were not told until the day before the massacre, lest the secret should leak out to the MacDonalds. Tradition relates that one of the soldiers, who was billeted on the house of one called MacEanruig mor nam Feadan ("big Henderson of the chanters"), asked his host to accompany him on a walk on the evening on which he learned the grim purpose he was meant to serve in the glen. On coming to a boulder by the path, the soldier told Henderson to stand still, as he had something to say to the stone. Stepping over to it, he addressed it thus: "Grey stone of the Glen, you have every right to be there, but if you knew what is to

KINGSHOUSE, STOB DEARG AND GLEN COE

[To face page 32

GLEN COE

happen to-night you would not remain there." His soldier's oath forbade him to reveal more. Henderson meditated on these remarks during the evening, and related them to young MacIain, son of the Chief, who was always warning his father and brother that the soldiers were in the glen for no good purpose. The result was that Henderson and MacIain's sons did not go to bed on the fateful night, and were thus able to escape as soon as the shooting commenced. Old MacIain, the Chief, refused to believe the story, and paid the penalty with his life.

Another story tells of a small party of soldiers, in search of fugitives, sighting a woman and child some distance off escaping into the thick mist of falling snow. The officer in charge ordered one of the soldiers to pursue them and kill them both, while the remainder searched elsewhere. When the soldier, who happened to be an Inverness-shire Highlander serving in the army, overtook the woman and child he found a dog trotting ahead of them. Instead of killing the fugitives he indicated a shelter among the rocks, and told them to hide there, as that place had already been searched. In order to produce evidence to his officer that he had carried out his order the soldier killed the dog and wiped his bayonet in its blood.

The sequel to this story is that many years afterwards this same soldier, when an old man, and long retired from military service, found himself storm-stayed in Glen Coe while on his way to the Lowlands. He was given hospitality by one of the crofters, and during the evening's *ceilidh* by the peat fire the conversation turned to the massacre. The old soldier mentioned that, much against his will, he had been forced to participate in that evil deed. His host, boiling with indignation that he had entertained such an enemy, vowed to himself there and then that he would kill his guest before morning to avenge his kinsmen. However,

C

the old soldier continued by saying that, personally, he had a clear conscience, as he killed no one, and related his action with the woman and child. His host, springing to his feet, and holding out his hand in gratitude, exclaimed: "That woman was my mother and that child was me, that you saved. Many a time my mother told me the story and prayed for your welfare. You are welcome to my hospitality as long as you like to stay."

An Appin version of this story, and probably the correct one, says that the old soldier told his tale while sojourning for a night in the old inn at Portnacroise, near the picturesque Castle Stalker. The innkeeper at that time was Donald Stewart, whose father had been a crofter in Glen Coe at the time of the massacre and was one of those killed by the soldiers. The woman whom the old soldier saved was Donald Stewart's mother and Stewart himself was the helpless babe of the story.

After his gruesome deed in Glen Coe, Glenlyon was drafted with his regiment to Flanders, where he gave distinguished service and rose to the rank of Colonel before his death. A story relating to his grandson, Colonel Campbell, indicates, however, that the guilt of the massacre weighed on the conscience of his descendants. On this occasion Colonel Campbell, while serving in Canada, was ordered to superintend the execution of a British soldier condemned to be shot. The soldier had left his sentry post to rescue his sweetheart, an Indian maid, whom he saw drowning when her boat capsized. Near the eleventh hour a reprieve was granted, but, in order to chastise the soldier as much as possible, Colonel Campbell was told to carry out the full proceedings until the final moment, and until then keep the reprieve secret. The orders were carried out until the prisoner was blindfolded, and the soldiers had their muskets levelled at him, awaiting

Colonel Campbell's signal to fire—the waving of a white handkerchief. At this stage Colonel Campbell put his hand into his pocket to take out the reprieve and read it, but alas!—

> "He, in a fatal moment's absent fit,
>   Drew forth the handkerchief and not the writ;
>   Wept o'er the corpse, and wrung his hands in woe,
>   Crying 'Here is thy curse again—Glen Coe! Glen Coe!'"

Thomas Campbell, the poet, erroneously ascribes this incident to the commander of the troops at the massacre, but it really relates to his grandson, and occurred in 1771.

The MacDonalds who were slain in the massacre were buried in Eilean Munde ("St. Munn's Island") in Loch Leven, opposite Ballachulish. MacIain, the Chief, is said to have been buried in the chapel which is now in ruins on the island. His two sons escaped from the massacre, and sped up the track through Glen Coe and over the hills at the Devil's Staircase, not halting until they reached friendly shelter at Fersit, on Loch Treig. They returned later to Glen Coe, along with other survivors of the massacre, and perpetuated the family of the chief. Their descendants retained possession of the glen until the year 1893, when it was purchased by Sir Donald Smith, the pioneer of the Hudson Bay Company and Canadian Pacific Railway, who, in 1897, became Lord Strathcona and Mount Royal.

In a magazine article, published a few years before his death, Sir Harold Boulton, the well-known writer of Scottish songs, made the following surprising statement: "A most curious episode in connection with the Massacre of Glen Coe took place in the early 'eighties, as I well remember. Lord Archibald Campbell, son of the eighth Duke of Argyll, conceived the quixotic idea that the Campbells should make restitution or do penance for their share in that atrocious historical episode. He planned and, I believe, executed a pilgrimage of expiation, and a march of the Campbells up the glen with the pipers playing laments for the murdered MacDonalds.

"For fear of a mistake on the part of those outside the Campbell clan as to the purely honourable intention of this curious parade, I understand a large force of police had to be mobilized to prevent disturbances. I fear that few people beyond the well-intentioned Lord Archibald felt the better for this demonstration."

As this garbled account of the incident appears to have been accepted without verification, and repeated by some other writers, it seems only fair that the true facts of the case should be made known. During the first week of September 1893 Lord Archibald Campbell arranged to give an outing to his famous Inveraray Pipe Band, before they attended the Argyllshire Highland Gathering of that year at Oban. He was very enthusiastic in encouraging the art of piping and also sought to revive the playing of the *clarsach*, or Celtic harp. The route selected by his Lordship for tour by the pipe band, which was under the command of Pipe - Major Charles Maitland, was, starting from Inveraray, through Glen Aray to the head of Loch Awe, traversing the Pass of Brander to Achnacloich, where they boarded the steamer and sailed to the head of Loch Etive. Coaches conveyed the party through rugged Glen Etive by Kingshouse, and drove through Glen Coe to Bridge of Coe, where they were met by Sir Donald Smith, proprietor. Here the pipe band gave stirring selections of bagpipe music to a large crowd which had assembled to hear them, and no untoward incident arose to mar the proceedings. Apparently some time before the outing Lord Archibald, with every good intention, had made inquiries as to the likely reaction by the people of Glen Coe to his pipe band playing a lament for the massacred MacDonalds.

He was advised not to risk arousing any unhappy memories, and therefore when the band set out they had no intention whatsoever of playing laments in Glen Coe for the massacred MacDonalds. As to the outing being "a pilgrimage of expiation," such an idea was never entertained.

In 1935 the National Trust for Scotland purchased the main portion of Glen Coe for £1,350, to preserve it as a national possession and prevent its desecration by unseemly buildings or otherwise. In 1937, through the generosity of friends of the Trust and members of Mountaineering Clubs throughout the country, the ancient Royal Deer Forest of Dalness was purchased and handed over to the Trust to be maintained as a National Forest Preserve. It is to be retained, as far as possible, in its present primitive condition, with free access for the public at all times. This area lies to the south and east of the Trust's previously acquired property in Glen Coe and adjoins it for several miles, forming a great wedge of rugged mountainous country between Glen Coe and Glen Etive. It extends to about twenty square miles and contains the famed Three Sisters of Glen Coe and the Herdsmen of Etive. On the east it adjoins the Deer Forest of Blackmount. Every true Scotsman must feel a genuine thrill of emotion and pride when he realizes that, at last, the spirit of Scotland is aroused and is active in preserving, as national property, historic and scenic areas of his country: more power to the cause.

On the south bank of the River Coe, at the foot of the glen, stands a graceful, slender cross of red granite, on a little *cnoc*, bearing the following inscription:

"This cross is reverently erected in memory of MACIAIN, CHIEF OF THE MACDONALDS OF GLEN COE, who fell with his people in the massacre of Glen Coe of February 1692, by his direct descendant, ELLEN

BURNS MACDONALD of GLEN COE, August 1883. Their memory liveth evermore."

A short distance to the south of the cross is the boulder known as "Henderson's Stone," which, tradition says, is the stone to which the soldier addressed the warning on the eve of the massacre.

These stirring events of the past invest Highland scenery with human interest, and for this reason they are worth preserving. But to carry any bitterness into present-day associations from events of which the perpetrators are long since dead is to forfeit one's claim to being fully civilized. No man is responsible for the actions of his ancestors—good or bad. Let every man be judged on his own merit.

Standing sentinel at the mouth of Glen Coe, where it meets with the waters of Loch Leven, is the conspicuous conical hill, or mountain, called "The Pap of Glen Coe" (2,430 feet), with rich woodland clothing its lower slopes. On a clearing, upon this hill-side, stands Glencoe House, built by Lord Strathcona about fifty years ago, and commanding one of the finest views in the west Highlands. Though still very commodious, it has been reduced from its original size, when it had three hundred and sixty-five windows— one for every day of the year. Its original red-tiled roof, which made it incongruous in this fine Highland setting, has also been replaced by a roof of Ballachulish slates, as it should always have been. This mansion was purchased recently from the Hon. Mrs. Kitson, granddaughter of Lord Strathcona, by the Argyll County Council, for use as a maternity home.

Near to the shore of Loch Leven, below Glencoe House, the old road and the new road unite, and bend eastward along the loch-side, high above its waters, for about ten miles to Kinlochleven, and thence, through Nether Lochaber, to Fort William.

CHAPTER II

NETHER LOCHABER

THE district of Nether Lochaber lies between Loch Leven and Fort William, or, to quote the more poetic phrase of its best-known writer, it lies "'Twixt Ben Nevis and Glen Coe." Though a main road skirts it by the shore, it has a rugged and little-explored hinterland, which includes the famous deer forest of Mamore. Travelling from the south, we enter Nether Lochaber and, incidentally, pass from Argyllshire into Inverness-shire, when we cross the River Leven at Kinlochleven, a town of modern growth, cupped in the hollow of high hills, at the head of Loch Leven.

The rural atmosphere of this site has been dispersed since the North British Aluminuim Company erected a factory here in 1907. Though quite a comfortable little town, Kinlochleven appears alien to its surroundings, and looks just what it is, a piece of the industrial Lowlands transferred to the Highlands. The town lies partly in Argyllshire and partly in Inverness-shire, owing to the boundary line (the River Leven) passing through it.

On crossing the River Leven we turn westward along the north shore of Loch Leven, putting the industrial atmosphere of the little town behind us, and travel along the foot of the green wooded slopes of the bens of Mamore Forest, a famous sanctuary of the deer, over which King Edward VII stalked several times. If we were to climb northwards over this lofty range we should ultimately descend into Glen Nevis.

A short distance from Kinlochleven a rough road

branches off to the right, and up the wooded hill-side. This road commences in a long steep incline of several miles, and continues in stiff gradients and zigzags for about fourteen miles over lonely hills and high moorland, past Loch Lundavra and Blarmachfoldach, to Fort William. It is "rough going" all the way, over a land of mountain-hare and moorcock, but is a splendid road for the tramper, presenting some unique hill-framed vistas of Ardgour and Lochaber. From the summit of the final descent to Fort William there is a wide panorama of the head of Loch Linnhe and the western end of the Great Glen. This road is not one of General Wade's roads, as is often stated, though it is an old military road. It was constructed under the direction of Major Caulfeild, Wade's successor in road construction, about 1751, to link with the "Devil's Staircase" at Kinlochleven. The only genuine Wade road in Lochaber is the old road from Fort William to Fort Augustus via High Bridge.

A remnant of Argyll's forces toiled over the Lundavra route when escaping from the battle of Inverlochy, with still much enemy territory to traverse. (There was probably a track, but no *road* here at that time.) They were pursued by some of the MacDonalds of Montrose's army to a spot between the old Toll House at Blarmachfoldach and Loch Lundavra, but having had a good start the Campbells escaped. To mark the spot where they turned, the MacDonalds erected a large stone, which is called *Clach nan Caimbeulach* ("the stone of the Campbells"). There is a cairn of stones near to this relic, said to have been erected some time in the past to indicate the exact position of *Clach nan Caimbeulach*, as there are a number of somewhat similar large stones in the vicinity. According to traditional custom every Campbell or sympathiser with Argyll who passes this way should throw down the topmost stone of the cairn, while every MacDonald or admirer of Montrose should, with equal duty, add a stone to the cairn.

Loch Lundavra stands five hundred feet above sea-level, and on one of its little islands the famous Macbeth, of Scottish history, is said to have resided and met his death.

This story is supported by Skene in his *Celtic Scotland*, where he says that the island was in a sheet of water in Mamore Forest. In olden times this loch was reputed to harbour a water-bull, which used to emerge occasionally and graze with other cattle in order to lure one of them to its watery home.

Blarmachfoldach, the isolated little settlement on this road, is one of the fast-disappearing places in the Highlands where the Old New Year—the 12th of January—is still rigidly observed in preference to the modern New Year's Day, the 1st of January. This custom has been held here from time immemorial. On the stroke of midnight all entrance doors are opened to welcome the New Year and the "first-footers," and are kept open until all the celebrations are over. With the Gaelic greeting, *Bliadhna-Mhath-ur* ("A Happy New Year"), the little community greet one another, and usually hold a *ceilidh* (a social gathering) at which songs and stories are contributed in the traditional style of olden times.

On the north side of the road, where it dips down finally to Fort William, there is a moorland known as "The Little Field of Battle," where some of Argyll's men made a stand after Inverlochy. Leading through this moorland is an old road to Glen Nevis. It is known as the "Famine Road," as it was constructed to give employment to the local people during the great potato famine, caused by "blight," in 1846.

If, instead of following the Lundavra road, we proceed by the main road from Kinlochleven to Fort William by the shore of Loch Leven, we commence by

passing through several picturesque woodlands, whose
fresh foliage frames the mountain and loch scenery in
beautiful vistas. Opposite the entrance to Glen Coe
we come to Callart House, with its ivy-clad walls in a
verdant setting by the shore. It is a comparatively
modern building, having been built by Sir Duncan
Cameron of Fassifern, who acquired the estate by
purchase towards the end of the eighteenth century,
when the old Cameron of Callart family, the oldest
cadet family of Lochiel, left the district. Sir Duncan's
daughter married Campbell of Monzie.

An interesting story is told of Mary, a daughter of
the laird of Callart during the seventeenth century.
Her name is usually given in the Gaelic, Mairi of
Callaird. This young lady had incurred the displeasure
of her father by associating too freely with the tenants
of the estate and giving them presents. As punishment,
Mary's father locked her in her room and kept her there
for several days. During her seclusion a Spanish ship
arrived in Loch Leven, with silks and satins for trading
purposes, and, naturally, all the members of the Callart
household visited the ship, with the exception of Mary,
as her father refused to allow her to leave her room.
On their return from the ship Mary could hear them
discussing their purchases, and one garment in
particular seemed to be greatly admired. It was a
magnificent silk robe which they all tried on in turn.

On the following morning Mary was surprised at
the silence in the house. As the day wore on, and she
could hear no sound of voices or movement, she tried
to force open the door of her room, but was unable
to do so. While pondering her situation, Mary heard
people speaking beneath her window and, looking out,
found one of them to be Donald Cameron, of Ballachulish, with whose family she was very friendly. He
shouted up to Mary that it was known in the neighbourhood that the *Black Plague* was in the house, conveyed

by some of the purchases from the Spanish ship, and that the occupants were all dead or dying. He had orders to burn the house to the ground, with everyone in it, dead or alive. As recompense for her past kindnesses to his family, however, Donald agreed to convey a message to Mary's sweetheart, Diarmid, son and heir of Campbell of Inverawe, and delay the burning until his return. He told her to remain in her room and not to seek contact with any other part of the house.

On Diarmid's arrival, Mary's escape was achieved under cover of darkness by means of a rope thrown up to her, but before meeting him she was bid wash herself in the burn which flowed past the house, and put on a change of clothing, which he had brought for her. Immediately Mary left the house it was set on fire, and burned to the ground.

News of the plague at Callart had reached Loch Awe in advance of Mary and Diarmid, so that Diarmid's father would not allow them to enter his house when they arrived. Speaking from an upper-floor window, he told them they would require to spend a month in isolation, in a bothy on the side of Ben Cruachan, but before doing so he made them take the vows of matrimony. On completing their term of isolation satisfactorily, the young couple returned, and were welcomed to Diarmid's ancestral home.

Diarmid died, when quite a young man, from wounds received at the battle of Inverlochy. He is buried in the precincts of the Priory of Ardchattan on Loch Etive-side, an old Campbell burial-ground, but a still earlier burial-ground of the MacDougalls, the ancient Lords of Lorn. There are two poetic versions of the story of Mary Cameron of Callart, one by an old Clan Cameron bard, who also wrote *Mary's Lament for Her Husband*.

It is said that when old Callart House was burned it contained a considerable amount of valuable silverware and money, but the fear of the plague was so great that no one would go near the ruins. During the centuries that have passed since the event the ruins have crumbled, and become obliterated by earth and vegetation, until now only a heap of moss-clad stones near to the present Callart House indicate the site of the old building. The treasure, if treasure there be, in the ruins has remained intact, as a tradition which has held sway in the district states that whoever digs up the treasure will also dig up the germs of the Black Plague.

During last century, Campbell of Monzie, laird of Callart, and grandfather of the present proprietrix, cherished a desire for some time to search for the treasure in the old buried ruins. Ultimately he engaged a number of workmen from Onich to excavate on the site. At the end of their first day's work they had dug a large trench, but had found no valuables. Monzie told them to come back the next day and they would trench another part of the site. On their arrival next morning, to continue the job, the workmen received a surprise when Monzie told them to fill in the first trench and dig no more. Why Monzie changed his mind so suddenly no one has ever found out. He refused to discuss the subject. Did he receive warning in a dream that night of his first excavations?

A mile or so beyond Callart the road leads through a wooded region to the crofting township of North Ballachulish, with its rich meadow-lands, at the narrows of Loch Leven. On the opposite side of the narrows rises the pine-clad knoll where James Stewart of Glen Duror, "James of the Glen," was hanged for having been accessory to the murder of Colin Campbell of Glenure in 1752. He was not accused of being the actual murderer, as is often stated. This event, known as the *Appin Murder*, is a *cause célèbre* of Highland history, and has been made famous beyond the bounds of the Highlands by R. L. Stevenson in his *Kidnapped* and *Catriona*. As to the identity of the actual murderer, the least said the better. If ever there was a coward he was one. Indeed, he was a double-dyed coward, because he shot an innocent man in the back and also allowed an innocent man to hang for the crime. It was no hot-headed murder but treacherous, premeditated assassination. To attempt to whitewash the culprit, as is sometimes done, by saying that he wished to give himself up on the day of the execution of James Stewart, and that he had to be bound with ropes to prevent him doing so, is absurd. The time for the guilty man to surrender was when James was arrested or, at the latest, when James was on trial at Inveraray. A few Appin people alive to-day are believed to be aware of the identity of the actual murderer, passed on to them as an hereditary secret. For family and neighbourly reasons, however, they are not likely to betray their trust by revealing the secret, least of all to the few *Sasunnaich* who appear to be the only ones who claim to have had the secret revealed to them.

From North Ballachulish there is a very fine view towards the west, looking out through the entrance to Loch Leven, where it widens into Loch Linnhe, with the high hills of Ardgour and Sunart rising in serried ranks in the distance. It is a scene which appeals whether sparkling under a summer sun and azure sky or when the drifting mists soften the outlines, but perhaps best of all when it forms the golden gate of sunset.

Close to the shore, where the fronds of brown seaweed float in the translucent gravel shallows, we wend our way westward to the little village of Onich, a veritable sun-trap in a sylvan setting, at the northern portal of Loch Leven. There are a number of pretty villas here, in addition to the crofters' houses, indicating that its sunny situation has appealed to visitors. Onich was the parsonage of the Rev. Alexander Stewart, better known in the Highlands by the pen-name of *Nether Lochaber*, whose fascinating accounts of the natural history and folk-lore of this district are very interesting. He was a fluent writer in Gaelic as well as in English, and translated into English many Gaelic poems. A memorial, in the form of a fine Celtic cross, stands above the roadway as a token of the esteem in which he was held by West Highlanders.

From Onich the road leads through a little valley of heather and bog-myrtle, with an occasional birch- and rowan-tree, across the peninsula of Cuilcheanna, from which projects a long, dangerous sandbank stretching out into the mouth of the loch. Cuilcheanna House was at one time the residence of Dr. Norman MacLeod, the famous divine.

On the western shore of Cuilcheanna we find ourselves at the narrows of Loch Linnhe at Corran, where the snow-white lighthouse and its outbuildings rise from the fresh green platform of a *raised beach* on the further shore, about a quarter of a mile distant. At this point, we can either follow the road along the east shore of Loch Linnhe to Fort William, or else cross the ferry and travel along the Ardgour side of the loch to Camas-nan-Gall, opposite Fort William, and there recross the loch by ferry. Let us follow the latter road. In Ardgour we are outside the present-accepted bounds of Lochaber, but are merely on the opposite shore of Loch Linnhe. The Ardgour road is more varied, more picturesque, and much more secluded than the road on the Fort William side of the loch. There is little traffic of any kind on it; indeed, the whole district of Ardgour is very sequestered and will appeal strongly to the tramper who wishes to get off the beaten track. It is a wild, unspoiled, mountainous solitude of more than one hundred square miles, and is likely to remain unspoiled for a long time owing to its being isolated from the surrounding districts by long deep lochs which prevent any main road passing through it. Though not generally realized, Ardgour and the lesser district of Sunart form almost an island, being bounded on the north and east by the long arm of the sea forming Loch Linnhe and Loch Eil, on the south by another arm of the sea, Loch Sunart, and on the west by the long stretch of fresh water forming Loch Shiel. Only three narrow necks of land, or tarberts, prevent these water boundaries from being continuous, and the highest watershed is only forty feet above sea-level.

A very swift current flows through the narrows at Corran and sets up strong whirlpools at certain states of the tide. In days gone by, before the general introduction of steamships, Corran Narrows had an evil reputation. Sailing vessels caught at full ebb- or full flood-tide were frequently swept ashore, and at low tide the remains of several wrecks used to be visible. About seventy years ago a local rowing-boat was capsized in this turbulent tide with the loss of four Ardgour men.

There is a pretty little gravel bay at Corran, from which the place derives its name — Gaelic *corran*, meaning "a cutting hook, or sickle." In a picturesque setting in the wooded surroundings stands Ardgour House, seat of MacLean of Ardgour, chieftain of an old branch of the Clan MacLean. This title was in dispute in the Law Courts for two years (1936–38) between Miss Catriona MacLean, eldest daughter of the late chieftain, who died in 1930, and a kinsman, Lieutenant-Commander Henry Hugh MacLean. Giving his judgment, the Lord Lyon King-of-Arms stated that the Lords of the Court of Session had held that Chieftainship was not a legal status that the law recognized, but was merely a social distinction which was not in his power to impose upon a clan if they declined to recognize it. The Lord Justice-Clerk regarded the finding of the Clan MacLean Association in favour of Lieutenant-Commander MacLean as Chieftain of Ardgour as immune from challenge before any tribunal. The Lord Lyon merely gave his ruling regarding the coats-of-arms of the disputants.

Until the middle of the fifteenth century the lands of Ardgour ("the height of the goats") belonged to the Clan MacMaster. Unfortunately for them, their chief incurred the enmity of the all-powerful MacDonald, Lord of the Isles, some say by passing a slighting remark, which resulted in the MacLeans dispossessing them of their lands.

Here is the story that is told of how the MacLeans came into possession of Ardgour. A young warrior, named Ewan MacLean, who was a grandson of the first MacLean of Duart, was in Ireland visiting the home of his ancestors when he heard that the Lord of the Isles was distributing land to his friends. Thinking he was entitled to something, Ewan set out with a few followers to interview the Lord of the Isles. On arrival, however, MacDonald told him that all the land had been already distributed, but, admiring Ewan's abilities as a warrior, he told him he could have the land of Ardgour, belonging to the MacMasters, if he was prepared to fight for it. This reply was sufficient for Ewan, who lost no time collecting his followers and sailing his galley up Loch Linnhe to the home of the Chief of the MacMasters, which stood near to where the present Ardgour House stands. Knocking at the door, Ewan demanded, abruptly, food and bed for himself and his warriors. MacMaster was not in the habit of being bullied by strangers, and commenced to tell Ewan so in no uncertain terms, but Ewan cut him short by lunging at him and sheathing his dirk in MacMaster's heart. The son and heir escaped from

WESTWARD, FROM BALLACHULISH

[To face page 48

STRONCHREGGAN, ARDGOUR

the house, but Ewan pursued and slew him at Corran Ferry. From that time the MacLeans have possessed Ardgour, though during last century the Earl of Morton purchased the northern part. The descendants of the Boyds and Livingstones who came over from Ireland with Ewan still reside in Ardgour.

Northwards from Corran the road leads along the skirt of a steep green hill-side bare of trees, and at a short distance from the shore. Close to the road is the little burial-ground of Killevaodain, where rests the bones of Ewan MacLachlan, the Gaelic poet and scholar. Though buried here, he was born on the opposite side of the loch, at Torracalltuin of Coruanan.

Two little cottages, with their fields of varied-hued crops, are the only sign of habitation until, about five miles from Corran, we come to Inverscaddle Bay, where the united waters of the River Scaddle and the River Cona enter Loch Linnhe. It was at Inverscaddle that Colonel John Cameron, of Quatre Bras fame, was born in 1771. Stretching back into the heart of Ardgour are the long, deep and lonely Glen Scaddle and Cona Glen, drained by the rivers of the same name, and separated by Druim Leathad nam Eas, which, from Loch Linnhe, appears like an enormous upturned boat. With the exception of the local game-keepers and shepherds, few people ever explore these glens, which remain the undisputed haunt of deer and hill fox. Above the bay, and set against a background of steep wooded hill-side, is Conaglen House, the Highland residence of the Earl of Morton. The prominent peak towering over this mansion, a little to the west, is Stob Choire a Chearcaill (2,527 feet), whose summit is the "weather-glass" for a wide area around the shores of Upper Loch Linnhe and Loch Eil.

In the entrance to Inverscaddle Bay is the rock on which Colonel Alastair Ranaldson MacDonell, fifteenth Chief of Glengarry, was killed when attempting to save

D

his life by leaping from the steamer *Stirling Castle*, which struck this rock and was wrecked here on the night of 14th January 1828. In leaping ashore his foot slipped, and he fell forward heavily on his head, sustaining injuries from which he died a few hours later. This Chief of Glengarry was the last Highland chief to live in full feudal splendour. He always wore Highland costume, with eagle feathers in his bonnet denoting his chiefship of the clan, and had his *tail* of attendants wherever he went. Like the majority of Highland chiefs and lairds, he was known by his territorial name — Glengarry. This custom was necessary in the Highlands in order to distinguish the different families of the same name and clan. Glengarry took a prominent part in the grand reception given to George IV on the occasion of the royal visit to Edinburgh in 1822. His bard was the famous Alan MacDougall, *Ailean Dall* ("Blind Alan"), who was arrayed in full professional robes when Glengarry was entertaining friends. Sir Walter Scott knew this Chief of Glengarry well, and, of course, his nature would appeal to a romantic like the Wizard. He is believed to be the prototype of Fergus MacIvor in *Waverley*. Glengarry had a very fiery temper, and on one occasion fought a duel and killed a grandson of Flora MacDonald, the Jacobite heroine. Only the forensic skill of his lawyer, Henry Erskine, saved him from the scaffold.

Northwards, from Inverscaddle, we tramp through cool avenues of fir, oak, ash and birch on a fine country road overlooking a steep rocky shore, birch, bracken and mossy turf growing right down to the rock-face overchanging the loch. Only at wide intervals do we find little inlets of shingle backed by grassy clearings in the woodland.

At Stroncreggan there is a broad grassy plain stretching back from the shore into the mouth of a wide heather- and bracken-clad glen, where the road

dips down to a low level. From now onwards the
landscape is open, and affords a splendid view of Ben
Nevis and the Great Glen, as we travel along close to
the shore by the skirts of Meall an t' Slamain and
through the scattered shore clachan of Trislaig. Here,
a few crofters' cottages snuggle at the foot of the hill-side,
with the smoke from their chimneys rising lazily into
the calm air, and long fields of flower-starred meadow,
corn and potatoes stretching down to the road. Through
the fields a collie comes racing, barking his defiance
at the stranger, but the more placid cows, grazing by
the roadside, merely lift their head, give a lazy look
and continue munching the grass.

From Trislaig we climb a little incline in the road,
and descend to the pretty little sheltered Camas-nan-
Gall ("bay of the stranger"), with a row of neat
cottages near the clean gravel shore, and backed by
green fields in a woodland clearing. It is a favourite
anchorage of small craft owing to the good shelter it
offers from the prevailing winds.

From Camas-nan-Gall we can cross by the ferry-boat
to Fort William, the capital of Lochaber.

CHAPTER III

FORT WILLIAM AND BEN NEVIS

THE thriving little Highland town of Fort William, or *An gearasdan* ("the garrison"), as it is called by old natives of Lochaber, occupies a picturesque setting at the head of Loch Linnhe. Built on the green hill-side which rises from the waters of this long arm of the sea, where they turn westward to enter the bounds of Loch Eil, it has a wide and varied outlook. The population is only about three thousand five hundred, but it seems quite an imposing town after the sparsely populated regions through which one approaches it, either from north or south. The town shelters in the shadow of Ben Nevis, being only about two miles from it, though the Ben cannot actually be seen from the town, owing to the rounded green mass of the Cow Hill intervening. Yet, one can hardly imagine Fort William without picturing Ben Nevis as its background.

The name of the town—Fort William—is derived from the fort which was built here during the seventeenth century to keep in check the turbulent Highland clans, especially the Camerons. The position of this fort was of strategic importance for the purpose, as it commanded the western end of the Great Glen and could receive supplies by sea without fear of interference by the Highlanders. In conjunction with Fort Augustus, midway through the Great Glen, and the fort at Inverness, at the eastern end of the glen, it raised a Government defence right across Scotland, and through the heart of the lands of the Highland clans. It was built on a spit of land where the River Nevis enters Loch Linnhe, thus giving it only one side available for attack by land.

The first fortified structure here was erected by General Monk, Cromwell's emissary, in 1650, though, for the first forty years or so, it was merely a fence and rough earthworks around the houses of the troops. It was fit to accommodate two thousand soldiers. Monk called it the Garrison of Inverlochy, as Inverlochy was the nearest settlement to it with a place-name. In 1690 General Hugh Mackay, commander of King William's troops in Scotland, made it a substantial fort of its kind, but on a smaller scale than Monk, by constructing ramparts twenty feet high, moat glacis, ravelin, and a bomb-proof magazine for the storage of arms and ammunition. He mounted fifteen twelve-pounders, taken from the warships which conveyed the building materials, and made accommodation for a regular garrison of two field officers, two captains, four subalterns and ninety-six privates, though in time of trouble many more soldiers were billeted here. There must have been over a thousand troops in the fort when it was besieged in 1746, for in the journal of an officer in the fort at that time (vide *Prince Charles Edward and the Forty-five*, by Winifred Duke, p. 202) it is stated: "Capt. Scott having ordered 12 men out of each company, amounting to about 150 men, to make a sally. . . ." This statement means thatt here were about twelve companies in the fort. Again, the same journal states: "We made a sally with about 500 men."

When the building was completed, MacKay named it Fort William, in honour of the King. The adjoining little village of rude huts, which had been built by local inhabitants who wished to trade with the soldiers, he named Maryburgh, in honour of the consort of William and in keeping with the name of the fort.

Towards the end of the eighteenth century the name Maryburgh began to be superseded by the name Gordonsburgh, in honour of the Huntlys, who were overlords of the district. Writing in the old (Sinclair's)

Statistical Account of Scotland, in 1793, the parish minister
says: "Maryburgh, or Gordonsburgh, is the only
village of note in the parish (Kilmallie) and is situated
upon the seashore, south side of Locheile, within a few
yards to the south-west of Fort William. Anciently,
the place where it stands was called Auchintore-beg.
The village was then built on the ground where the
esplanade is now. It was after the accession of the
Prince of Orange to the British throne that it obtained
the name of Maryburgh, in honour of his consort.
For some time past it has been indiscriminately called
Maryburgh and Gordonsburgh, from the family of
Gordon whose property it is."

In 1834 the name of the town was again changed,
to Duncansburgh, by Sir Duncan Cameron of Fassifern
(brother of Colonel John, of Quatre Bras), who became
superior of the town in that year.

Despite these early names, the name of the fort has
survived as the name of the town. Its original name
is sometimes given as Inverlochy, but the settlement of
this name was probably near the site of the present
ruins of Inverlochy Castle, about a mile to the north of
Fort William, or perhaps a little nearer the mouth of
the River Lochy. The word "inver" means a confluence of waters. In this case referring, evidently, to
the confluence of the River Lochy and Loch Linnhe.
The name would therefore be applied to a settlement
near the mouth of the Lochy, which is separated from
the present town of Fort William by the River
Nevis. The origin of the present town of Fort William
was, evidently, the huts which sprung up around the
fort. The early settlement referred to by the writer
in the *Statistical Account* ("on the ground where the
esplanade is now," 1793) was, probably, one or two
huts of fishermen or small crofters, but insufficient in
number to have a definite place-name.

In a letter written by Captain Burt, one of General

Wade's assistants, during the eighteenth century, the following passages occur: "The town was elected into a Barony in favour of the governor of the Fort, for the time being, and into a Borough bearing the name of Queen Mary. It was originally designed as a sutlery to the garrison in so barren a country, where little can be had for the support of the troops.

"The houses were neither to be built with stone nor brick, and are to this day (1725–27) composed of timber, boards and turf. This was ordained to the end that they might the more suddenly be burnt, or otherwise destroyed, by order of the governor, to prevent any lodgement of an enemy that might annoy the fort, in case of rebellion or invasion." That they actually were burned during the siege of 1746 is evident from a statement in the *Glasgow Journal* of 31st March 1746: "Fort William. That place Governor Campbell has bravely defended; and to prevent the rebels sheltering themselves near the fort has caused burn the town of Maryburgh."

A description of the fort is given in the manuscript of a journey in Scotland, in the summer of 1787, by the Rev. James Bailey, Vicar of Otley, in Yorkshire, thus: "The plan is nearly the same as that of Fort Augustus: but it is somewhat larger. It is precisely of the same architecture, viz., of the age of William, from whom it derives its name and by whom it was, in part, erected. The four angular turrets are strong and handsome: and the masonry of the whole is substantial and well executed. The ditch is of formidable depth: and may be filled at pleasure from the waters of the Nevis, or emptied by sluices into the Lynne Loch. The Bridge is uniformly drawn up at ten in the evening (excepting when the Fort-Major is absent, whose return is always awaited) and a strict and regular sentry is unremittingly preserved. Within the quadrangle are wooden pent-houses which might occasionally serve as barracks, and I was told that, if necessary, a thousand or twelve hundred men might be accommodated here.

"The armoury is splendid, and is enriched with many curious specimens of ancient Scottish and Islandish armour; amongst which are said to be the swords of Banquho and of Fleance; as are also the two sceptres, fantastically carved; the stubborn vouchers of the Royal presence at Inverlochy."

"The neighbouring village of Maryburgh," he says, "does not contain more than an hundred inhabitants."

It was from Fort William that the final orders were issued for the massacre of Glen Coe in February 1692. A detachment of troops, under Lieutenant-Colonel Hamilton, set out for Glen Coe early on the morning of the massacre to assist in that gruesome deed, but the severe snowstorm which was raging prevented them arriving until the whole sorry business was over. The fort successfully resisted a siege by the Jacobites during both the Fifteen and the Forty-five. In 1715 General Gordon, who raised the clans in the west, attacked the fort with his full force of five thousand men, but failed to force its surrender. After this siege General Wade strengthened the structure, in 1719. A company of Prince Charlie's forces had it under siege in 1746 from 3rd March until 4th April, but failed to subdue it.

An unfortunate incident occurred at the fort after Culloden, when the Highlanders were surrendering their arms and swearing allegiance to the Crown. Three men from Glen Coe arrived at the fort one evening for this purpose, when there happened to be a jovial feast in progress owing to the absence of the Governor. The Deputy Governor had been dining well but not wisely, when the orderly entered the august presence and, announcing the arrival of the Glen Coe men, asked what he would do with them. "Oh, hang them," was the thoughtless retort of the officer. On rising, on the following morning, the officer was horrified to see three corpses hanging in the yard and to realize that his hasty answer on the previous evening had been obeyed literally.

It was to Fort William that James Stewart, "James of the Glen," was conveyed and imprisoned when he was arrested for having been accessory to the murder of Colin Campbell of Glenure, the Government factor, in Appin, in 1752. From Fort William, James was conveyed to Inveraray for trial, and after a verdict of "guilty" had been pronounced he was taken back to Fort William while preparations were made for his public execution. Finally, he was conveyed to the little hillock at the south side of Ballachulish Narrows, and hanged.

A local worthy who gave considerable trouble to the troops of the fort, by raiding the stores and munitions of their patrols, was Sergeant Mor Cameron, who had served in the French army and fought with the Jacobites in 1745, for which he was outlawed. He organized a band of outlaws and became the Robin Hood of the West Highlands. Of him, several interesting and amusing stories are told in Lochaber. He was ultimately betrayed by a farmer in Rannoch, in 1753, and charged with cattle theft and murder. Though he vehemently denied the latter charge he was executed and his body hanged in chains.

The fort continued to be garrisoned by troops of the regular army up till the beginning of the Crimean War in 1854. At the end of the war it was garrisoned by a part of the 71st Highlanders. The last to occupy it was a company of the Lancashire Militia. In 1864 the fort was dismantled, and the buildings sold to Mrs. Cameron Campbell of Monzie, Superior of the town, the barracks were made into dwelling-houses and the moat into gardens for the tenants. With the advent of the railway to Fort William, in 1894, the ground of the fort was purchased by the railway company, and the buildings, with the exception of one block, were demolished to make room for engine-sheds. The main gateway was taken from the fort and re-erected over the entrance to the local burial-ground, called "The Craigs," in 1896.

The block of buildings retained by the railway company was occupied by their employees until 1935, when it was condemned by the Local Authority as being unfit for habitation, and is now demolished. Part of this building was occupied by the governor of the fort in the olden days, and in one of its rooms Colonel Hill interviewed MacIain when he desired to take the oath of allegiance, and later drew up and signed the warrant for the massacre of Glen Coe. This room of grim memories was about eighteen feet square and panelled with native pine. In 1936 the panelling was removed, and presented by the railway company to the local West Highland Museum, where it has been utilized to panel one of the exhibit rooms. After being re-erected in this room the panelling was painted a bright green, which has evoked caustic criticism from many visitors, who complain that it has spoiled the historical atmosphere of the room. It is now, cynically, known as the "green-room." A notice in defence of the colour, however, hangs on the door, stating: "This room was painted in order to reconstruct as exactly as possible its original appearance when built (1707). The paint is the exact shade of the original paint found on the ground wood underneath many layers of paint and paper." One recent entry in the visitors' book, which must echo from the heart of many visitors, is: "If this was the original colour of the governor's room, I am not surprised that it led to a massacre."

Fort William was the first town in Britain to have its streets and dwellings lit by electricity produced solely by means of its own water-power. The streets were at first lit by oil-lamps, but about 1890 gas-lamps were introduced, the gasworks being situated between High Street and the site of the present railway station. The gas-lamps were removed in 1895 and, after about a year's interval, when the lighting went back to oil-lamps, were replaced by electric light, the streets being first lit by electricity on 22nd August 1896. Thus Fort William was an early pioneer of electricity for lighting, much earlier than important towns in the Lowlands. During my boyhood, in Lochaber, I used to be greatly surprised when on a visit to Glasgow to find many of the city shop-windows lit by comparatively dim gas-light, after being accustomed to the brilliant electric-lit shop-windows of Fort William. The electricity supply of Fort William was controlled by a private company until 1937, when it was taken over by the Town Council. In May 1947 control was transferred to the North of Scotland Hydro-Electric Board.

Northwards from the pier runs the main street; broad enough for the occasional carts, vans and coaches when it was constructed, but now rather narrow for the greatly increased traffic, caused principally by the modern highway from the Lowlands through Glen Coe and Fort William to Inverness. In Cameron Square, which widens off to the right, is the exceptionally interesting West Highland Museum, founded in 1922, and well worthy a more pretentious and permanent building. Here we can study at leisure many objects of Highland antiquarian interest, such as weapons of war, claymores, dirks, muskets, etc.—coins, maps, tartans and ancient domestic utensils like the *cruisie*, or early oil-lamp, the *cas chrom*, or foot-plough, and grinding querns, also fine specimens of the bird and animal life of the district. Also preserved in the museum are the "Visitors' Books" from the hotel which used to be on the summit of Ben Nevis. Lochaber being the heart of the Jacobite country, it is only natural that the museum should have a unique collection of relics relating to that romantic movement. Here are pay-notes as issued to the men of Prince Charlie's army, and the dies from which they were printed, also many interesting letters and other documents signed by the chief participants in the Jacobite risings. One very interesting exhibit is a secret mirror-portrait of Prince Charlie, which consists of a wooden plate painted with, apparently, meaningless daubs of various colours in crescent-shape. When the reflection is viewed in a vertical cylindrical polished steel mirror, that rests on the plate, a distinct portrait of Prince Charlie appears. It was used on the table, in the dark days after Culloden, when drinking a toast to "The King over the Water." Highlanders owe a deep debt of gratitude for the gathering together and preservation of these precious relics to the late Mr. Victor Hodgson, of Onich, the originator and enthusiastic supporter of the museum, of which he was elected Honorary Curator.

In the centre of Cameron Square is a monument to Dr. William Kennedy, the local physician, who died in 1851. It is worthy of note that Dr. Kennedy contracted the illness which caused his death—typhus —while attending the poverty-stricken family of the notorious "MacPhee the outlaw," who had his home, or rather his "stronghold," on an island in Loch Quoich. After several futile attempts, MacPhee was arrested by armed officers and imprisoned. His wife and family came to reside in Fort William, and owing to their extreme poverty they all lived in a single-apartment hovel in the poorest part of the town. Ultimately typhus developed among them and, being unable to help themselves, Dr. Kennedy treated and nursed them, even going the length of cleaning their hovel. Alas! his devotion was the cause of his death. He contracted their disease and died, like many medical men, a martyr to his profession.

A short distance beyond Cameron Square is an open space, laid out in grass plots, called "The Parade." It was on this stretch of ground that the troops of the fort paraded for muster, hence the name. Here, on that bitter early morning of snowstorm in 1692, the detachment of soldiers had roll-call before setting out for Glen Coe on their grim errand. The railway line, to the west, intersects the site of the fort. It was also on The Parade, on a winter's morning of December 1793, that the first men of the Cameron Highlanders, to the number of seven hundred and fifty, mustered for roll-call by "Old Archie Maclean," their first Adjutant. After being inspected and addressed by Sir Alan Cameron, of Errachd, who raised the regiment, they marched off from Lochaber, with Sir Alan at their head, the pipers leading, and playing the well-known march "*Gabhaidh sinn an rathad mor*" ("We will take the High Road").

Two monuments stand conspicuously on The Parade. One is a fine bronze statue, on a granite base, of Donald Cameron of Lochiel, twenty-fourth Chief of his clan, who died in 1905. The other is the local War Memorial of the Kaiser's war, a plain but potent reminder of the worthy part played in that grim conflict by the young men of Fort William. In that war no less than one hundred and twelve lads of this little town made the supreme sacrifice. Again, during Hitler's war, many sons of Fort William returned to Lochaber no more. In the words of Allan Ramsay it was:

> "Farewell to Lochaber, and farewell my Jean,
>   Where heartsome with thee I've mony a day been;
>   For Lochaber no more, Lochaber no more,
>   We'll maybe return to Lochaber no more.
>   These tears that I shed they are a' for my dear,
>   And no' for the dangers attending on weir,
>   Tho' borne on rough seas to a far bloody shore,
>   Maybe to return to Lochaber no more."

The wailing Highland lament of *Lochaber no More*
sounds so eerily on the pipes that it had to be forbidden
during the Peninsular War, on account of its depressing
effect on the spirits of the troops.

A few minutes' walk beyond The Parade, and on the
left-hand side of the road, is the old burial-ground,*
called The Craigs, which originated as a cemetery
for the troops of the fort. There are many old
stones in it, on which the inscription is indecipherable;
some of them probably never had an inscription.
The most conspicuous memorial is the monument
erected, in 1847, to the memory of Ewan MacLachlan,
Gaelic scholar and poet. The date of his birth is
given on the monument as 1775, though the record of
his baptism is dated 15th March 1773. Within The
Craigs also lies Donald MacBane, who was an active
participant in the battle of Mulroy, which is described
in Chapter VI, and whose account of the fight is the
main source of information. He became one of the
most famous swordsmen in Scotland. His tombstone
was broken many years ago and is now lost.

At the time of the Disruption, when the Free
Church congregations were refused sites on which to
build churches, the Fort William congregation at first
worshipped in The Craigs burial-ground, seated on
the graves of their kindred. Times had changed from
the olden days of *creach* and clan feud, and the Church
had a stronger grip on the people than the clan chiefs.
One minister, a Mr. Macrae from Kintail, when
assisting at a communion service in The Craigs, was
blunt enough to say in his address: "People of Lochaber, seed of the thieves and the murderers, you are
there sitting on the graves of your fathers, where their
bodies are rotting and their souls are roasting in hell."
This expression indicates the power that the ministers
had developed over the people since the clan chiefs lost

* The modern burial-ground of Fort William is in Glen Nevis.

authority, for if Mr. Macrae, or anyone else, had uttered these words in Lochaber in the heyday of the clan system a dozen dirks would have been buried in his body, there and then.

The arch at the entrance to The Craigs is of interest for three reasons. It formed the gateway to the fort in the days when it was garrisoned. As already mentioned, when the fort buildings were demolished by the railway company, this gateway was removed to its present situation. The gateway is also of interest as it spans the old General Wade road from Fort William to Fort Augustus, which passed through the centre of the burial-ground. This road is one of the five genuine Wade roads in Scotland.* Many old roads in the Highlands are described as "Wade" roads, but though to him the drafting of the greater part of the system of roads throughout the Highlands may be ascribed, he, personally, superintended the construction of only five main roads, the remainder of his idea being carried out by others. Again, the gateway at The Craigs is of interest as it was here that the first men of the Cameron Highlanders, the 79th, were sworn in, when Alan (later, Sir Alan) Cameron of Errachd raised the regiment in 1793.† During his fifteen years' connection with the 79th, Sir Alan took a

---

* (1) Fort William to Fort Augustus. (2) Fort Augustus to Inverness. (3) Inverness to Dunkeld. (4) Crieff to Dalnacardoch. (5) Dalwhinnie to Fort Augustus. Vide *Wade in Scotland*, by J. B. Salmond.

† Succeeding to the number of a regiment that had been disbanded some nine years before, the regiment came into being as the 79th. In the Army Lists for 1794 to 1804 the 79th is styled the "Cameronian Volunteers"; 1805 to 1806, the "Cameronian Highlanders." In the List for 1807 the designation "Cameron Highlanders" first appears, and in 1873 it is gazetted "The Queen's Own Cameron Highlanders." It was certainly a mistake, probably an English one, applying the name "Cameronian" to the 79th. This name has always been applied to the Lowland regiment, the 26th, or Scottish Rifles, raised in 1689 from amnestied survivors of those who had followed Richard Cameron, the famous Lowland Covenanter. The 26th were the enemies of the House of Stuart, while the Clan Cameron were its staunch supporters.

fatherly interest in his men, and was familiarly called
by them "Old *Cia mar th'a thu*?" ("How are you?"),
a question he was constantly putting to them in Gaelic
as he asked after their welfare. The regiment has
a record of military service of which it may well
be proud. Toulouse, Peninsula, Waterloo, Alma,
Sebastopol, Lucknow, Ashanti, Tel-el-Kebir and the
Great War are but a few of the names on its Roll of
Honour. The Cameron Highlanders were again to
the fore on the various fronts of Hitler's war. In *The
Eve of Waterloo* Byron has written:

"And wild and high the 'Cameron's Gathering' rose!
  The war-note of Lochiel, which Albyn's hills
  Have heard—and heard, too, have her Saxon foes:—
  How, in the noon of night, that pibroch thrills,
  Savage and shrill! But with the breath which fills
  Their mountain-pipe, so fill the mountaineers
  With the fierce native daring, which instils
  The stirring memory of a thousand years;
  And Ewan's, Donald's fame, rings in each clansman's ears!"

His Majesty King George VI is Colonel-in-Chief of
the Cameron Highlanders.

The tartan of the Cameron Highlanders is a combination of the Cameron and MacDonald tartans.
The reason for it being so is that, when the regiment
was raised, the Chief of the MacDonells of Keppoch
gave liberal assistance and recruited many of his clan
for service. It is usually stated that both Sir Alan
and Keppoch agreed that neither the reddish tartan
of the Clan Cameron nor the reddish tartan of the
MacDonells of Keppoch was a suitable contrast to the
regulation scarlet tunic; that Mrs. Cameron, Errachd's
mother, and sister of Keppoch of Culloden, solved the
problem by suggesting that they should utilize the clan
tartan of the MacDonalds (of whom the MacDonells
are a branch), which has a dark green background, and
superimpose upon it the yellow lines of the Cameron

THE OLD FORT, FORT WILLIAM

[To face page 64

BEN NEVIS, FROM GLEN NEVIS

(Showing the track up the Ben)

tartan, thus achieving a suitable colour combination with both Errachd and Keppoch represented in the tartan. A lesser known reason for the uniform kilt of the Cameron Highlanders not being of Cameron tartan is that from 1792 until 1795 (the regiment was raised in 1793) Errachd and Lochiel were at loggerheads owing to their bitter dispute in the Law Courts. Lochiel had accused Errachd of attempting to obtain actual possession, instead of a lease, of the farm lands of Errachd by illegal means, which Errachd denied. The verdict of the courts was given in favour of Lochiel. Thus Alan neither sought nor received assistance from Lochiel when recruiting. He may therefore have wished to have a tartan of his own design for the regiment, as it was an exceptional step to pass over the clan tartan for a regiment bearing the title, "Cameron Highlanders." The tartan designed for the regiment has become known as the "Errachd Cameron" tartan, though, like the tartan of the Black Watch, or "Forty-second," it is a regimental rather than a clan tartan. Therefore, the only persons legally entitled to wear it are members of the Cameron Highlanders, irrespective of what name they bear. This tartan is not the prerogative of Cameron clansmen.

Within The Craigs, to the left of the gateway, is a rock from the shelter of which Jacobite guns fired on the fort during its siege of 1746.

On the opposite side of the road from The Craigs is the Victoria Park, where the sporting events of Fort William have been held for many years, though for several years after the fort was demolished, in 1864, the Lochaber sports were held within its quadrangle. Until 1936 the surface of the Victoria Park was rather uneven, just as nature had made it, but during the winter of 1936 extensive alterations were carried out, and it is now as level as any professional sports ground.

The principal event of the year in the Victoria Park

E

is the well-known Lochaber Gathering—locally called "The Games"—which is held in August, and at which almost every eminent Scottish athlete, piper and Highland dancer has competed at some time. The Lochaber Gathering still retains a strong local element, thus preserving the true spirit and function of Highland Sports Gatherings, and the banning of all side-shows from the grounds of Victoria Park is an action to be commended. Some of the most widely advertised Highland sports meetings debase the name and spirit of Highland gatherings by paying little heed to local talent, but relying on the big "pot-hunters" and absurd gaudy displays to attract large crowds of spectators, mostly English and foreign, and many of whom don't know the difference between a caber and a clarsach.

A short distance beyond the Victoria Park the road forks, one part leading onwards into Glen Nevis by the south bank of the River Nevis, while the main road bends northwards across the new red granite bridge which spans the deep cutting of the river. The old bridge is also in use, but traffic has been diverted from it to the new bridge, which is stronger and avoids a nasty S-bend in the road on the north side, where frequent accidents occurred in the past. The old Nevis Bridge is usually described as a Wade bridge, but J. B. Salmond, an authority on Wade roads, says: "From High Bridge, Wade took a straight line to Fort William. His road crosses the present road about two miles from the fort, and then comes in by the present bridge over the Nevis. Wade may have had a bridge here, but of it there is no record."

Immediately we cross the Nevis Bridge a rough country road branches off to the right along the tree-clad north bank of the river, and leads for about a mile to Achintee farm, at the foot of Ben Nevis, where the track up the Ben commences.

Naturally, Ben Nevis is the most conspicuous and renowned feature of Lochaber. Monarch of British mountains, it rises in a massive pile to a height of four thousand four hundred and six feet above sea-level, but it is not easy to comprehend its height owing to the considerable height of its close neighbours. It really consists of two mountains, one rising above the other. The lower portion is a bulky mass which rises in one vast sweep from almost sea-level to a height of two thousand three hundred feet, and is called Meall an t' Suidhe, pronounced *Melantee*, and meaning "the hill of rest." Ben Nevis proper rises from the rear of Meall an t' Suidhe in another huge mass, with a blunt rounded summit. It was only in 1870 that Ben Nevis was surveyed and declared to be the highest mountain in Britain.

Ben Nevis has not the dramatic appearance of the sharp-peaked Alps or even the Coolin of Skye, but its massive bulk, its rounded contours and its wide-flowing skirts give it a venerable appearance, like an aged law lord sitting in judgment. This comparison is even more pronounced when the Ben is clad in the regal colours of autumn and the early snows have draped his broad shoulders in an ermine cape. The steep western slopes of the mountain—the most conspicuous side—appear more or less smooth and rounded, but on its north-eastern face vast precipices, with an average height of one thousand five hundred feet, extend for about two miles, where there is always snow in the crevices. The best view of Ben Nevis, and the one showing the precipices to advantage, is from upper Banavie, about two miles to the north-west, though the whole Ben Nevis *massif*, or group of mountains, is best seen from the high moorland road above Spean Bridge, from which point the various ridges and peaks appear converging towards an imaginary apex. The photograph facing page 128 was taken from this viewpoint.

On it, Ben Nevis is the long, dark ridge on the right.

There is considerable divergence of opinion regarding the derivation of the name Ben Nevis, each suggestion having its own merits. Perhaps the most appropriate one is that of Dr. Alexander MacBain, author of the *Gaelic Etymological Dictionary*. He adopts the form *Neibheis*, the root of which, *neb* or *nebh*, he associates with clouds and water. The "cloudy mountain" is a very appropriate name for Ben Nevis, as its summit is seldom free of clouds. Professor Rhys also refers to the root in a somewhat similar manner as "cloudy."

Alas, the vandal hand of man has scarred the most conspicuous and most imposing side of Ben Nevis in a hideous and, apparently, permanent manner. In 1934 the British Aluminium Company, which has a factory at Kinlochleven, completed a vast scheme for utilizing the waters of Loch Treig to generate electricity at a Hydro-Electric Station near Fort William. They bored a tunnel, fifteen feet in diameter, along the skirts and beneath the surface of the Ben Nevis group of mountains for about fifteen miles, through which they have led the waters of the loch to Fort William, the longest tunnel in the world. They did not bore through the centre of the mountain group *from one side to the other*, as one is liable to infer from the dramatic descriptions of the scheme given in the Press. The undertaking was commendable, and merits credit, except for the position chosen for the exit of the tunnel at the Fort William end. It has been taken out through the most conspicuous and most imposing side of Ben Nevis at a height which makes it conspicuously visible for many miles around. From this exit huge pipe-lines have been led down the mountain-side to the power-house and aluminium factory erected at the foot. Thus has been committed one of the most flagrant acts of vandalism in Britain. Of all the mountains and hills in Britain why choose the monarch of them all to deface? If it was absolutely necessary that the Ben Nevis group of mountains should serve this purpose, surely the pipe-lines could have been led down before reaching the Ben, such as down the slopes of Carn Mor Dearg. If engineering requirements necessitated the downfall of water being in its present position, the company should have been compelled to carry it down *underground* to near the base of the mountain. Naturally, this method would have added to the expense of the scheme, but it would have been well worth the cost, and would have made the company realize that the district has an æsthetic value as well as a commercial value. Now that the pipes have been laid in their exposed position, surely they could be camouflaged by coating them with some colour which would blend with the mountain-side. The factory at the foot of the Ben —though, no doubt, built to fulfil engineering require-ments suitably—is like a heap of pots and pans in front of a Rembrandt. Thirdly, the outflow from the factory has been led in an open channel near to the venerable ruins of Inverlochy Castle, where it tends to shatter the romantic atmosphere of this historic site. Though the onward march of the world's progress will never be stayed by sentimental considerations, due regard should be paid to rural scenery when encroached upon by engineering undertakings.

The climb up Ben Nevis by the rough track is more a test of endurance than a difficult climb, and can be attempted with every hope of success by any ordinary healthy person, provided they go shod properly: this climb will make short work of light or shoddy footwear. One requires stout boots or shoes, well shod with "tackets" or "sparables." The average time taken from Achintee to the summit is three and a half hours and about two and a half hours for the descent. The record for the *double* journey, however, starting and finishing at Fort William post office, was, for many years, two hours, ten minutes, nineteen seconds!— set up in 1903 by Ewan MacKenzie, of Achintore, a roadman employed at the old Observatory. The distance he covered was about fourteen miles, with a rise and descent of over four thousand four hundred feet. Until the closing of the Observatory, in 1904, foot-racing up Ben Nevis was conducted annually, the competitors being mainly local men. After that time the race was abandoned, until 1937, when it was revived. The race is now open to all comers, and in 1939 D. Mulholland, a stranger to the district, astonished everyone by breaking MacKenzie's record and setting up the present record from the post office of two hours, three minutes, forty-three seconds for the double journey.

During the summer of 1911 a Ford motor-car was driven up and down the Ben Nevis track, the first motor-car to do so, and no mean feat when one considers the rough and narrow nature of the route.

The best record of all, however, is surely that of Mr. Clement Wragge, an English scientist, who climbed Ben Nevis *every day* during the summers of two successive years (1881 and 1882) for the purpose of taking observations. His scorn of bad weather earned him the nickname of "Inclement Wragge," and what makes his feat even more worthy is that there was no track up the Ben at that time. It was mainly as a result of Wragge's work that the Observatory was built.

The track up the Ben was constructed by the Directors of the Observatory in 1883, and commences at Achintee farm in Glen Nevis, but there is a second route, though no track, up the north-west slopes of Meall an t' Suidhe, behind the Ben Nevis Distillery. The gradient is not steep but it is a rough scramble. This route is the best one for viewing the great northern precipices, where snow lies in the rock crevices usually

all the year round.   In order to obtain a close view of
these precipices a short climb should be made into the
corrie called Allt a' Mhuilinn.   The grandeur of the
scene will amply repay the exertion expended.   This
western route up the Ben joins the track from Achintee
at the lochan which lies in the hollow between Meall
an t' Suidhe and the Ben.   By the eastern shore of this
lochan, called Lochan t' Suidhe (pronounced *Lochantee*),
there are several peculiar marks sunk into the rock
surface strongly resembling the hoof-marks of a large
horse: perhaps there is, or was, a water-horse here!

A short climb above where the two routes unite at
the lochan there used to be the half-way hut, where
observations were taken when the Observatory was in
service.   Here, also, the toll of one shilling was collected
for the pleasure of climbing Ben Nevis.   As receipt, the
climber received a ticket, which was not considered
complete until he had reached the summit and visited
the hotel for the purpose of having his ticket stamped
"Ben Nevis Summit" and the date.   There is now no
trace left of the half-way hut.

As we proceed, the track becomes very rough,
resembling in many parts a dried-up river-bed rather
than a road.   Even this comparison is not sufficient,
for a river-bed has rounded gravel and boulders,
whereas here they are angular and sharp.   Vegetation
gradually dies out and the ascent becomes steeper, the
track mounting in sharp zigzag gradients, some of
which are as steep as one in five.   We feel the air
becoming appreciably sharper, until on reaching the
wind-swept and boulder-strewn summit there is almost
certain to be a widespread coating, or large patches, of
snow, even if a summer sun is scorching down on the
low ground.   Minute lichen are the nearest approach
to plant life here.

There is always a certain amount of satisfaction in
having reached the highest point of one's country,

though one may be only a "wender" up the track that is disdained by the "ascenders" and "suspenders." These latter adventurers will find plenty of corries, precipices and chimneys off the beaten track to test their skill. Indeed, several mountaineers have lost their lives while climbing on Ben Nevis. The only real danger to those who keep to the track is the descending of thick mist, which sometimes comes down very suddenly. As evidence of the severe conditions which occur on Ben Nevis, even during the mountaineering seasons, Frank S. Smyth, the famous Everest climber, says in his book, *The Spirit of the Hills*: "I have crawled on hands and knees over the ice-bound plateau of Ben Nevis in the teeth of a snow-laden hurricane worthy of Everest at its worst."

If the atmosphere is clear, one is amply rewarded for the exertion of the climb by the very extensive panorama of scenery stretching to a far horizon in every direction from the summit. It is like looking down on a very large relief-map, the most striking feature being the amazing number of mountain peaks in the scenery. In 1927 an indicator was erected on the summit, by the Scottish Mountaineering Club, which assists the climber to identify the numerous peaks, lochs, and islands. Old Observatory records state that one day out of six is clear on the summit, and that April is usually the best month.

On the north-eastern face of the Ben there is a magnificent precipice with a vertical rise of about one thousand eight hundred feet. There used to be a rough wooden platform, with guard-rails, projecting a few feet over the precipice, from which one could obtain a genuine thrill when viewing this awful depth, especially when mist-wreaths swirled in the up-draught like serpents in agony. Like the half-way hut, the last trace of this platform disappeared many years ago. It was erected by the observers for throwing out their rubbish, and the chasm it overhung was, in consequence, named "Gardy-loo Gully."

On the summit of Ben Nevis a Meteorological Observatory was built by public subscription, and officially opened by Mrs. Cameron Campbell of Monzie, the then proprietrix of the mountain, on 17th October 1883. It was connected first by telegraph, and afterwards by telephone, with the post office at Fort William, and also with the low-level Observatory there. The Observatory remained in service, supplying valuable meteorological observations, until October 1904, when it was closed down owing to lack of financial support.

The hotel, or hostelry (really a large wooden hut), on the summit was open from June till September, and had accommodation for about a dozen guests. Meals were supplied to climbers at charges much above the average, but reasonable when the difficulty of obtaining supplies is considered. It remained in service until the end of the summer of 1915, when the young men and women of Britain had parts to play more grim than mountain-climbing.

The geological history of Ben Nevis is very interesting, and should appeal to all open-air enthusiasts, as geology is really the science of scenery and can be told in outline in simple language. The rocks of which the mountain is composed were formed during the Old Red Sandstone Period, which has been already mentioned in connection with the Moor of Rannoch and Glen Coe. Though Ben Nevis, as we know it, was never a volcano, the great majority of its rocks have solidified from a molten condition. The mountain and its spurs consist of three well-defined concentric zones:

First: An outer discontinuous ring of granite, which includes the whole of Meall an t' Suidhe, the lower western slopes of Carn Mor Dearg, and curves round to the north-east to include Aonach Mor.

Second: An inner continuous ring of granite, of later date and finer texture than the outer ring, which includes Carn Mor Dearg (excepting its lower western slopes), and forms the skirts of the Ben in upper Glen Nevis, including southern Carn Dearg. The dividing line between it and the older granite passes a short distance to the east of Lochan t' Suidhe.

Third: A central cap of about two thousand feet of andesite lavas and volcanic breccias, which form Ben Nevis proper—that is, the portion from the level of about where the half-way hut used to be to the summit, including western Carn Dearg. The great precipices are in the lavas, especially where the heart has been eroded away facing north-east. These lavas do not rest on the granite, but on a thin layer of conglomerate and shale overlying an unknown thickness of crystalline schists.

As was mentioned in the description of the Moor of Rannoch, granite is a *plutonic* rock, which means that it solidified deep underground. Lava is a *volcanic* rock, which means that it solidified at the earth's surface. These facts are apparent from the size of the crystals composing granite and lava: the larger the crystals the longer was the process of cooling which allowed them to grow, and vice versa.

At the time the rocks which form Ben Nevis came into existence, the surface of Scotland was a vast plateau, which in Lochaber must have been higher than the present summit of Ben Nevis, and the surface rocks here were of schist.

Owing to enormous pressure from beneath, vents, probably fissures, developed in the earth's crust in this region. Through these vents, large flows of lava were ejected and spread over the landscape, forming a deep and widespread covering. About the same time as the lavas were erupted, immense masses of granite were intruded into the under side of the earth's crustal rocks and solidified there, deep beneath the surface. This intrusion of granite now forms the outer, discontinuous zone of Ben Nevis.

Some time after the granite had solidified a large central block of it subsided into the molten mass, or *magma*, beneath, and the resulting cauldron was filled by a second intrusion of granite. This second intrusion granite now forms the inner, continuous zone of Ben Nevis. During this second intrusion of granite many volcanic veins, or *dykes*, were injected into the outer granite.

Before the inner, or second, intrusion granite had time to solidify, the roof of schist and its load of lavas over this cauldron sank down into the liquid granite, buckling into basin-form with the dip inwards. It is estimated that this block of schists and lavas must have dropped over one thousand five hundred feet.

Gradually, the inner granite solidified underground, while on the surface of the landscape the denuding agents of nature—rain, frost, ice and wind—proceeded with their work of erosion. So great has been the erosion since Old Red Sandstone times that all the surface rocks of lava and schist have been stripped off, and the granite, which was formed deep underground, is now exposed at the surface. But the block of surface schists and the lavas resting on it, which subsided into the granite, now project upwards from the granite like a huge nodule, as the core of Ben Nevis, and form its highest part, the result of differentiated weathering. This block of lavas, which forms the upper half of Ben Nevis (from about the site of the old half-way hut to the summit), and the mountains of Glen Coe (which also owe their preservation to subsidence) are the only surviving parts of the once widespread covering of lavas.

During the time of the Pleistocene Ice Age (about two or three million years ago), this region, which was more or less like its present configuration, was covered

by a huge ice-sheet, which advanced towards the
Atlantic in a south-westerly direction. The striation
of the rocks in Lochaber by the ice, which is still clearly
visible in many parts, indicates the direction of the
flow.

Even an elementary knowledge of geology adds
greatly to the pleasure of exploring scenery, as, mentally,
we try to unravel the methods by which nature has
formed the various configurations of the landscape. In
a district like Lochaber it adds an appropriate background for the stirring tales of human interest.

CHAPTER IV

GLEN NEVIS AND INVERLOCHY

WITHIN a mile of Fort William is the entrance to one of the finest glens in the Highlands, namely, Glen Nevis. It presents a remarkable variety of scenery, ranging from sylvan glade and farm-land to rugged gorge and pine-clad rocky eminence, and throughout its length the crystal-clear waters of the River Nevis rush along their rocky bed, churning around boulders and dashing over cataracts on their way to the sea. Fortunately, this glen has not yet been marred by the imprint of a mechanical age, with the exception of the original winding road being macadamized for about five miles. Otherwise the glen is as nature made it—long may it remain so. The ubiquitous motor-car does, of course, traverse this road, but though one may *see* from a motor-car, one cannot *feel* the true spirit of scenery. The glen, with its hills and recesses, its woodlands and scenes of stirring memories, requires to be explored on foot and at leisure in order to be appreciated fully. It winds for about seven miles into the heart of rugged mountains, commencing in a wide, but steep-sided valley and narrowing gradually until it forms a wild ravine. Where the road fades out at the head of the glen, a bridle-track continues high along the mountain-side and through a deep gorge for about another three miles.

The whole northern side of the glen is bounded by the massive slopes of Ben Nevis, while on its southern side are the high and lonely ranges of Mamore Forest. Along the river banks and on the lower slopes of the mountains are many fine birch woods and conspicuous clumps of old Scots pine. Throughout its length we rove in close contact with scenes that etch themselves on the mind, and many of which have very interesting human associations. For centuries it was inhabited by a branch of Clan Cameron, but these Glen Nevis Camerons are now non-existent in the glen. Miss Macgregor, Secretary of the West Highland Museum, Fort William, herself a descendant of this family, informs me, however, that they are by no means extinct and that there are still alive a number of descendants of the last chief, though now widely scattered from their ancestral home.

In olden times, Glen Nevis, with its fine streams of crystal-clear water dashing down the hill-sides and its secluded recesses with clumps of thicket, provided excellent sites for the illicit distilling of whisky, or *uisge beatha* ("water of life") in the *poit dubh* ("black pot") of private stills. It was really a staple commodity in the Highlands at one time, and, as many a crofter could pay his rent only by the profits from his still, landlords were inclined to turn a blind eye to this illegal occupation. That this unlawful branch of "The Trade" is not just a thing of the distant past in the Highlands became apparent when as recently as 1936 a private still in Glen Nevis was raided by police and excise officers. It was found in full working order, with the "distiller" in attendance. He was arrested and fined heavily for the offence.

Very often the brew from the old private stills was real rank stuff. An old Lochaber man when recalling his first dram from one of them remarked: "Man, yon was the stuff, when it touched my throat I thought I was shot."

Setting out from Fort William we enter Glen Nevis by the road which branches off from the main highway before the latter crosses the Nevis Bridge, and leads along the south bank of the river. The entrance is through an avenue of tall larch, birch and oak, whose widespread branches form a delightfully cool, leafy canopy during the heat of summer. Down on the left-hand side the River Nevis churns and gurgles, between its foliage-clad banks, on its winding course to Loch Linnhe.

Soon after entering the glen we come to a wide, deep pool in the river, at the foot of a low but voluminous waterfall, called the Roaring Mill, where, in the limpid water, the speckled trout dart about, their colour blending so closely with the spotted gravel and rock that only by their movements are they revealed.

Beyond the Roaring Mill there is a large boulder by the roadside, called *Clach Shomhairle* ("Samuel's Stone"), which, tradition says, turns round on its axis three times on a certain day each year, and anyone who finds it on the move will receive a correct answer to any three questions he may ask. On the opposite side of the river from Clach Shomhairle is Achintee farm, where the track up Ben Nevis commences. At this part the glen widens, rising in broad curves, with the fir and heather slopes of the Cow Hill on the right and the grassy, boulder-strewn skirts of Meall an t' Suidhe sweeping upwards on the left. Far up on these slopes white specks indicate the mountain sheep nibbling the short grass.

Onwards from Clach Shomhairle the road leads through mossy ground to the farm-lands of Glen Nevis House. Up on a mound, to the south of the road, is a little burial-ground, called *Tom-eas-an-t-slinnean* ("knoll of the waterfall of the shoulder"), overshadowed by tall beeches and elms, where lie the old Camerons of Glen Nevis, who bore the patronymic of MacSorlie ("Son of Samuel"). In a corner of this burial-ground, and almost hidden among the nettles, there used to be an old iron coffin, or mort-safe, a relic of the days of the body-snatchers, who were liable to break open anything less vulnerable than iron in their gruesome business. It is now preserved in the West Highland Museum in Fort William. Behind the graveyard a hill track leads up the slopes of Ben Riabhach (or Ben Riach) through rich larch plantations, and continues round the back of the Cow Hill to join the Lundavra road above Fort William. It is well worth climbing for the sake of the splendid views it presents of Meall an t' Suidhe and Ben Nevis, and also of Glen Nevis. The tremendous masses of these mountains are impressed upon the observer from Ben Riabhach much more strongly than from any other viewpoint.

When traversing the lower part of Glen Nevis the most conspicuous feature is the shining silver-grey quartz and schist peak of Sgor a Mhaim (3,601 feet), which, together with Stob Ban, rises straight ahead. Sgor a Mhaim is a conspicuous object from parts of Lochaber far from Glen Nevis, and its whitish summit is sometimes, erroneously, assumed to be due to a coating of snow.

Through a fine avenue of beech and sycamore by the river-side we come to Glen Nevis House, standing in a small plantation of tall beech-trees. It was here that Lochiel and Keppoch made their headquarters when they laid siege to the fort at Fort William in 1746. The house is reputed to be haunted by a little old woman in grey, but who she is no one knows. Though it was in existence at the time of the Forty-five, this house is not regarded as the home of the MacSorlie chiefs. They are believed to have lived in a house which stood upon a little knoll called Dun Dige ("the moat hillock"), a few hundred yards farther up the glen, and now clad with a small grove of beech-trees.

When the Government troops were scourging the Highlands, after Culloden, Lochaber being inhabited by staunch Jacobites felt the full brunt of the punish-

THE ROAD INTO GLEN NEVIS

[To face page 80

GLEN NEVIS

ment. On one occasion word was conveyed to Mrs. Cameron, of Glen Nevis House, that a band of soldiers were in the neighbourhood wreaking vengeance, and were likely to visit her home. She had the presence of mind to gather all the silverplate, china, and other valuables in the house and, having wrapped them carefully, had them buried deeply outside the garden wall. She then betook herself, her children and a few personal maids to a spacious cave far up the glen. Naturally the soldiers were greatly chagrined when they found the house stripped of its valuables, and took revenge by burning and plundering throughout the glen. Somehow, they located Mrs. Cameron's place of refuge, and threatened her with dire punishment if she did not disclose the whereabouts of the valuables, but she refused absolutely to tell them and, baffled, they had to leave her. On leaving the cave, one of the soldiers noticed that she had something bulky underneath her plaid which she guarded carefully. Thinking that it might be some silverware, or other valuable, he caught hold of her and slit open her plaid with his knife, but instead of material treasure the rent plaid revealed her infant son, a few months old. Taking her plaid and a silver brooch as trophies, the soldiers at last departed. The knife-thrust of the soldier had wounded the child slightly in the neck, but he recovered all right and ultimately became laird of Glen Nevis, though he bore the scar of the wound till his dying day. Naturally, after peace had been restored in the Highlands, the buried valuables were dug up and found to be none the worse for their temporary interment. This version of the story is as related by Dr. Stewart, in *Nether Lochaber*, but a more prosaic, and probably more correct, account appears in the *Lyon in Mourning*, volume one, thus : "Mrs. Archibald Cameron communicated to Bishop Forbes a lamentable story of how her sister, Glennevis's wife, was stripped by Cumberland's men, under

F

Caroline Scott, and only permitted to keep a single petticoat. Her little son's gold buttons and gold lace were cut off his coat, and the child was wounded by the knife."

A short distance further back from the road than Dun Dige there is a glacial boulder called Clach an Turraman, which, it is said, used to be so delicately balanced that a gentle push would set it rocking. Alas, it either rocked too far on one occasion, or else its bearings have become worn, for it no longer moves. The last time I visited it I found a decayed wooden log projecting from its base, which seemed to have been used as a lever by someone who was determined to test the boulder's rocking powers.

A short distance into the glen beyond Clach an Turraman there is a little green eminence called the Hillock of Evil Counsel. Until the timber shortage of Hitler's war, it was clad with a fine grove of Scots pine. This hillock derives its name from the following event. During the time of the clan feuds, a MacSorlie chief wished to make peace with his old enemies, the Clan Chattan, and invited some of its senior members to a meeting in his home in Glen Nevis, to discuss the situation. His action was not approved by many of his clansmen, but they had to obey their Chief. The meeting duly took place and lasted the greater part of the day. It was quite successful, conditions being agreed upon by both parties, and when the time came to bid adieu to the guests in the evening MacSorlie called upon his piper to give them a "send-off" tune on his pipes. The piper, however, gave vent to his indignation at entertaining the men of Clan Chattan by playing the war pibroch of Clan Cameron, *Come Hither, Children of the Dogs, and You'll Get Flesh*. No apology of the Chief could wipe out this insult, and the members of Clan Chattan left the house vowing vengeance. On reaching the hillock mentioned above, they halted and took counsel, deciding to take revenge that very night. Marching slowly up the glen, as if making for home, they proceeded until darkness hid them from view, when they halted. At midnight they returned stealthily to the habitations of the Mac-Sorlies, who, though they may have expected revenge, thought the Clan Chattan men would return home and summon their fellow-clansmen before doing so. Falling upon the sleeping inmates of Glen Nevis, the men of Clan Chattan spared neither man, woman, nor child, and finally set fire to the houses. MacSorlie, the Chief, was one of the first to be killed, but one of his clansmen grasped Iain, the infant heir, and some of the family heirlooms, including a silver spoon, and fled with them up the glen to a cave. Here he made his home, and tended the infant carefully for some time, living on game which he trapped. He kept his whereabouts a secret, but his wife, who had believed him killed in the massacre, traced him ultimately to the cave by following her dog, which visited the cave regularly. On being discovered, the clansman fled north with his charge to a part of the Highlands where he was not known, lest the Clan Chattan men should attempt to trace the infant heir. There, he brought up young MacSorlie until he was a sturdy boy. When he deemed the boy able to assume his rightful heritage he took him back to Lochaber. Disguising himself as a beggar, he called at the house of Inverlair, where resided the sister of the murdered Chief, and asked for food for Iain. Being given a bowl of porridge, he, to the amazement of the lady of the house, proceeded to feed the boy with a silver spoon. On coming closer, the lady recognized the heirloom spoon and saw the resemblance in the boy to her dead brother. Upon the clansman relating his story, and producing other items of identity, she gladly accepted the boy as her nephew and had him educated to the best of her ability. When Iain reached the age of seventeen the whole story was told to him, and he was readily accepted by the clansmen as the rightful laird of Glen Nevis. Remembering that the perpetrators of the massacre were members of Clan Chattan, no further chief of the MacSorlies would allow a cat in his house.

Beyond the Hill of Evil Counsel the beeches and pines give way to a more open region of deer-grass and heather, and about half a mile further on a conspicuous rounded green hill rises fairly steep on the right-hand side of the road to a height of about one thousand feet, called Dun Dearduil. There are really two somewhat similar hills here: Dun Dearduil is the first one on our way. On its summit are the remains of a vitrified fort, one of those structures which has puzzled archæologists for many years. Parts of the fort uncovered by turf show the vitrification clearly. The name of this hill fort in Glen Nevis recalls Deirdre, the tragic beauty of Celtic tradition, as Dearduil is an alternative way of spelling her name, though the spelling of the name of the hill has been disputed. Some authorities claim that the name does not refer to Deirdre, but should be spelt *Dun dearg suil* ("hill of the red eye"), meaning that it was once a beacon hill from which messages were signalled along the glen in times of trouble.

A mile or two beyond Dun Dearduil, the glen, and consequently the road, bends round towards the north-east, where the few houses stand that constitute the settlement of Achriach. Here, the road crosses the Nevis by a light wooden bridge, where the river is confined in a narrow gorge, through which it rushes and plunges over a waterfall, called the Lower Falls of Nevis, into a seething cauldron below. Near Achriach there is a rude little burial-ground on the hill-side called Achnacon ("the field of the dogs"), which is seldom visited.

After crossing the bridge, the road becomes very rough and the scenery grim and rugged. The glen narrows considerably, though still towering high on either side, making one feel dwarfed by the immensity of the mountain barriers and the solemnity of the *atmosphere*. The road climbs along the steep side of the ben, and the river is lost to view far down in its tree-fringed channel. Here, we are surrounded by solitude and natural grandeur which our elevated position enables us to appreciate fully.

On this rugged road, not far from Achriach, one of the Glen Nevis chiefs is said to have been murdered during the early part of the seventeenth century by a dwarf of evil repute, called Iain Beag MacAindrea, while drinking from his wooden *cuaich*. The dwarf, who was an expert archer, had a grudge against the Chief for some imaginary suffering. Lying in wait for him, he shot an arrow which transfixed the head of the Chief and the cup, and then made good his escape.

When the friends of the murdered Chief saw how accurately the arrow had been shot their suspicions at once fell on the celebrated archer, though none of them had ever seen him, but they knew him by repute. They set off immediately for his home, seeking vengeance. MacAindrea was sitting at the fireside when the angered clansmen forced their way into the house, but with shrewd presence of mind his wife made use of his very diminutive size by telling him to go out and fetch his father. Thus the MacSorlies in their innocence allowed the dwarf to escape, but he did not allow them to escape. Climbing a tree near the door of his house, he shouted to the MacSorlies that Iain, his father, was waiting for them outside. As they rushed from the doorway he shot them one at a time with his arrows. Though Iain's home was in Strath Spey, he was a frequent visitor to Lochaber, and there are several tales in the local traditions about him. It was said that "a fox is an idiot compared to MacAindrea."

MacIain, in his *Clans of the Scottish Highlands*, gives a
different version of this story. He says that the archer
was a MacLachlan, who had a quarrel with the Chief
of Glen Nevis, and that the incident occurred in Glen
Nevis when the Chief was drinking milk from a coggie
at a fold where the maids were milking the cows.

About a mile beyond Achriach, but on the hill-face
on the opposite side of the glen from the track, there
is a spacious cave with an eerie reputation. It is
called Uamh Shomhairle ("Samuel's Cave"), and is
the cave to which the clansman carried the heir of Glen
Nevis on the night of the massacre by the men of Clan
Chattan. It was also in this cave that Mrs. Cameron,
of Glen Nevis House, hid after burying her valuables
in 1746. At this part of Glen Nevis it is difficult to
realize that one is within a few miles of a town, everything seems so wild and elemental. The scene—of huge
boulders, heaps of coarse gravel, clumps of heather,
scattered pine and birch clinging to the misty mountain-
sides, and crystal cataracts dashing down the rocky
fissures—wafts one's thoughts far from the fume and
fret of an industrial civilization.

Where the rough road fades out high on the hill-side,
near the head of the glen, a narrow bridle-track
continues along the steep slopes, hundreds of feet above
the river-bed, and turns abruptly southwards through
a grim gorge, where the cliffs on either side rise close
together and soar sheer high overhead. A false step
on this track would mean a sudden end on the boulder-
strewn bed of the river far below. From this elevated
situation there is a thrilling view as we look backwards
down into the rugged mountain ravine. At the
southern end of the gorge the track dips down to a
fragile rope-bridge across the river, leading into a huge
amphitheatre of mountains, towering to the sky around
a grassy plain through which wind the swift waters
of the Nevis.

About a mile beyond the rope-bridge we come to the foot of *An Steall* ("the waterfall"), or the Upper Falls of Nevis, where a beautiful cascade falls like a bridal veil over a sheer rock-face from a *hanging valley*, about five hundred feet above the grassy flat in the bosom of Glen Nevis. A lone shepherd's hut, near to the waterfall, serves but to emphasize the solitude and impressiveness of this scene. In winter-time this lonely abode is often cut off from all communication.

We have now reached the limits of Glen Nevis, but shall appreciate it quite as much on the return journey, as we shall obtain different views of it in a different lighting, with the longer shadows and richer glow of afternoon or evening. The tramper who wishes to continue further than the head of the glen may follow a lonely track leading for about seventeen miles through the mountains to the head of Loch Treig and Corrour, but it is not a route for the tenderfoot.

INVERLOCHY

On the green bank of the River Lochy, a short distance from the western slopes of Ben Nevis, stands the venerable ruin of Inverlochy Castle, around which is centred the early history of Lochaber. Its hoary walls have witnessed scenes of splendour and scenes of carnage, and radiate a thrilling atmosphere to those who can see with the mind as well as with the eye. From Fort William it is reached by following the main road across the Nevis Bridge and continuing for about half a mile.

On crossing the Nevis Bridge we pass the Glenlochy Whisky Distillery and the township of Inverlochy, built to house the employees of the Hydro-Electric scheme. On the right-hand side the steep slopes of Meall an t' Suidhe sweep upward to the clouds from the moorland at the foot, on which stands the unseemly buildings of the British Aluminium Hydro-Electric factory. On the left the wide grassy plain, known as the Black Parks, stretches away to the shores of Loch Linnhe. A short distance beyond where the road crosses the railway a little green hillock rises on the left, called Tom-na-faire, or Tom-na-h-aire (usually pronounced *Tomnahara*), meaning "the watch hill." It is said that on the summit of this hillock, in the year 1730, took place the last execution of a clansman for cattle-stealing, which shows that, as late as this date, Lochiel held the power of "pit and gallows" over his clansmen, though at that time there was a sheriffdom at Inverness.

In olden days the *creach*, or foray, when raiders confiscated the cattle of a neighbouring clan, was regarded as quite a legitimate business by the wilder Highland clans, though several clans were notorious for the frequency of their creachs. There is an old saying in the Highlands about the reivers: "If Badenoch is bad enough, Lochaber is twice as worse." General Wade, in his Report to the Government on the state of the Highlands in 1724, before he commenced his great road-building scheme, states: "The clans in the Highlands the most addicted to Rapine and Plunder are the Camerons on the West of the Shire of Inverness, the Mackenzies and others in the Shire of Ross who are Vassals to the late Earl of Seaforth, the McDonells of Keppoch, the Broadalbin Men, and the McGregors on the Borders of Argyleshire."

During the eighteenth century some of the clan chiefs endeavoured to lessen the barbarous customs of the Highlands, and no one did more in this way than Donald, nineteenth Chief of Lochiel (who, later, became the staunch ally of Prince Charlie). He threatened dire punishment on any of his clansmen found guilty of cattle-stealing.

Shortly after Lochiel had issued this decree, one of

his clansmen stole a young bull belonging to a local
laird, who, having traced the animal to the clansman's
croft, had him arrested and taken to Achnacarry for
trial by Lochiel. The Chief found the clansman
guilty and sentenced him to death. The thief was
brought to Fort William and lodged in the prison, and
a few days afterwards was taken to Tom-na-faire and
hanged, in front of a large concourse of Lochaber
natives. His friends had pled earnestly with Lochiel
to revoke the sentence, but the Chief was adamant. It
is said that while lying in Fort William prison, previous
to his execution, the condemned man composed several
verses of poetry describing himself as bound with
ropes, and calling upon his kinsmen to avenge his
death.

A short distance beyond Tom-na-faire a branch
road curves round to Inverlochy Castle at a point
where there used to be several houses. Overlooking
this road, and near the castle, is a rustic little burial-
ground beside a low rocky eminence. Old Lochaber
folk say that no one is entitled to be buried here except
descendants of those who fought in the battle of Inverlochy in 1645, but they admit that this rule has been
broken for many years.

There before us stands the mellow ruin of Inverlochy
Castle. In its pristine power it echoed not once but
often with the tumult of battle, the rejoicings of the
victors and the wailings of the vanquished. Many
eminent personages in the olden history of the Highlands have passed through its portals, some of them
guests of honour and others captives of war.

The most impressive view of the castle is from the
west bank of the River Lochy, when the sun is low in
the evening sky. In the foreground, the smooth but
swift waters of the Lochy sweep by, while shaggy
Highland cattle browse on the banks or wade in the
shallows. Rising from the greensward on the further

bank of the river, the old grey walls of the castle glow in the rays of the setting sun amid the verdant foliage of fringing sycamores. Around its base, and in its unkempt courtyard, straggling sheep nibble the grass, while in the twilight of its towers and dungeons eerie bats flutter around. Towering in the background is the mighty mass of Ben Nevis, silent sentinel through æons of time. No sound disturbs the solemn atmosphere save the faint bleat of a sheep or the splash of a salmon in the river.

The history of the settlement at Inverlochy goes back into the mists of antiquity. Tradition says that the first castle here was built by the Picts in one night, and as the buildings of that early race were of wattles and turf, the time taken to erect it may be correct, and the tradition may refer to an early building on this site. Hector Boece, in his *History of Scotland*, the first attempt to set forth a formal full-length history of our country, published in Latin in 1526, and translated into English by Holinshed in 1580, tells us that King Edwin, the second of that name, not only built a castle but a city at Inverlochy, some years before the commencement of the Christian era, "which city was much frequented with merchants of France and Spain, by reason of the great abundance of salmons, herrings and other fish which was taken here." The River Lochy is certainly one of the finest salmon streams in Scotland, and many herring are caught in Loch Linnhe at certain times of the year, while most other salt-water fish are plentiful in Loch Linnhe and Loch Eil. Boece further states that Inverlochy was at last "so defaced by the warres of the Danes that it never was able to recover her prestine renoune." Though Boece's *History* is crude in parts, fabulous and incredible in others, historians generally believe that there was an important settlement at Inverlochy from a very early date. It is reputed to have been the place where the ambassadors of Charlemagne, King of France, and Achaius (Angus), King of the Picts, signed a treaty in 790 for their mutual protection against the depredations of the English. This King Angus is believed to have been the first to introduce the cult of St. Andrew into Scotland and the first to use the Scottish national flag —a white St. Andrew's Cross upon an azure background—representing a white cross of vapour which appeared in the sky and proved a good omen to him on one occasion.

In several recent books on Scotland, and even in the *Official Guide* to Fort William, occurs the erroneous statement that Inverlochy Castle was the residence of Banquo, Thane of Lochaber, and that close by there is a road called Banquo's Walk. Banquo's residence, however, was not at Inverlochy but at old Tor Castle, about three miles further north, and Banquo's Walk is close to it, as stated clearly in the *Old Statistical Account of Scotland*. Banquo's Walk is well known to the inhabitants in the vicinity of Tor Castle.

The present ruin of Inverlochy Castle is of quadrangular shape, about ninety feet square, with a massive round tower of three storeys at each corner, the walls being pierced by loopholes. Within each tower there is a crumbling stairway in the thickness of the wall. The screen walls between the towers are about thirty feet high and about ten feet thick. There is a main gateway towards the east and one towards the west, in each of which there is a recess for a portcullis, and there is evidence that the castle was surrounded by a moat. Three of the towers are the same size, but the one towards the south-west, called Comyn's Tower, is larger. It derives its name from the Comyns, or Cummings, who were lords of Lochaber and Badenoch for about two hundred and fifty years—from about 1080 to the accession of Bruce, of whom the Comyns were bitter enemies, as they had strong claims to the throne of Scotland. It is estimated that the castle would require from five hundred to six hundred men to defend it. The castle, which is now in ruins, was built, probably, about the end of the thirteenth century by one of the Comyns, who are said to have built it at the command of Edward I, of whom they were partisans, and who appreciated the strategic value of the site. After the fall of the Comyns, by the accession of Bruce, the castle fell into decay, but was restored and strengthened by George, Earl of Huntly, when he was made overlord of Lochaber in 1505, after the abolition of the Lordship of the Isles. The Gordon family settled a garrison in the castle to keep the neighbouring clans in check.

The first battle of Inverlochy was fought here in 1431, between Donald Balloch, with his island clansmen, and the Royalist forces of King James I, under the command of the Earls of Mar and Caithness, during the desperate struggle of the Lords of the Isles to maintain their independence against the King.

In 1427 James had summoned Alexander, third Lord of the Isles, and a number of his vassals to Inverness, under the pretext of discussing peace terms. Instead of discussions, however, he imprisoned them all and executed most of them, though he allowed the Lord of the Isles to go free, thinking, no doubt, that he had taught him a salutary lesson. In revenge for this treacherous deed, Alexander led an army against Inverness two years later, and burned the town, for which act he was captured and imprisoned in Tantallon Castle.

In 1431, during Alexander's imprisonment, his young cousin, Donald Balloch, then only twenty years of age, roused the island clansmen and arranged for the help of his uncle, Alastair Carrach, of Tor Castle, for an attack upon the Government forces, who were stationed at Inverlochy under Mar and Caithness.

Sailing up Loch Linnhe, Donald landed his men near Inverlochy and attacked it from the south. By previous arrangement, Alastair Carrach and his clansmen attacked it fiercely at the same time from the north. Though the Royalist forces were greatly superior in numbers they were completely routed, leaving more than one thousand dead on the field, including the Earl of Caithness. Donald followed up his victory by ravaging the lands of the Camerons, who had fought on the King's side, and giving a large portion of them to the Macleans. It was, probably, at this time that the Macleans settled in Ardgour, though they may not have come into actual possession of it until the incident related in Chapter II.

This battle is commemorated in the stirring "Pibroch of Donald Dhu," or in the Gaelic spelling, *Piobaireachd Domhnull Dubh*, which, the MacDonalds claim, refers to Donald Balloch. This pibroch was adopted by the Cameron Highlanders as their march tune, and consequently it is often assumed that the Donald Dubh referred to is the famous Cameron Chief who fought at Harlaw in 1411, and for the Royalist forces against Donald Balloch at Inverlochy, and from whom succeeding Cameron chiefs have derived their patronymic *Mac Domhnull Dubh* ("Son of Black Donald"). The consensus of opinion, however, seems to favour the MacDonald claim regarding this tune.

The most notable event associated with Inverlochy Castle is the battle fought here on 2nd February 1645, when the Marquis of Montrose, with his Royalist Highlanders and Irish levies, completely routed the Covenanting forces of his great enemy the Marquis of Argyll. On that Sabbath morning, Ben Nevis looked down upon Lochaber's greatest scene of slaughter, as broadsword, dirk and Lochaber axe wrought their bloody work amid the wild war-cries of clansmen.

During the preceding months of December and

January, Montrose and his men had played havoc in the Argyll country, in their campaign to restore the fallen fortunes of Charles I. Leaving the ravished country-side, they set out northwards for Inverness, intending to take that town. When proceeding up the Great Glen, Montrose learned that Seaforth was advancing southwards against him with five thousand men. Montrose's own army at this time amounted to about fifteen hundred men.

At Kilcumin (Fort Augustus) word was brought to Montrose that Argyll, with three thousand Campbell clansmen and Lowland levies, had reached Inverlochy hot on his tracks, plundering as they progressed, and intending, no doubt, to take Montrose in the rear. The person who conveyed this news about Argyll to Montrose was Iain *Lom* MacDonald, the Keppoch bard. Though Iain was well known and respected in Lochaber, Montrose was doubtful of his news at first, and suspected a trap, but when convinced of the truth of the report he decided to turn back immediately, and take Argyll by surprise.

After an amazing march, over mountain passes deep in the snows of winter, Montrose and his army arrived on a clear frosty moonlight night at the mouth of Glen Nevis. Several recent writers, including John Buchan (Lord Tweedsmuir) in his biography of Montrose, say that Montrose marched from Glen Roy along the northern skirts of the Ben Nevis group of mountains to Inverlochy, but according to the tradition which has long been current in Lochaber, and which I often heard related when a boy there, Montrose cut through the Ben Nevis mountains from Roy Bridge to the head of Glen Nevis, and travelled down this glen. Drummond-Norie in his *Loyal Lochaber*, and W. T. Kilgour in his *Lochaber in War and Peace*, both give the Glen Nevis route, and both these writers were well acquainted with Lochaber. By coming at Argyll's forces from the mouth of Glen Nevis, Montrose was not only taking them by surprise in the rear, but he was blocking their only avenue of escape back to their own country. If Montrose had come to Inverlochy by the northern skirts of the Ben Nevis mountains his full forces would be in view of the Campbells, as he says, in his dispatch to his sovereign, that the night of his arrival "was moonlight and very clear," and surprise would therefore have been impossible. He would require to attack them by a flank movement, thus leaving open to them an avenue of escape to the south if they were defeated. The most authoritative advocate of the route by the skirts of the Ben Nevis group was Dr. A. Cameron-Miller (vide *Celtic Monthly*, November 1910), the well-loved physician of Lochaber for many years, and a reliable antiquarian, and who, incidentally, was family physician to my own home during my boyhood, but the weight of evidence seems to be against this opinion. John Buchan states that the Campbells did see Montrose's army, but thought it was some contingent of Highland raiders. This opinion seems unlikely if Montrose had come, as Buchan says, by the northern side of Ben Nevis, as Montrose had fifteen hundred men including cavalry, and they were within a mile of Inverlochy when they halted for the night. At the northern side of Ben Nevis they would be seen clearly from Inverlochy, whereas in Glen Nevis, even if they were seen, only the advance guard would be visible, and this small portion might have suggested to the Campbells that they were only a band of raiders. The best evidence in support of the Glen Nevis route is that of Montrose himself, who says in his dispatch: "The difficultest march of all was over the Lochaber mountains, which we at last surmounted and came upon the back of the enemy when they least expected us." Near the Upper Falls of Nevis, in Glen Nevis, there is a large flat boulder known as "Montrose's

Seat," a name which lends evidence to Montrose having passed this way.

Those who oppose the Glen Nevis route use as their main argument the fact that there was deep snow in the mountain passes. Anyone who has traversed mountain passes in summer and winter, however, knows that if the snow has a firm surface the winter traverse is often easier than in summer, when loose screes, bog and boulders add to the difficulty. From Montrose's "moonlight and very clear" we can assume, reasonably, that there was some degree of frost, which would make the snow firm. Thus the main argument against the Glen Nevis route fails. Regarding the difference in distance of the two routes, the great benefit of the surprise element of attack from the recess of Glen Nevis would outweigh the shorter but much more exposed route by the northern skirts of Ben Nevis.

> "For six weeks past the northern clans, led by the great Montrose,
> With fire and sword had ravished all the country of their foes:
> Clan Diarmid felt their vengeance sore, and swore by Cruachan Ben,
> To give their foemen's flesh to feed the eagles of the glen.
> And now on plund'ring thoughts intent, they rest by Lochy's shore—
> Three thousand Campbells, sworn to serve their chief, Mac-Cailean Mor;
> Little they dreamt the great Montrose, with all his loyal men,
> A thousand gallant Highland hearts, lay hidden in the glen." *

On the night before the battle Argyll retired to his galley, which was lying at anchor in Camas-nan-Gall, in Loch Eil, opposite Inverlochy, and for this action he is often accused of cowardice, but the accusation is quite unwarranted. If the Campbells did not realize that it was the forces of Montrose whom they saw in the distance, as most writers assert, then it cannot have been

* W. Drummond-Norie.

INVERLOCHY CASTLE AND BEN NEVIS

[To face page 96

BEN NEVIS, FROM BANAVIE

fear of Montrose that made Argyll leave Inverlochy. The probable reason for his departure was more likely to have been that, whether or not the Campbells knew that they were opposed to the forces of Montrose, Argyll was not a soldier of experience, and his presence during the expected battle would have embarrassed his military leaders. He had a very experienced commander for his forces in Sir Duncan Campbell, of Auchinbreck. Again, Argyll's officers would no doubt counsel him to leave for, no matter what the result of the battle might be, they would want the cause of the Covenanters to be carried on, and, therefore, would not wish to risk the life of their uncrowned king. This policy did ultimately prove successful, despite their defeat at Inverlochy. Argyll proved himself no coward when he went to his execution with the greatest fortitude in 1661, eleven years after Montrose had met a similar fate.

Montrose rested his men overnight but attacked early on the following morning. He placed his Irish levies on the wings and his Highlanders in the centre. Those Highlanders comprised the men of Atholl, Appin, Glen Coe, Clanranald, Glen Garry, and a number of Camerons from Brae Lochaber and Nether Lochaber, who had come of their own free will without any orders from their chief, who took no part in the battle. A number of Camerons from Western Lochaber took no side until they saw how the tide of battle was flowing, when they joined with Montrose. Lochiel had to be careful, for though he, probably, favoured Montrose, he was married to a daughter of Campbell of Breadalbane, and his son, who later became the famous Sir Ewan, was under the guardianship of Argyll at Inveraray for his education at the time of the battle.

Auchinbreck, or *Auch-nam-breac*, arranged his men with the Campbell clansmen in the centre and his Lowland levies on the wings.

G

The battle commenced a short distance south-east of the castle, that is towards Glen Nevis. Argyll's forces lined the ridge at Tom-na-faire overlooking the present highway, having left about fifty men to guard the castle against a surprise attack by the enemy. Montrose and his men occupied the almost-parallel ridge to that of Argyll, which stretches across the mouth of Glen Nevis to the east of the railway,* where one would expect him to be if he came out of Glen Nevis. As the Campbells were pressed back by the forces of Montrose, the final scenes of the battle developed on the plain to the south of the castle, which is now bisected by the Fort William to Mallaig railway.

In his dispatch Montrose says: "A little after the sun was up both armies met, and the rebels [the forces of Argyll] fought for some time with great bravery, the prime of the Campbells giving the first onset as men that deserved to fight in a better cause. Our men having a nobler cause did wonders, and came immediately to push of pike and dint of sword, after their first firing. The rebels could not stand it, but after some resistance at first began to run, whom we pursued for nine miles, altogether making a great slaughter."

No quarter was given the Campbells as, being hereditary enemies, the Royalist clansmen had old scores to wipe out, and Montrose's Irishmen were really half savages. So beastly was the behaviour of these "wild Irishes," throughout the campaign of Montrose, that even his Highlanders, who were certainly no faint-hearts, were disgusted on several occasions. *Cruachan*, the war-cry of the Campbells, was a cry of death at Inverlochy, when the waters of the River Lochy and Loch Eil were dyed crimson with the blood of the sons of Diarmid as they were slaughtered while trying to escape.

* *Vide* article entitled "Montrose in Lochaber—1645," by Dr. A. Cameron-Miller, Fort William, in *Celtic Monthly*, November 1910.

Montrose's Irishmen were commanded by the famous, or notorious, Alastair MacDonald—young Coll Ciotach (often spelt "Colkitto" by *Sasunnaich* writers) —who is known among the Royalist Highlanders as *Alasdair an gaisgeach* ("Alastair, the Hero"), but by the Campbells he is called *Alasdair mosach* ("Dirty Alastair"), owing to the excesses of his men in ravishing the Campbell country. He was undoubtedly a fearless soldier and skilful leader of irregular troops, but the beastly behaviour of his men at the sacking of Aberdeen and the massacre of Lagganmore, in Lorn, are two indelible stains on the brilliant campaign of Montrose.

The losses on Montrose's side at Inverlochy were trivial, the only men of note killed being MacDougall of Reray, reputed the most handsome man in the Royalist army, and Sir Thomas Ogilvie, who died shortly after the battle. The Campbells, on the other hand, are said to have lost over fifteen hundred men, including their commander, Auchinbreck. Though a Campbell, Auchinbreck was an uncle of Alastair MacDonald, his enemy. It is said that Auchinbreck was taken prisoner and brought before Alastair, who asked him if he preferred death by hanging or by the sword. Auchinbreck's reply has become a saying in the Highlands—"*Da dhiu gun aon roghainn*" ("two evil alternatives that give no room for choice"). Being a soldier, he said he preferred death by the sword, whereupon Alastair drew his sword and smote off his head. Another version has it that, after the battle was over, Alastair asked one of his officers if he knew aught of his uncle, Auchinbreck. The officer replied: "He lies on yonder field with his back to the ground. See if you can bring him back to life!"

Argyll, or *MacCailean Mor* ("son of big Colin"), to give him his Gaelic patronymic, was not the only eminent non-combatant during the battle. Ian Lom, the bard, who had accompanied Montrose from

Kilcumin, made no attempt to fight, and when asked
by Montrose why he behaved thus, Iain replied: "And
if I were killed, who would there be to sing of the great
victory?" And sing he did in a very stirring poem,*
full of the satire for which he was famed. Later on,
Iain was appointed Poet Laureate by Charles II, and
awarded a pension—the first and only Gaelic poet to
receive this honour.

The characters of Montrose and Argyll were
diametrically opposed to one another, and make an
extremely interesting study. Montrose was the
brilliant man of action, while Argyll was the prosaic
intellectual, though his clansmen retained the martial
spirit of the Gael and were fierce warriors. Montrose
was at his best in the campaign of war, while Argyll
was more at home among the intrigues of State, and
the Argylls liked to "fish in drumlie waters." To a
martial race like the Scots, especially the Highlanders,
the romantic campaigns of Montrose and Prince
Charlie make a much greater appeal then the parchment dealings and marriage alliances of the Argylls.
Nevertheless, if the Argyll method of warfare, by the
pen more than by the sword, lacks romance, it has
certainly proved effective, as is evident by the wide
extent of the present territory of the Campbells at the
expense of their neighbouring clans. Though men of
action provide the high lights of history, it is the
intellectuals who have most influence on its ultimate
course. Again, it is to be remembered that something in human nature makes us partial to a martyr,
irrespective of whether or not we agree with his
policy.

Lest any reader should think that I am prejudiced in
any way in favour of the Campbells, let me say that I
have good reasons to be of the opposite persuasion. I
have a strong strain of MacDonald blood in my veins,

* See page 103.

the greatest enemies of the Campbells. Also, ancestors of mine, by the name of Lamont, felt the vengeful might of *MacCailean Mor* during the ruthless campaign of the Campbells in Cowal, in 1646. They had to flee to Islay, and change their name to the non-committal one of Brown, in order to escape pursuit and persecution for the power of the Campbells reached far.* In their endeavour to exterminate the clan, and confiscate their territory, the Campbells slaughtered in cold blood about two hundred and fifty unarmed Lamonts, including many of the principal members of the clan, at Dunoon, a massacre that makes "Glen Coe" pale into insignificance. They also proscribed the name Lamont. Another of my family scores against the Campbells is that no clan has suffered more from the spreading tentacles of the Campbells than the one of which the Argyllshire MacCullochs are a sept, namely, the MacDougalls; their territory and even their ancient title—Lord of Lorn—have passed into possession of the Campbells. Nevertheless, there is no sense in allowing sentiment to blind one to hard facts.

An old motto of the Campbells is *I Byde my tyme*, and surely it was never more remarkably fulfilled than in the case of Inverlochy. The Campbells received the greatest defeat in their history here, yet the Lord Abinger family, who have been in possession of Inverlochy estate for the past century, are collateral descendants of Sir Duncan Campbell, of Auchinbreck, who had command of the Campbell forces, and was killed in the battle. The greater part of the estate and the modern castle of Inverlochy were sold by Lord Abinger in 1945.

Early in the nineteenth century the estate of Inverlochy was purchased by Sir James Scarlett, who was created the first Lord Abinger, in 1835. He was born

* Most of the Browns and Blacks of Argyllshire and the Western Isles obtained their names in this way.

in Jamaica, of English descent, and married the daughter of Peter Campbell of Kilmory, of the family of the Campbells of Auchinbreck, cadets of the house of Argyll. He built the modern castle of Inverlochy, or Torlundy as it is called locally, which stands about two miles to the north of the ruined castle. Lord Abinger's second son was a worthy descendant of his Highland ancestors. It was he, the Hon. Sir James Yorke Scarlett, G.C.B., who led the heavy cavalry charge at Balaclava on the morning of 25th October 1854, the bravery of which was overshadowed by the famous charge of the Light Brigade which took place later on that day. A daughter of this Lord Abinger married Lord Chancellor Lord Campbell, and was created a peeress in her own right as Baroness Stratheden.

Restoration of the ruin of Inverlochy Castle was commenced at the beginning of the present century by the fourth Lord Abinger, but was left unfinished when he died in 1903. During restoration, a complete skeleton was found sealed up in the northern extremity of the parapet passage, and a number of cannon balls were found embedded in the walls.

The little settlement of Inverlochy was the home of Alan MacDougall, better known as *Ailean Dall*, the blind Gaelic poet, before Alastair MacDonell, Chief of Glengarry, took him under his care and appointed him his official bard. Alan was originally connected with the MacDonalds of Glen Coe, and, in addition to his bardic qualifications, was a skilled fiddler.

The following verses, given by Mark Napier in his *Memorials of Montrose*, are a condensed translation of Iain's Lom's poem, *The Day of Inverlochy*. They are not a literal translation (the original poem consists of twenty-one four-line verses), but they convey the vigour and even the sentiments better than any literal translation which has appeared. The original poem in Gaelic is given in MacKenzie's *Beauties of Gaelic Poetry* and in Drummond-Norie's *Loyal Lochaber*.

Heard ye not! heard ye not! how that whirlwind, the Gael—
To Lochaber swept down from Loch Ness to Loch Eil,—
And the Campbells, to meet them in battle-array,
Like the billow came on,—and were broke like its spray!
Long, long shall our war-song exult in that day.

'Twas the Sabbath that rose, 'twas the Feast of St. Bride,
When the rush of the clans shook Ben Nevis's side;
I, the Bard of their battles, ascended the height
Where dark Inverlochy o'ershadow'd the fight,
And I saw the Clan Donnell resistless in might.

Through the land of my fathers the Campbells have come,
The flames of their foray enveloped my home;
Broad Keppoch in ruin is left to deplore,
And my country is waste from the hill to the shore—
Be it so!   By St. Mary, there's comfort in store!

Though the braes of Lochaber a desert be made,
And Glen Roy may be lost to the plough and the spade,
Though the bones of my kindred, unhonour's, unurn'd—
Mark the desolate path where the Campbells have burn'd—
Be it so!   From that foray *they never return'd!*

Fallen race of Diarmid! disloyal,—untrue,
No harp in the Highlands will sorrow for you:
But the birds of Loch Eil are wheeling on high,
And the Badenoch wolves hear the Camerons' cry—
"Come feast ye! come feast, where the false-hearted lie!"

CHAPTER V

THROUGH THE HEART OF LOCHABER

THE River Lochy and the western reach of the Caledonian Canal, which follow, more or less, parallel courses, may be regarded as winding their way through the heart of Lochaber, for in the peaty moorland which lies between these two waterways is the traditional site of the loch from which the district derives its name.

Setting out northwards from Fort William, we cross the Nevis Bridge and continue, past the ruin of Inverlochy Castle, until we come to the bridge over the clear and swift-flowing waters of the River Lochy, about a mile and a half from Fort William. The present bridge is a rather ungainly concrete structure, appearing like a staging thrown across upturned drain-pipes. It was erected by the County Council in 1929 to replace the graceful suspension-bridge, built by Donald Cameron of Lochiel in 1848, which had become unable to cope with the greatly increased traffic on this route.

Near to the eastern end of the bridge is the old Ben Nevis Whisky Distillery, which produces the famed "Long John's Dew of Ben Nevis." Originally, the distillery was a smaller establishment at Millburn, a few miles off, which drew its waters from a stream descending the steep slopes of Ben Nevis, and consequently its whisky was named "Dew of Ben Nevis." Subsequently, the present distillery was built, and the name "Long John" became attached to the title of the blend of whisky, as that was the nickname of the distiller (John MacDonald), who was a man six feet four inches in height. He was a great-grandson of the Keppoch chief killed at Culloden.

On crossing the Lochy Bridge the road runs straight as a tautened tape-line for about a mile across Corpach Moss, or the Blar Mor ("the great plain"), where the lapwing utters its plaintive *peeweep!* as it circles and swoops overhead, and the shrill-piping snipe darts about among the tufts of marsh-grass. This wide, flat stretch of swampy moorland is not much above high-water-level of Loch Linnhe. The surface is composed of peat, resting on a deep bed of gravel, which overlies hard boulder clay deposited by the glaciers which filled the Great Glen during the last Ice Age. For many years the local inhabitants made good use of the peat in the Blar Mor, but since the Kaiser's war the quick and cheap transport of coal to the Highlands has almost ousted the use of peat in this region. Many a happy day of boyhood have I spent in my bare feet at the cutting, drying and stacking of the peats here during spring and summer. In autumn they were wheeled home in barrows, to serve as fuel during the long winter nights, when their fragrance permeated the village.

The Blar Mor is believed to occupy the site of the loch from which the district derives its name—Loch-aber, and it is quite reasonable to suppose that a loch existed here at one time. When the glaciers of the Great Glen, during the last Ice Age, began to melt and retreat, their earth and rock debris was, probably, deposited as a *terminal moraine* across the mouth of the glen—that is, from the present site of Fort William to Corpach. This barrier would act as a dam, preventing the accumulating waters, formed by the melting ice, from mingling with the waters of Loch Linnhe, thus a glacier lake would be formed. There is still a narrow track of arable land covering this barrier between the Moss and Loch Linnhe. Later on, the waters of this lake would gradually seep through the debris barrier, and little channels would also form to drain them into Loch Linnhe. Thus the glacier lake, or Loch Aber, would dwindle in size until it would disappear and leave a swamp, or marsh, behind.

The term "Aber" is generally accepted as meaning "a confluence," similar to "Inver," whether of two streams, or of a river with the sea. As applied to Lochaber, it might mean the confluence of the River Lochy and Loch Linnhe, or the confluence of Loch Linnhe and Loch Eil. Several eminent authorities, however, including Dr. Alexander MacBain, believe that the second part of the name should really be "Apor," an old Gaelic word meaning "marsh," hence Loch Apor, "the loch of the marsh." In Adamnan's *Life of St. Columba*, written in the seventh century, mention is made of Stagnum Aporum ("the loch of marshes") in connection with a poor man who resided on its shores, and for whom Saint Columba made a stake for killing wild animals and blessed it, so that the poor man should always have meat for his family. We know that Saint Columba passed up the Great Glen on his journey from Iona to Inverness, where he converted the pagan King Brude to Christianity. Writing in the sixteenth century, Hector Boece says, "Lochquhaber took the name of a great mere of water, into which the river of the Quhaber falleth and passeth through the same." Boece may be referring to traditions regarding Loch Aber when it was a fair size, and his River Quhaber may mean the present Lochy. During the year 1760 Richard Pococke, Bishop of Ossory, Ireland, and the first systematic explorer of unknown regions of Scotland, visited Lochaber. In his letter describing his visit he says, "A little to the north of this [Fort William] is a very small lake called Loughaber, which gives name to that part of the Shire of Inverness." Evidently the waters of the loch had diminished greatly before Pococke saw it. It would be unreasonable to assume that the whole district should be named after the loch had it never been greater in size, and therefore in importance, than when Pococke visited it. A rather fanciful derivation is given in the *Old Statistical Account of Scotland*, 1793. The contributor on Lochaber states, "Lochaber, or *Loch nu capper*, signifies the 'Lake of Horns.' Indeed, it deserves not the name of lake, being a small pool in the moss of Corpoch. The tradition is that the deer, in the routing season, fought about this lake and lost their horns. Hence the whole country has received its name." I was told by an old Lochaber man that the final waters of Loch Aber were situated between the present railway and Caol Farm, which lies to the south.

To the west of Blar Mor, and overlooking it from a higher level, is the little village of Banavie, on the banks of the Caledonian Canal. Here there is a series of eight locks elevating the canal seventy-two feet in height, which Telford, the engineer of the canal, christened "Neptune's Staircase," and which still bears that name. Two substantial, bow-fronted, white-washed houses on the western bank of the canal at this part were designed by Telford, both of which appear in the photograph of "Ben Nevis, from Banavie." During last century Banavie was an important halting-place for travellers in the Highlands when the steam-boats made their terminus at Corpach, at the entrance to the canal, about a mile to the south, instead of, as now, at Fort William.

Banavie came into existence as a village by the settlement here of the workmen employed at the construction of Neptune's Staircase. Quite a number of these workmen had been crofters who were evicted from Glen Dessary and Loch Arkaig-side by the trustees of the Lochiel estate. Some of the evicted crofters from these districts also found employment at the construction of the canal at Corpach and some of them emigrated to the colonies.

On the hill-side, to the west of the village, stands the schoolhouse, and below it, on the opposite side of the road, there is an inconspicuous little whitewashed cottage and barn worthy of notice. This cottage was the local post office for many years. At the time of the Disruption the present barn was the home of the crofter, the present cottage not then being in existence. This humble abode was occupied during that stirring time by the widow and young family of John MacMaster, a noted teacher of the Society for the Propagation of Christian Knowledge. The previous tenant had been evicted from the district for smuggling whisky. Mrs. MacMaster reared her family on the meagre produce of the little croft and a pension of one shilling and sixpence per week, awarded to her for her husband's services. She was a very religious and independent-minded woman, and when the order was issued that no one was to give shelter to the Rev. Mr. Davidson, the secessionist minister from the Parish Church at the Disruption, she readily made accommodation for him in the *ben* end of her humble home. Here he lived while he conducted his religious services in the open air, a site for a church being denied to him and his congregation. Mr. Davidson had been minister of Kilmallie Parish Church since 1835 when he succeeded his father-in-law, the Rev. Mr. MacGillivary. For many years after the Disruption, until the death of Mrs. MacMaster, her cottage, which would be thatch-roofed at that time, was a resort for the religious worthies of the old school in the Highlands. Many of the stalwarts of the Disruption movement, including the noted Dr. Candlish of Edinburgh, sojourned beneath its roof-tree and discussed the tenets of their belief around its peat fire.

Turning northwards from Banavie, we can either follow the main road or the banks of the canal. This latter route is the most picturesque and most interesting, but is for the tramper only, as all vehicles are prohibited.

Following the eastern bank of the canal, we obtain what is regarded locally as the finest view of Ben Nevis. From the top lock of the canal there is an uninterrupted view of the Ben, across the Blar Mor, from its moorland base to its snow-clad summit, its great northern precipices appearing to advantage with their dark shadows and snow-filled crevices. Stretching north-wards, the whole massive range of the Grampians dwindles into the distance. Away to the south appear the bens of Mamore Forest, Appin and Ardgour, with Loch Linnhe stretching to the Firth of Lorn, and the snow-white lighthouse at Corran Narrows gleaming in the distance.

Beyond Banavie we wend our way along the canal bank, thickly clad with whin, hawthorn, and bramble, until we pass Mount Alexander farm. A few minutes' walk beyond this farm, a cart-track, which we should follow, leads down the side of the canal bank to the bank of the River Lochy, where the latter bends sharply towards the east. Here, on a large island of shingle with a number of trees towards the centre, there was, at one time, a large heronry. This cart-track dwindles into a mere sheep-track as we proceed north-wards close to the river, with its clean, bleached shingle-bed, towards a little tree-clad spit of rock projecting into the current. The dark pool formed by the river eddy at this point is called *Buinne a Chait* ("the cat pool"), and a short distance through the trees back from the river there is a little clearing called *Dail a Chait* ("the cat field"). These place-names originate from a story that is told of a Cameron chief who resided in old Tor Castle during the fifteenth century. The ruin of this old castle appears through the trees on the brink of a high cliff rising from the rocky bed of the River Lochy, a short distance ahead. It is not easy to detect from the south when the trees are clad with foliage, though the modern hotel of Torcastle appears clearly set among rich woodlands a short distance beyond the ruin.

The story is said to relate to the twelfth Lochiel, Chief of Clan Cameron, called *Ailean nan Creach* ("Alan of the Forays"), owing to the numerous cattle-lifting raids which he led. Alan was a bold and reckless man, fearing neither God, man, or devil, but some time before his death he repented for the evil life he had led and decided to consult the oracle of the *Tigh Gairm* ("house of invocation") in order to learn how he could atone for his evil ways. He sought the advice of a local witch as to the rites he required to perform. According to her instructions, he built a hut in the little field called Dail a Chait, which we have mentioned, and to this hut he retired with a gillie, or servant-man, and a cat. Having kindled a blazing fire within the hut, he proceeded to run a spit through a non-vital part of the cat and, hoisting it over the blaze, told his gillie to keep roasting it alive while he guarded the door with his claymore. The wild screeches of the tortured animal attracted all the cats in Lochaber, who, super-naturally gifted with the power of speech, threatened to tear Alan in pieces if he did not release his victim. Had Alan lost his nerve, or quailed before them, his doom, and that of his companion, was sealed, they would have been torn to shreds. But Alan showed utter defiance, and kept the infuriated cats at bay with his claymore, shouting to his gillie in Gaelic: "Hear you this, or see you that, turn the spit and roast the cat." The united screams of the feline tribe sounded as if hell had broken loose, but still Alan defied them and ordered the torture to continue. Suddenly, a gigantic black cat appeared and, having ordered his maddened brethren to keep silent, asked Alan why he tortured the animal. Alan replied: "I will release it if you will tell me how I can obtain forgiveness for my past misdeeds." The great black cat said: "You can atone and be forgiven by building seven churches in the Highlands, one church for each of your great forays." On hearing this verdict, Alan ordered his gillie to release the tortured cat. Immediately the half-roasted animal escaped from the hut it let out a terrific screech and, dashing through the trees, plunged into the Lochy at the place now called the Cat Pool, followed by the whole feline tribe. They swam with the strong current down the river reach to the bend further south, where, having now cooled, they landed and dispersed.

Alan proceeded to build the seven churches according to his instructions, and these are reputed to be Kilmallie, Kildonan, Kill-a-Choireil (near Roy Bridge), Kilchoan, Arisaig, Morven, and Kilkellen at Laggan. The church on Eilean Munde, in Loch Leven, is sometimes said to be one of the seven.

Some writers give the site of Alan's hut as being near the centre of Corpach Moss, but the place-names relating to the incident are well known to the local people and are as already described, and not near Corpach Moss.

The story of the Tigh Gairm and church-building is usually ascribed to "Alan of the Forays," and is said to have taken place during his old age, but according to history Alan was killed in a fight with the Mac-Intoshes and MacDonells of Keppoch, when only thirty-two years old. Thus he had no old age, and would not have much time for repentance and church-building. The incident more probably relates to Alan's son, Ewan, the thirteenth Chief, who was also a fearless man and notorious raider. It was he who rebuilt Tor Castle and made it the residence of the Cameron chiefs. During one period of Ewan's life he developed a melancholy state of mind owing to deep grief at the loss of his eldest and favourite son, Donald. He resolved to give up his wild ways of living and devote himself to the works of religion and peace. It was evidently to this period in his life that the incident of the Tigh Gairm relates. Apparently, Ewan's spell of religious fervour lasted only for a few years, for soon again he was raiding and fighting as fiercely as before. Indeed, though he lived to a good old age, his turbulent life caused him to end his days on the scaffold.

The ruin of old Tor Castle on its elevated site above the river is now almost hidden by a screen of trees, while at the foot of the cliff on which it stands the Lochy whirls and boils in dark rocky pools. In olden days, when firearms were unknown, this castle must have been a strong refuge. It appears in the well-known painting entitled "A Salmon Stream," by James Docharty, A.R.S.A., which hangs in the Glasgow Art Galleries. The ruin is believed to stand on the site of the original Tor Castle, which is attributed to Banquo, Thane of Lochaber, during the tenth century, who figures in Shakespeare's *Macbeth*. Banquo's son, Fleance, is said to have fled to Brittany when his father was murdered. Later on, his descendants returned to Britain in the train of William the Conqueror, and some of them settled in Scotland. One of them was Walter, who became High Steward of Scotland and was given the hand of Marjorie, daughter of Robert the Bruce, for his bravery at Bannockburn, and became the progenitor of the Stuart dynasty. There is, of course, another history of the founding of the Royal House of Stuart.

The second Tor Castle was built in the eleventh century by Gillicattan Mor, one of the earliest chiefs of the old Clan Chattan Confederation, which included many septs, and became the principal residence of the Clan Chattan chiefs for many years. The Mac-Intoshes, one of the principal clans of the Confederation, though not originally a Lochaber clan, came into possession of Tor Castle along with the chiefship of

TOR CASTLE, NEAR BANAVIE

(Suggested appearance based upon measurements of the ruin)

From *Invernessiana* by C. Fraser MacIntosh of Drummond

[*To face page* 112

BANQUO'S WALK, NEAR TOR CASTLE

LOCH LOCHY, NEAR ACHNACARRY

LOCH ARKAIG

[To face page 113

Clan Chattan and the lands of Glen Loy and Loch Arkaig in 1292, by the marriage of Angus MacIntosh, sixth Chief of the MacIntoshes, to Eva, only child of Dougall Dall MacGille Chattan, Chief of Clan Chattan. Angus and his wife resided in Tor Castle until 1308, when they removed to Badenoch.

A few years after Angus MacIntosh left Tor Castle, the Camerons, whose possessions in this region, at that time, lay mainly to the east of the loch and River Lochy, occupied the lands of Glen Loy and Loch Arkaig, as they said these lands had been deserted by the MacIntoshes. When Angus's son, William, inherited the chiefship of the MacIntoshes he tried to drive the Camerons from their acquired territory by force, but failed to do so. This dispute developed into one of the most bloody clan feuds in the Highlands, lasting from generation to generation until the close of the seventeenth century, and almost ruined the two clans. Though the MacIntoshes could not drive the Camerons from the lands of Glen Loy and Loch Arkaig, they still regarded themselves as the rightful owners, and selected as their title "MacIntosh of Tor Castle," as that was the ancient residence of the Clan Chattan chiefs, a title they wished to retain, even though not residing there. Even the present chief's cousin is styled—"Mackintosh of Mackintosh-Torcastle" and style of Clan Chattan which "style of Torcastle" was derived from the principal fortalice of the Clan Chattan lands of Glen Lui, Loch Arkaig, Glen Spean and Glen Roy and was in a contract with Ewan Cameron of Lochiel 15th June 1664.

Tor Castle fell into decay after Angus MacIntosh left it, the Camerons not having any use of it though occupying the adjacent territory, but when John, first Lord of the Isles, granted the lands of Glen Spean and Mamore to Alastair Carrach (1380–1440), his fourth, and youngest, son (by his second wife), Alastair,

H

built a new Tor Castle, or perhaps rebuilt the Mac-
Intosh residence, and made it his home. The Lord of
the Isles also conferred on Alastair the Lordship of
Lochaber, a title granted to an ancestor by Bruce
when the latter, on his accession to the crown of Scotland, expelled his enemies, the Comyns, who were the
ancient Lords of Lochaber. The Camerons would
not, or dared not, object to Alastair residing in Tor
Castle as they were vassals of the Lord of the Isles.
This Alastair Carrach became the progenitor of the
MacDonells of Keppoch. The MacIntoshes were also
vassals of the Lord of the Isles, but in 1429, during the
struggle with James I, both the Camerons and the
MacIntoshes withdrew their allegiance, which contributed materially to the overthrow and abolition of
the Lordship of the Isles in 1493.

When the Lord of the Isles was overthrown, and
consequently the lands of the Keppoch MacDonalds,
or MacDonells, were declared forfeit, Queen Mary
bestowed the Lordship of Lochaber on the Earl of
Huntly. He, in turn, granted to the Camerons "the
lands of Lochiel and the fortalice of Tor Castle."
These lands of Lochiel had previously been held by
the MacDonalds of Clanranald, a branch of the
Lordship of the Isles. Huntly also granted the
Keppoch lands to the MacIntoshes, but though they
held this territory by charter, the Keppoch chiefs held
it by the sword, and defied them to take possession.
Those were the days of—

> The good old rule, the simple plan,
> That they should take who have the power
> And they should keep who can.

The Keppochs kept their territory until the overthrow of the clan system after Culloden in 1746.

At the beginning of the sixteenth century, Ewan,
thirteenth of Lochiel, and son of Ailean nan Creach,
rebuilt Tor Castle and made it his residence. It

remained the seat of the Cameron chiefs until the time of the famous Sir Ewan, seventeenth of Lochiel (1629–1719), who built a mansion for himself at Achnacarry, some time after 1665. Ludovick Cameron, youngest son of Sir Ewan, and uncle of Lochiel of the Forty-five, resided at Tor Castle. He acted as Young Lochiel's * Major throughout the Forty-five campaign and died in exile in France. After the Forty-five, Tor Castle was left unoccupied, and gradually crumbled into the ruin which now appears among the trees overlooking the River Lochy.

The present mansion of Torcastle, situated amid beautiful surroundings, is comparatively modern, having been built at the beginning of last century, and was used for some time as the residence of Lochiel's factor. In 1947 it was opened as a first-class hotel, and is already a popular residence, especially with fishers.

About half a mile north of Tor Castle there is a beautiful secluded woodland avenue by the bank of the River Lochy, called Banquo's Walk, where few feet ever tread nowadays. Here, it is said, the Thane of Lochaber sought seclusion when he desired peaceful meditation, and it would be difficult to find a more ideal retreat for that purpose. With the exception of the residents of Torcastle, and the neighbouring crofters, there are few people, even in Lochaber, who are aware of its actual location, though the name may be familiar. There are good reasons for it being so little known, as it is well off the beaten track and no road leads to it. It commences abruptly, suggesting that part of its original length may now be obliterated and overgrown with vegetation. It is not easy to locate, as it is screened from approach by a high, thickly wooded bank, and is itself among the trees.

* He was called "Young" Lochiel for, though ruling the clan, and being about fifty years old when he led them in the Forty-five, his father was alive, but in exile in France for participating in the Rising of 1715.

Banquo's Walk is no mere cart-track, but is an avenue about thirty feet broad carpeted thickly with the autumn leaves of centuries and with a mossy earth bank on either side, the whole embowered by the rich foliage of beech, sycamore, oak and birch. It is fully a quarter of a mile long, close to the swift-flowing Lochy, but only at intervals through the trees and banking is the river visible. I do not know of any place which so prompts a pensive mood as this secluded retreat, indeed there is a pregnant *atmosphere* about it which is difficult to define. Over some scenes there seems to brood an indefinable *influence* which penetrates the observer. It may be the reflection of our thoughts which we project on to the scenery, but those who commune with nature alone frequently are not likely to admit that this explanation accounts fully for the phenomenon. Of such a place is Banquo's Walk, at least in my experience. If you would see this avenue at its best, visit it during autumn, when the dense foliage which embowers it and its mossy banks glow in russet, gold, crimson and elfin-green, thrown into high light and shadow by the long beams of sunlight which penetrate its twilight; when the only sound is the rustling of the leaves in the breeze and the music of the near-by river in its rocky bed.

From Tor Castle we can continue along the canal bank to Gairlochy, but in order to visit some places of interest let us join the main road by passing under the canal through the near-by culvert.

Proceeding northwards along the road from the Sheangain Burn we are at a high level, and therefore obtain an extensive view of the surrounding scenery. In about half an hour's walk we come to Strone farm, on the right-hand side, beyond which there is a long, steep decline in the road. Strone farm was occupied at one time by a famous member of Clan Cameron, namely Alexander Cameron, the Lochaber bone-setter, who died in 1875, an octogenarian, at Strone.   He was a well - known sheep farmer but was much more renowned for his remarkable natural gift of manipulative surgery in the treatment of dislocations, sprains and broken bones, somewhat similar to our modern osteopaths.   He practised his art without charging any fee for many years, but ultimately his services were in so much demand that he made a small charge to cover his travelling and other expenses.   He was successful in relieving many sufferers whose cases had been misunderstood or wrongly treated by medical practitioners.   His fame became so widespread that when his farming business necessitated his visiting Glasgow, Edinburgh, Perth, and other towns, the local Press advertised the date of his visit.   He was often asked to visit patients who were unable to travel, at places all over Scotland, though his own modesty prevented his skill from being even more widely known. He was a fine type of Highlander, of splendid appearance, high principles, deep piety and a staunch clansman.   His son, John, who succeeded him at Strone, inherited his father's skill and was equally successful in his treatment.

At the foot of Strone Brae a road leads off to the left into lonely Glen Loy (laoigh—"a calf"), with bare hill-sides at the entrance, but densely wooded further on.   On an eminence a short distance into this glen, and nestling among tall trees, is the white-walled Errachd House, ancient home of the Errachd branch of Clan Cameron, who trace their descent from Ewan Cameron, son of the thirteenth Lochiel, by his second wife.

The first laird of the present Errachd House was "out" with Mar in 1715, and gave his life in the cause at Sheriffmuir.   His son, Donald, had the honour of being placed second in command of the Camerons in the Forty-five.   After Culloden, he was a fugitive until the Act of Indemnity was passed, in which he was one of those pardoned, when he returned to Glen Loy.

The son of Errachd of the Forty-five was Lieutenant-General Sir Alan Cameron, who served with distinction in the first American war, in Egypt, Sweden, and Spain, and all through the Peninsular War, and in 1793, in the short period of three months, raised the Cameron Highlanders, who, later, had "The Queen's Own" attached to their title. Sir Alan was born a short time before Prince Charlie landed in Scotland, and was carried in his mother's arms to the door of Errachd House to see the Prince's clansmen march past at the outset of the campaign. Thus early, Alan made his acquaintance with warfare.

Beyond Glen Loy the road winds along the heather-clad hill-side, with the Caledonian Canal and the River Lochy running parallel courses in the moorland beneath, and the Ben Nevis group of mountains rising beyond until, in a short time, we see the bridge over the canal at Moy. Here, Prince Charlie and his army rested on the fourth and fifth nights of their march from Glenfinnan,* and here Murray of Broughton received his official appointment as secretary to His Royal Highness. It was also at Moy, at Dalmuccomer, that Viscount Dundee, *Ian Dubh nan Cath* ("Black John of the Battles"), gathered together the Highland clans in the Stuart cause, in 1689, before leading them to victory over the Government troops at Killiecrankie, though Dundee himself was killed in that famous battle. While the clans were mustering, Dundee resided in Moy House, which is no longer in existence.

* The heavy-baggage party appears to have camped at Errachd, and not at Moy with the remainder of the army. Errachd is about one mile short of Moy. In a manuscript in the possession of the Keppoch family, containing notes on the campaign, set down by a grandson of Keppoch of the Forty-five, from an account received from the narrator's own father, who was a participant, it is stated: "Third stage Errachd, passing by the moss of Corpach; a few guns were fired from the garrison of Fort William." A local man would not mistake Errachd for Moy.

It is also said that Gormsuil, the famous Lochaber witch, made her home at Moy House.

A mile or so beyond Moy the road passes high above the little village of Gairlochy, where there are two locks uniting the waters of the Caledonian Canal with those of Loch Lochy, the most westerly of the three lochs stretching through the Great Glen. The loch is about ten miles long from Gairlochy to Laggan, the next stretch of canal.

Through rich woodlands of oak, hazel and birch we skirt the shore of Loch Lochy, where it widens out from Gairlochy, passing by a clearing on the left where the Cameron clansmen mustered before marching off to Glenfinnan to join Prince Charlie. This gathering ground is now covered thickly with long bracken. Through quivering foliage appears the rounded green mass of Clunes Hill rising from the loch, its base richly clad with pine and fir. Presently, at a little bay in the loch, a private road leads off to the left, through a little valley to Achnacarry Castle, the residence of Lochiel, Chief of Clan Cameron. The castle is an imposing square pile of comparatively modern structure, standing close to the River Arkaig in the shadow of Ben Bhan, which rises to the south. The building was commenced at the beginning of the nineteenth century, but was not completed until 1837.

The name Achnacarry is derived from the Gaelic *achadh na cairidh*, meaning "field of the weir." Though it has become well known since the Forty-five campaign, the only mention of it in history, previous to that time, relates to the memorable occasion in the history of Lochaber, in 1665, when the Camerons, led by the famous Sir Ewan, met their hereditary enemies, the MacIntoshes, on the banks of the River Arkaig, both clans in battle array. The Camerons and their allies numbered about twelve hundred, while there were about fifteen hundred MacIntoshes. During the two days which they spent throwing up enbankments, and preparing for a decisive fight, young Campbell of Glenorchy, who later became the first Earl of Bread-albane, arrived on the scene. (Sir Ewan's mother was a Campbell of Glenorchy.) Acting as mediator, he achieved a peaceful settlement between the two clans. By this agreement the Camerons obtained legal possession of "the lands of Glenlui and Locharkaig," which the MacIntoshes had long disputed, on payment of a sum of money to the latter clan. Thus ended the internecine feud between these two clans, which had lasted for about three hundred and sixty years.

The first castle at Achnacarry was built towards the end of the seventeenth century by Sir Ewan Cameron, seventeenth chief, to which he removed from Tor Castle. This castle built by Sir Ewan was the one which was burned by the Hanoverian soldiers on 28th May 1746, after Culloden. Lord Macaulay, the historian, describes it as, "A large pile built entirely of fir wood and considered in the Highlands a superb palace," but there is reason to doubt that it was composed entirely of wood. There is a ruin of a stone building near the stables of modern Achnacarry Castle which is reputed to be part of the old castle. The present Lochiel, K.T., however, regards this belief as erroneous. He told me that the old castle was built on an entirely different site, some distance from these ruins. He believes that the ruins are part of a building existing previous to the old castle, and that it must certainly have been there when the Gentle Lochiel planted the beech avenue to the old castle, as it has turned the avenue slightly out of line. The fact that this ruin is of stone suggests that the old castle would also be of stone. The reason for the entire disappearance of the old castle, apart from its being burned, was probably that which accounts for the disappearance of many old stone buildings in the

Highlands — namely, that when a new building is erected, the stones from the old one are often utilized in the new structure.

The avenue of tall beeches at Achnacarry, mentioned above, is said to have been in course of being planted by Lochiel when Prince Charlie landed in Scotland. As the first part of the avenue had been planted before the arrival of the Prince, its trees were spaced at regular intervals, but when Lochiel decided to join the standard of the Prince he had the last lot of trees inserted hurriedly without any alignment. He intended to arrange them properly when he returned after the campaign. Alas, he never returned to Achnacarry, with the result that the avenue now shows the equally-spaced and erratic-spaced beeches.

Clan Cameron, of whom Lochiel is the Chief, is one of the oldest and most renowned of the Highland clans. They were always to the fore in the fight for the Royal House of Stuart, and had their full share of inter-clan warfare. The name Cameron is generally believed to be derived from the Gaelic *cam sron*, meaning "crooked nose," a distinguishing feature of some early chief, just as the name Campbell is derived from the Gaelic *cam beul*, meaning "crooked mouth." This derivation, however, displeases many Cameron clansmen, some of whom claim that the name is more likely to be derived from a place-name.* The clan badge of the Camerons is the oak, of which there are many fine specimens in Lochaber.

Leaving legend aside, the first Cameron chief is believed to have been Angus, who married Marion, daughter of Kenneth, Thane of Lochaber, and sister of Banquo. He is said to have saved Banquo's son,

* Dr. Cameron Lees in his *History of the County of Inverness* puts forward a summary of evidence in favour of Clan Cameron being of Lowland origin, originating, probably, from the district of Cameron, or Cambron, in Fife.

Fleance, from the cruelty of Macbeth. In any case, there is definite mention in history of a Cameron chief during the reign of Robert II (1371–90). The clan originally consisted of four main branches—the Mac-Martins of Letterfinlay, the Camerons of Lochiel, the MacGillonies of Strone, and the MacSorlies of Glen Nevis. The MacMartins appear to have been the early chiefs of the clan, and the Lochiel family the oldest cadets. Since the fourteenth century the Lochiel family have held the chiefship, through the marriage of Donald, their leader (the famous Donald Dubh), to the heiress of MacMartin of Letterfinlay. This marriage not only united the Lochiel Camerons and MacMartins, but resulted in the majority of the MacMartins adopting the name Cameron. The early possessions of the clan lay on the east side of the Loch and River Lochy. Their more modern territory, from Loch Arkaig to Loch Eil, belonged at that time to the Clan Chattan and the MacDonalds of Clanranald. According to tradition, Clan Cameron is said to have once formed one of the Clan Chattan Confederacy, but to have broken away after the famous battle of the North Inch of Perth.

Though the Cameron chiefs have always wielded a powerful sway in the Highlands, Sir Ewan, who built the first castle at Achnacarry, was probably the most famous of them all. In the Highlands he was called Eoghann Dubh, or Black Ewan, owing to his swarthy complexion. Born in February 1629, at Kilchurn Castle, Loch Awe, at that time the home of his maternal grandfather, Sir Robert Campbell, Ewan was brought up at Letterfinlay until he was twelve years old. His father having died during his infancy, Ewan, when he passed his twelfth birthday, was placed in charge of the Marquis of Argyll to be educated, and to act as a hostage for the good behaviour of Clan Cameron. At the age of eighteen Ewan left Inveraray, where he had

been attending the school, for Lochaber, and soon
made his presence felt.   Both by his stature and bearing
he was well endowed for the rôle of Highland chief.
He and his clan became a sore thorn in the flesh of
Cromwell's soldiers, and it was mainly to curb their
activities that the fort was built at Fort William.   On
the restoration of Charles II, Ewan was knighted for
his services to the Stuart cause, and when Viscount
Dundee raised the Highlanders in revolt against
William of Orange, in 1689, Sir Ewan was his principal
adviser, and fought with him at Killiecrankie, when
the furious charge of the Highlanders completely
routed the Government forces.   It is said that Lochiel
was the only member of his clan at that battle who
possessed a pair of shoes, but immediately before the
charge he cast them off and led his clansmen barefooted.   According to Pennant, Sir Ewan, in 1680,
killed with his own hands the last wolf that was seen
in the Highlands, but this claim is also made for other
Highlanders.   Sir Ewan's wolf was probably the last
seen in Lochaber.*

Stories of second sight are quite common in the
Highlands, and it is said that Sir Ewan exhibited this
supernormal faculty in his old age.   On the morning of
22nd December 1715 he awakened from a sound sleep
and said to his wife that King James had landed in
Scotland, and they must celebrate the occasion.   His
wife at first thought that he was in a delirium, but he
was so clear-headed and emphatic that she had his
commands carried out to prepare and light a bonfire,
and all at Achnacarry toasted the King's health in
uisge-beatha.   Sure enough, word came soon afterwards
that James had landed secretly at Peterhead on the

* There is a memorial at Lothbeg, in Sutherland, said to be near the
spot where the last wolf in Sutherland was killed in 1700, while Perthshire claims that the last wolf in Scotland was killed in Rannoch about
1710.

morning on which Sir Ewan had announced it. Sir
Ewan died in 1719, in his ninetieth year, and was
buried in Kilmallie churchyard on Loch Eil-side,
having shared to the full in the stirring events of his
day. Macaulay, the historian, styled him "the Ulysses
of the Highlands."

Sir Ewan's grandson, Donald, who was Prince
Charlie's staunch supporter, and one of his most
influential and trusted counsellors throughout the
Forty-five campaign, was probably the next most
famous chief of the clan. He became known as the
"Gentle * Lochiel" owing to his natural refinement
and courtesy. No man knew better the slender chance
the Rising had of success, and no one realized more
fully the calamity that its failure would mean to the
Highlands, yet he sacrificed his all in his loyalty to
the House of Stuart. He suffered severely with his
Prince after Culloden, and died in exile. After the
Forty-five the Cameron lands were forfeited, but were
restored to Donald, twenty-second Chief of Lochiel,
subject to a fine of £3432, by the 1784 Act of Indemnity.

The present Chief of the Camerons, Sir Donald
Walter Cameron of Lochiel, K.T., twenty-fifth Chief,
whose home, Achnacarry Castle, was damaged by fire
during the recent war, has worthily maintained the
noble traditions of his clan. During the Kaiser's war
he served with distinction, commanding and leading
into action the 5th Battalion of the Cameron Highlanders. He also raised the 6th and 7th Battalions for
service. His brother, Alan Cameron, was killed while
serving with the 2nd Battalion. During Hitler's war
Lochiel's three sons also upheld the military tradition
of their ancestors.

On the 24th of June 1938 the greatest gathering of
Cameron clansmen since the Forty-five took place at
Achnacarry, when seven hundred Camerons rallied at

* The word "gentle" here refers to "gentility" rather than meekness.

the ancestral home of their chief. On that occasion Lochiel announced that a proposal, which had his full consent, was under consideration to acquire the lands of the estate and to hand them over to a clan trust to be preserved in perpetuity as clan lands, lest economic conditions might necessitate their sale into alien possession.

Beyond the private road to Achnacarry Castle we cross the rapid-flowing River Arkaig, which is of short course but of rugged nature. It is only about a mile long, flowing from Loch Arkaig into Loch Lochy, in a bed of shingle and rock between thickly wooded banks.

Skirting a woodland of magnificent pines and firs, we come to a pretty little sandy bay in Loch Lochy at Clunes, where there used to be a pier for the private use of Lochiel, but which has fallen into decay. From this point there is a striking view of mountain, moor, loch and forest, all invested with romantic history. On the hill-side, the dark background of Scots pine and fir throws into vivid prominence the lighter tints of spruce and larch, while here and there gleams a clump of silver birch. In these woods Cameron of Clunes lived in a hut when a fugitive after Culloden, and in his rude abode he sheltered Prince Charlie for some time. It was in the permanent home of Cameron of Clunes on 20th September 1665 that Sir Ewan and the Chief of the MacIntoshes signed the treaty that ended their blood feud which had lasted for more than three centuries.

A short distance beyond Clunes the road bends towards the west, away from Loch Lochy, and leads through the famous "Dark Mile" in the woods of Torr a Ghallain, which clad a picturesque little valley. The short but fairly wide valley which stretches between high hills from Loch Lochy to Lock Arkaig is really divided by a little tree-clad ridge into two small parallel valleys. The River Arkaig flows through the southern one, while the Dark Mile leads through the northern one. Until the present century the Dark Mile was fringed and overhung with such dense foliage that even at midday it was almost twilight in this avenue. During the last few decades, however, especially during the Kaiser's war, so many trees were felled, and others collapsed during storms, that now it can hardly be recognized as a "dark mile," and the stranger may be excused if he fails to recognize it.

To readers other than those acquainted with Lochaber, and Jacobite students, the Dark Mile may be familiar by the reading of Miss D. K. Broster's well-known novel of this title. Indeed, I would strongly advise those who have not already done so to read Miss Broster's trilogy of Jacobite novels, *The Flight of the Heron*, *The Gleam in the North*, and *The Dark Mile*, as they deal mainly with the district of Lochaber, and portray the scenery and Highland character in a fascinating and accurate manner.

There is a little incline in the road as we enter the Dark Mile, called "Culcairn's Brae," which derives its name from the following incident, which took place here during the plunderings of the Highlands after Culloden.

A company of soldiers, under Captain Grant, one of Cumberland's officers, while on a punitive expedition on Loch Arkaig-side met a local young man called Alexander Cameron, carrying a gun on his shoulder. Captain Grant demanded to know why he had not surrendered his arms to the military authorities. Cameron replied that he lived in an outlandish region but was now on his way to surrender his arms. This answer did not satisfy Captain Grant, and he ordered Cameron to be tied to a tree and shot immediately. When Cameron's father learned of this outrage he vowed to take Captain Grant's life. Later, when

Grant and his men were returning from their expedition they met a company of soldiers under command of Major Munro of Culcairn, also returning from a similar outing.   Uniting into one body of men, they marched along Loch Arkaig-side, with Major Munro and Captain Grant walking together at their head.   When Cameron's father learned that the soldiers were returning he went into ambush in the Dark Mile, armed with a gun and, as Munro and Grant marched past, he fired to kill Grant and then made good his escape.   Either Cameron's aim was faulty, or else he mistook his man, for he killed Major Munro of Culcairn instead of Captain Grant.   This incident took place at the little incline in the road now called Culcairn's Brae.

Near the Loch Arkaig end of the Dark Mile, and on the south side of the road, lies the bleached trunk of Prince Charlie's Tree, now bare of bark but still preserved.   It was blown down during a storm at the beginning of the present century.   The tree was an ash, with a large hollow in the trunk from which an opening faced towards the west.   A story became attached to this tree that on one occasion the unfortuate Prince, during his fugitive wanderings, sought safety in its recess, when he was surprised suddenly in the Dark Mile by a detachment of redcoats; hence the name given to the tree.   This story, however, would seem to be an invention, as there does not appear to be mention of it in any of the many histories of the Forty-five.   If the tree existed in Prince Charlie's time it must have been over one hundred and fifty years old when it collapsed.   Consequently, the trunk was not likely to be hollow during the Forty-five, and even if it were so, the hollow would not be sufficiently large to accommodate a man.

Up on the wooded hillside to the north of Prince Charlie's Tree is Prince Charlie's Cave, where he and his companions, Dr. Archibald Cameron (brother of Lochiel), Cameron of Clunes and the Rev. John Cameron, found shelter for several days while fugitives.

A short distance beyond Prince Charlie's Tree and on the right-hand side of the Dark Mile there is a double waterfall where the waters of the River Cia-aig, from the high hills to the north of Achnacarry, come dashing down through thickly wooded banks into a deep pool, called the Witch's Cauldron, at the road-side.

The story relating to this pool is that, long ago, the Camerons of this district were sorely troubled by an unaccountable sickness among their cattle. Suspicion was aroused that someone was putting the evil eye on them, so they consulted an old woman seer who lived in Glen Loy. She told them their suspicions were correct and that the culprit was an old hermit woman who lived near the shore of Loch Arkaig. Only by killing this hag would the curse be lifted. The Camerons set off to carry out the deed, but when they reached the hermit's house they found it empty, save for a large, fierce, striped cat crouching in a corner. Drawing their dirks they dashed at the cat, but it sprang for the door and, though two of the clansmen stabbed it when passing, it escaped. The trail of blood, however, showed them the route it had taken and, tracking it through the heather and woodland, they came to the Cia-aig Falls, where they found the cat lying exhausted. As they made to bury their dirks in its body, and finish it off, the cat let out a frightful scream and leaped over the falls into the deep, dark pool beneath. When in mid-air it changed into the form of the old hag they sought, which action confirmed their suspicions, so, instead of helping her out of the water, they stoned her until she was drowned. From that day their cattle improved in health and there was no more illness among them.

Passing the waterfall, a rough road branches off to

BEN NEVIS GROUP, FROM ABOVE SPEAN BRIDGE

[To face page 128

GENERAL WADE'S ROAD ABOVE LOCH LOCHY

THE GLAS DOIRE HILLS AND LOCH LOCHY

BEN NEVIS, FROM CORPACH

[To face page 129

the left and is bridged over the River Arkaig where it leaves the Loch.   This road curves along the south side of Loch Arkaig into the lonely fastnesses of Glen Mallie. If you wish the real thing in untamed nature, tramp into this glen with its magnificent forests.   You will feel that the realm of business and machinery belongs to another world.   Here solitude reigns supreme, with heather hills and noble pines and firs—some of the finest specimens in Scotland.   This is a real haunt of red deer and golden eagle, as well as hill fox and wild cat.

Returning to the main road, we come to the foot of Loch Arkaig immediately we pass the divergence to the Glen Mallie road.   This loch is one of the most peacefully picturesque stretches of water in Scotland, and one which will always be associated with the fugitive wanderings of Prince Charlie.   The drooping, lacy foliage of silver birch and the coral fruit of the rowan overhang its heathery shores and mirror-like waters, which lead away into the distant mountains. A little pier, now crumbling in decay, was used by the present Lochiel's father as a wharf for his little steam-yacht, the vessel which carried Queen Victoria on her cruise of the loch during her tour of the Highlands in 1873.   The decayed and sunken hull of the yacht itself lies close to the pier.   Through frames of foliage at the loch-side appear a little tree-clad island, which contains the ruins of a chapel, and the old burial-place of the MacPhees of this district.   On it Sir Ewan Cameron of Lochiel held a few officers as hostages while he treated with the Government for favourable terms.   On a tree on this island an osprey, or sea-eagle, nested for a number of years at the beginning of the present century, but though the tree was protected by barbed wire some rascals succeeded in robbing the nest several times, with the result that the bird left, in 1908, never to

I

return. This is the last authentic breeding of an osprey in the British Isles.

About a mile beyond the foot of the loch we emerge from the woodlands of oak, ash and birch to the open hill-side at Achnasaul. It was here that Prince Charlie, after remarkable adventures on the west coast, met Cameron of Clunes to obtain information as to the whereabouts of Lochiel, in order to make arrangements for their escape to France. One of his companions describes his condition on this occasion: "The Prince at this time was in a small hut built for the purpose in the wood betwixt Achnasaul and Loch Arkaig. He was then barefooted, had an old black kilt coat on, a plaid, philabeg and waistcoat, a dirty shirt and a long red beard, a gun in his hand, a pistol and durk by his side. He was very cheerful and in good health. We continued in this wood and that over against Achnacarie (having three huts in different places to which we removed in turn) till, I think, about the 10th of August." There does not appear to be any evidence that the Prince wore the kilt when leading his army. He wore it only when a fugitive after Culloden.

From the heather- and bracken-clad hill-side above Achnasaul there is a thrilling view spread out of the lonely hills of Lochiel's forest, and the loch winding away to the west. By its northern shore a rough country road leads to its head at Kinlocharkaig, about twelve miles off. It was up there, at the head of Loch Arkaig, in Glen Camgharaidh, or Camgarry, that Prince Charlie and his faithful fugitive friends spent their last day in Lochaber. They were hastening to Arisaig to embark on the two French ships which had eluded the naval patrols, and were anxiously awaiting their arrival to convey them to France. Cluny, the MacPherson chief, and one of the Prince's staunchest supporters, preferred to seek safety in his native hills of Badenoch rather than sail into exile, so he bid them

all farewell at Glen Camgarry on the morning that
they set out on the last stage of their trek to Arisaig.

From the head of Loch Arkaig, narrow and lonely
Glen Pean leads away to the head of Loch Morar.
Also from the head of Loch Arkaig, Glen Dessary leads
away westward towards the head of Loch Nevis.
Through this glen there is a rough track said to be an
old military road. It is now seldom traversed, but
used to be utilized by drovers when taking their cattle
from the west to the Lowland sales.

There used to be a cadet branch of the Lochiel
family at Glen Dessary, and it was the oft-discussed
Jenny Cameron of Glen Dessary who was a conspicuous
spectator at the raising of the standard at Glenfinnan.
The local tradition is that, mounted on a white horse,
she led the men from the district around Glen Dessary
to Glenfinnan to join Prince Charlie, and returned
home after the ceremony. She is said to have under-
taken this duty as her brother, the head of the Glen
Dessary Camerons, was at that time abroad. Chambers
says that she had married an Irish gentleman by the
name of O'Neil, but was obliged by his brutal treatment
to divorce him and that she dropped the name O'Neil,
reverting to her maiden name. Owing to confusion with
another Jenny Cameron, a camp-follower of Prince
Charlie's army, who was captured by the Government forces at the Battle of Falkirk, gossips have
woven the story that Jenny Cameron of Glen Dessary
was the mistress of Prince Charlie and followed him
throughout his campaign. This insinuation, however,
seems to have been a malicious invention of enemies of
the Prince.

Principal Shairp's fine poem, *Glendessary, or the Sequel
of Culloden*, deals with the whole area from Loch Arkaig
to Loch Hourn, a romantic region which must be one
of the least explored parts of Britain. Few Highlanders,
let alone *Sasunnaich*, ever traverse it.

No account of Loch Arkaig would be complete without mention of the "Loch Arkaig Treasure," some part of which, according to tradition, still lies buried by the shores of the loch.

After Culloden, when the clan chiefs and their clansmen were widely scattered in their different places of escape, and a few days after the Prince had sailed for the Outer Hebrides, two French ships arrived at Borrodale, Arisaig, and landed seven casks containing 35,000 *louis d'or* to help in carrying on or reviving the Rising. This money was received by Murray of Broughton, who was a fugitive along with Lochiel, and entrusted by him to the care of Dr. Archibald Cameron, brother of Lochiel, for conveyance to Loch Arkaig. It was carried over the hills to Loch Morar and thence by boat to the head of the loch. From there it was conveyed through Glen Pean to Murlaggan, on the north side of Loch Arkaig. One cask had been stolen before leaving Borrodale but was recovered soon after the remainder had reached its destination.

On the arrival of this war chest, Lochiel sent word to all the fugitive chiefs to meet at Murlaggan on 8th May in order to discuss future action. The meeting was duly held, and the decision arrived at for each chief to proceed to his own territory and muster every conceivable man, and all meet at Achnacarry on 15th May. Each chief was given a certain sum from the war chest to help in recruiting men.

Meanwhile, however, the Duke of Cumberland, who had command of the Government forces, ordered Lord Louden to march into Lochaber with seventeen hundred men and stamp out any attempt at further insurrection. This move counteracted the arrangements of the clan chiefs and led to the final abandonment of any further opposition.

It was now thought advisable to hide the remainder

of the war chest in a place of security until an opportune time to use it.   It was therefore divided into two lots, one of 15,000 *louis d'or* and one of 12,000 *louis d'or*.   The first lot in bags of 1,000 *louis* was buried by the side of a burn in a wood opposite Caillich, by Murray, Dr. Cameron, Alexander MacLeod of Neuk, Sir Thomas Threipland and Major Kennedy.   The second lot was buried near the foot of Loch Arkaig by Dr. Cameron and MacLeod of Neuk.

Shortly after burying the hoard, Murray was arrested at Tweeddale while on his way south, and, whether or not Dr. Cameron had suspicions that Murray might reveal the site of the money to the Government (as he actually offered to do), Dr. Cameron dug it up and reburied it at different sites with his own son and another gentleman as witnesses.   Thus the Government troops never found it, though they searched diligently for it.

The money remained hidden until September, when the Prince and his friends passed along Loch Arkaigside on their way to escape to France, when Dr. Cameron revealed the site of the buried treasure to the Prince, Lochiel and Cluny MacPherson.   As Cluny decided to remain in hiding in Scotland, while his friends sailed for France, he was appointed guardian of the money.   It is said that, later, Cluny and a brother of Cameron of Glen Nevis unearthed the whole treasure and conveyed it to Cluny's own territory of Badenoch, where they reburied it.   Cluny was entrusted with the distribution of money from the hoard to the necessitous clans, but this distribution was the cause of much bitterness, each clan believing that it had not received as generous treatment as the other clans, and aroused many unpleasant accusations against Cluny by his enemies.

In 1749 Dr. Cameron arrived from France at Cluny's country on a secret visit, to obtain some of the money on behalf of the family of Lochiel, who were in exile in France, Lochiel having died in 1748. Dr. Cameron says that Cluny refused to give him any money except his expenses without orders from James, the Prince's father, and that he had to return to France in order to obtain this authority. Young Glengarry ("Pickle the Spy") says that Dr. Cameron did get 6,000 *louis d'or* from Cluny on giving him a receipt. On his second visit to Scotland, in 1753, Dr. Cameron was captured at Inversnaid, while on his way northward, and conveyed to London for trial. Being found guilty, under the Act of Attainder, he was executed at Tyburn on 7th June 1753, the last man to suffer death for complicity in the Forty-five. Horace Walpole says, in *Memoirs of the Reign of George II*, p. 333 : "Intelligence had been received some time before of Cameron's intended journey to Britain, with a commission from Prussia to offer arms to the disaffected Highlanders."

According to Lochaber tradition some part of the treasure still lies buried by the shores of Loch Arkaig, but this belief seems doubtful, owing to the large portions known to have been dispensed. When Cluny left Scotland finally for France he is believed to have taken the residue of the treasure to Prince Charlie. In a modern book, *Romance of the White Rose*, Mr. Grant R. Francis gives new evidence on the disposal of the treasure after it came into Cluny's possession, based upon a number of receipts discovered by him in 1928, among old documents in the Cluny Charter Chest, which seems to account for the whole sum of money, thus dispelling the tradition that some of it still lies buried on the shores of Loch Arkaig. In the *Scottish History Society Miscellany*, vol. vii, 1941, there is also a very interesting account of the treasure and its disposal.

CHAPTER VI

BRAE LOCHABER

THE district of Brae Lochaber, or the Braes of Lochaber, lies around Glen Spean and Glen Roy, that is the north-east part of Lochaber, and is the ancestral home of that staunch Jacobite clan the MacDonells of Keppoch. From Fort William the route to Brae Lochaber leads along the northern skirts of the Ben Nevis group of mountains and, to Spean Bridge, follows closely upon General Wade's old road to Inverness.

Passing the ruin of Inverlochy Castle, and the bridge over the River Lochy, we continue northwards, keeping to the east bank of the river. About a mile or so beyond the Lochy Bridge stands the imposing pile of modern Inverlochy Castle on a grassy eminence, backed by tall firs and pines, with a pretty little lochan and the sinuous River Lundy in the foreground. Locally, it is called Torlundy Castle. This castle was built by the first Lord Abinger (formerly Sir James Scarlett), who purchased the lands of Inverlochy in 1837 from the Earl of Aboyne, who had previously acquired this part of the Lochaber estate of his cousin, the Duke of Gordon, on the death of that nobleman. Part of the estate is still in the possession of Lord Abinger's successors. The castle, which he sold in 1945, was visited by Queen Victoria in 1873, when on her tour of the Highlands, during the time of the second Lord Abinger. Within the grounds, and a short distance from the castle, there is an ivy-clad mausoleum where lie the mortal remains of three Lords Abinger.

Beyond Torlundy, to Glen Spean, stretches a low-lying moorland, with few signs of habitation. Dotted all over this moor are little knolls, or *drumlins*, of boulder-clay covered with green mossy turf, and many *erratic* boulders borne from distant parts and dropped here by glaciers. One of these glacier knolls on the right-hand side of the road, opposite Achandaul farm, is called Torr na Bratach ("mound of the banner"), where, it is said, a party of Campbells escaping from the Battle of Inverlochy made a last stand.

The homestead of Achandaul itself is worthy of mention, for here lived Colonel Mitchell of the Gordon Highlanders, who took command of the regiment at Quatre Bras when Colonel John Cameron of Fassifern was killed. At the time the Gordon Highlanders were raised, the Duke of Gordon was overlord of Lochaber, which accounts for many of the original officers and men of the regiment being natives of the district.

Colonel Mitchell was severely wounded later in the battle, and at Waterloo the regiment was commanded by Major MacDonald of Dalchosnie, Kinloch Rannoch, Perthshire, the county abutting Lochaber on the east. The MacDonalds of Dalchosnie are descended from a son of the seventh Chief of Keppoch. It was Major MacDonald who led the regiment to victory in its famous charge at Waterloo against tremendous odds, which is said to have elicited from Napoleon the exclamation, "Les braves Écossais!" When the Gordons were nearing the enemy, the order was given for the Scots Greys (the only regular Scottish cavalry regiment) to charge in support of them, and together these two famous Scottish regiments dashed upon the foe and routed them, shouting to one another, "Scotland For Ever!" This thrilling military incident forms the subject of Lady Butler's well-known painting "Scotland For Ever," which hangs in the Leeds Art Gallery.

Achandaul was also the home for years of John

Cameron, son of the Lochaber bone-setter, and himself highly skilled in the treatment. He went from his father's farm at Strone to Fassifern, and thence to Achandaul.

About a mile or so before we reach Spean Bridge, a rough country road strikes down to the left at a point where this same road, but on the opposite side of the highway, passes under the railway. This road is worth following, for about a mile along its birch and hazel course is High Bridge, now in ruins, where the first shots were fired of the Jacobite Rising of 1745.

High Bridge was built in 1736 by General Wade, on three arches founded on rock, to span the narrow but deep and precipitous rocky gorge of the River Spean, as part of his Inverness to Fort William road, at a cost of £1,087. Previous to this time the Spean was crossed at the ford of Dalnabea, below Corrie-choille. This was the point crossed by Montrose and his men on their way to Inverlochy. A report from Fort William of the proceedings on the occasion of laying the foundation stone of High Bridge, dated 16th June 1736, states:

"Last Friday being the Anniversary of his Majesty's Accession to the Throne, our Lieutenant Governor, attended by the Officers of this Garrison, and several other Gentlemen, went to the River Speyn six miles from hence, where all the Materials are being prepared for a Bridge over that rapid and dangerous River, the first stone was laid, and the Healths of their Majesties, the Prince and Princess of Wales, the Duke and Royal Family, with many other loyal Toasts were Drunk, at the Instant our great Guns were firing on the happy Occasion of the Day. This Bridge is to be of three Arches; the Middle Arch fifty foot Diameter, the other two Arches forty feet each; the Hills through which the River runs being very high, the Causeway, for the better Access to the Road, on each Side, will be fourscore Feet from the common Surface of the Water, which is near Thirty Foot deep. The finishing this Work will complete a safe and easy Communication from this Garrison to those of Fort Augustus and Fort George, and likewise to all the Military Roads, which by his Majesty's Command have been carried on through the Highlands under the Care of General Wade. The Company returned and supped with the Governor, where the above Healths were repeated, and the Night ended with Bonfires, Illuminations, and all other Demonstrations of Joy."

The last repairs to the bridge were carried out in 1893, when an iron gangway was laid across its surface to relieve it of stress, but about 1913 the southern arch collapsed, and since then it has been deserted and left in ruin. It is a rather dangerous place to approach for close inspection, owing to the river banks being so steep and deep, and the surroundings a veritable jungle of birch, hazel, oak, and bracken. The ruins of the bridge itself are, naturally, also dangerous, especially as they are clad with mossy turf and several trees; but, even in its decayed condition, High Bridge can still arouse stirring thoughts of olden times.

The first engagement of the Forty-five occurred here, on 16th August 1745, when Captain Scott and his two companies of Government troops marched into an ambush at the northern end of the bridge. They were on their way from Fort Augustus to Fort William in order to strengthen the latter garrison, after the Government learned that Prince Charlie had landed in Scotland.

A party of Keppoch MacDonells, under the command of Donald MacDonell of Tirnadris, were guarding the bridge. Though there were only twelve of them, including a piper, they adopted the ruse of scampering about in the dense wood which at that time clothed this part, shouting and firing shots at different parts and calling on imaginary clansmen to gather and charge, which caused Captain Scott to think that the bridge was strongly guarded. Rather than get caught in a trap at this "bottleneck" in the road, he ordered his men to turn about and retreat. Tirnadris sent out express messengers to secure assistance, and thus a combined party of Highlanders overtook the Government troops near Loch Oich and forced them to surrender. A number of these prisoners were marched to Glenfinnan to be shown to Prince Charlie as representing the first victory of the Rising.

Keppoch, the Chief, was not present at the action at High Bridge, as he had set off for Glenfinnan some days previously, taking with him as prisoner Captain Switenham, an English officer whom he captured while on his way from Ruthven Barracks, in Badenoch, to inspect the defences at Fort William.

At the village of Spean Bridge we cross the River Spean by a stone bridge built in 1819 by Telford, high above its brown waters rushing and swirling among deep and dark pot-holes and crevices. Branching to the left is the road leading to Inverness, which rises steeply to a considerable height on a wide and wind-swept moorland, a haunt of curlew and moorcock, where the sun-warmed heather and grass breathe out fragrance. From the summit of this road there is a remarkably extensive and impressive view of Loch-aber. If one looks backwards, the whole group of the Ben Nevis mountains is seen in an uninterrupted view, with the tree-clad gorge of the Spean winding through the low stretch of moorland in the foreground. South-ward appears the gap between the hills of Ardgour and those of Nether Lochaber, in which lies Loch Linnhe. Westward the lonely mountains around Loch Arkaig rise in huge rounded masses. On a clear moonlight night, especially during winter when the mountains are covered with snow, this view of far horizons under s star-spangled sky is almost ethereal in its transparent tones of white, silver, blue and purple. No sign of life breaks the solemnity of the scene save an occasional glint of light from a crofter's cottage window.

From the summit of this moorland road, where it bends northwards, a branch road leads westward to Muccomer, and at Gairlochy joins the road from Banavie to Loch Arkaig. At Muccomer the waters of Loch Lochy flow through a deep channel and plunge over a low but seething waterfall, beneath the lofty road bridge, into the River Spean. This channel is really of artificial construction, having been cut during the building of the Caledonian Canal, as the waters of Loch Lochy required to be diverted from the original course of the river. From the Muccomer Falls onwards, the united streams are called the River Lochy. The original outlet of the River Lochy was near the course of the canal, and was filled in during the construction of the canal.

On the site of Muccomer farm, during the seventeenth century, the last battle was fought between the Camerons and the MacIntoshes in their long-standing feud.

The white-walled farm-house of Muccomer was the home, for many years, of Alexander Anthony Cameron, the famous Scottish heavy-weight athlete, who is generally regarded as the greatest heavy-weight athlete Scotland has ever produced. In Lochaber he is always referred to as "Muccomer." On his retiral from the sports arena he was holder of fifteen world's records in heavy-weight events, and few of these records have been surpassed since then. It is said that "Muccomer" inherited his strength from his mother's side of the family, and of his maternal grandfather a story is told in support of this assertion. On one occasion his grandfather found a neighbour struggling with his horse and cart, which had become bogged in a peat-moss while carting home the peats. Hastening to render assistance, he got behind the cart and, seizing the two projections, struggled for a few minutes and then gave it one hefty heave on to firm ground. Turning to his friend, "Muccomer's" grandfather exclaimed, "No wonder the horse could not get the cart out, I could hardly get it out myself."

The old graveyard at Gairlochy was the burial-place of the MacMartins of Letterfinlay, the oldest branch of Clan Cameron, and who, later, changed their name to Cameron. So numerous were the Camerons here at one time that a story is told of a traveller who, arriving late on a stormy night and being unable to find lodgings, shouted in at one window, "Are there no Christians here?" "No," came the answer, "we are all Camerons." Two place-names, *Leum an Taillear* and *Lochan Mhic-an-Toisich*, not far from the canal bank at Gairlochy, commemorate the exciting escape of a Cameron warrior, called *Taillear Dubh na Tuaighe*, from his MacIntosh captors.

The Inverness road, from which the Gairlochy road branches, leads northwards on a long, gradual decline from the high moor above Spean Bridge. From it, as it skirts Stronaba, there is a fine view, westward, of the wooded region of Achnacarry and the Loch Arkaig hills beyond. Until it reaches Glenfintaig House, at the entrance to Glen Gloy, this modern road follows the line of General Wade's old road, but here it sweeps down to the shores of Loch Lochy, while General Wade's road climbs up to a high level on the hill-side overlooking the loch. Wade's road crosses the waters of the Gloy Burn by a picturesque little bridge in a sylvan setting, called Low Bridge. It is well worth visiting, and the tramper should proceed up the hill-side by Wade's road, from which he will obtain an entrancing view of Loch Lochy and the

mountain scenery which surrounds it. To the west
the hills and mountains appear like huge billows
rolling up from the south in long slopes and abrupt
faces towards the north. There is also a lonely road,
which should appeal strongly to the tramper, leading
into Glen Gloy, close to the burn, or little river, whose
waters for crystal clarity I have never seen surpassed.
One will search it in vain for weeds of any kind. A
small military post was stationed at Low Bridge after
the Forty-five, consisting of a non-commissioned officer
and six men. In the miltary records the bridge is called
Nine Mile Bridge, as the Gloy was then known as the
Nine Mile Water. This Wade road we are traversing
was the one followed by Prince Charlie and his
Highlanders on their journey northward from Moy to
Invergarry.

A mile or so beyond Glen Gloy, Wade's road sweeps
down and, crossing the present road, disappears
beneath the waters of Loch Lochy, continuing northwards past Letterfinlay to the head of the loch at
Laggan. This part of Wade's road was submerged
when the waters of Loch Lochy were raised during the
construction of the Caledonian Canal.

By the road-side at Letterfinlay there is a crofter's
house which was built originally by Wade's soldiers as
quarters for the officers in charge of the construction
of his military road between Fort Augustus and Fort
William. Later it became an inn, which was much
frequented by drovers on their way with stock to the
southern markets. The inn subsequently became the
mansion of Letterfinlay estate until superseded, about
seventy years ago, by the present lodge.

Prince Charlie and his army bivouacked at Letterfinlay on the sixth night of their march from Glenfinnan, but the arrival of a messenger with the news
that Sir John Cope and his army were marching to meet
them caused the Prince to strike camp in the darkness

of night and, in a storm of wind and rain, proceed to Invergarry Castle.

About four miles beyond Letterfinlay we come to Laggan, where a short reach of canal connects Loch Lochy to Loch Oich. At Laggan we are passing from Lochaber into the lands of the MacDonells of Glengarry. Just at the head of Loch Lochy there is a piece of ground called Blar-nan-leine ("field of the shirts"), where a ferocious clan battle was fought on a summer day of 1544, between the Frasers and a combined force of Clanranald MacDonalds, Camerons and MacDonells of Glengarry, regarding the chiefship of Clanranald. So hot the day and so fierce the battle that the combatants stripped to their shirts. It was a real hand-to-hand combat with broadswords, dirks and Lochaber axes, a fight for extermination rather than victory, and developed into a veritable shambles. By sunset the three hundred Frasers were annihilated almost to a man, only four of them surviving, while of their five hundred enemies only ten remained alive.

We have followed the Inverness road from Spean Bridge to the northern bounds of Lochaber; let us now follow the road through Glen Spean from Spean Bridge.

Bearing to the right when we cross Spean Bridge we pass through the little village, with its snug houses, which calls for no special mention. About half a mile beyond, however, there is one house worthy of note, namely Tirnadris, standing on a raised piece of ground a short distance from the road on the left-hand side. This house gave to the Jacobite Rising of 1745 one of its most notable heroes, though the present house is not the one which stood at the time of the Rising. That one was burned by the Government troops after Culloden. The laird of Tirnadris, you will remember, had command of the small party of Highlanders who drew the first blood for Prince Charlie at High Bridge.

He served throughout the campaign until the battle
of Falkirk, where he was taken prisoner. After being
kept in Edinburgh for some months he was taken
to Carlisle, and tried for his share in the Rising. Being
found guilty, he was sentenced to death, and executed
on 18th October 1746, his head being affixed to a spike
on the Scottish gate of the town along with the head of
his kinsman, MacDonald of Kinlochmoidart, where they
remained for several years. It is said that the Government's reason for ultimately removing these gruesome
relics from their conspicuous position was that every
Highlander who passed this way saluted them reverently.

One dark and stormy winter night, about the year
1610, a wild-eyed fugitive clansman, in tattered kilt
and shirt, knocked at the door of Tirnadris House and
begged shelter for himself and four companions. The
laird of the house asked him who he was, as his bleached
kilt did not proclaim his tartan. "Mention of my
name is forbidden," said the clansman, but, drawing
back a fold in his kilt, he revealed that he was a Mac-
Gregor—a member of the clan who was at that time
outlawed. This revelation in itself might not have
hardened the laird's heart, but his sweetheart, a Miss
Colquhoun, of Loch Lomond-side, had died of grief
after the murder of her father and brothers by the wild
MacGregors. This grim memory caused the laird to
order the clansman and his companions to begone at
once, and he sent a messenger to Keppoch, the Chief,
informing him that these "broken men" were sheltering
on his land. Keppoch's oath to the Government
compelled him to track down the fugitive MacGregors.
They were found hiding in the wooded banks of the
burn which flows past Tirnadris House. As they
would not surrender, Keppoch and his men slew them,
and sent their heads to Edinburgh. Their headless
bodies were buried in a knoll in front of Tirnadris.

Parallel to the main road, and a short distance from

THE ANNAT BURN

[To face page 144

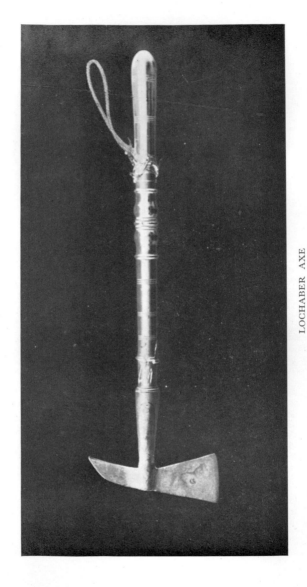

LOCHABER AXE

(Given to Cumming by Sir Ewan Cameron of Lochiel just before the famous skirmish with English troops at Achdalieu in 1654 and used by Cumming on that occasion with deadly effect)

it, across mossy moorland, the River Spean sweeps
through its rocky gorge. Along the greater part of its
course it cuts across the *strike* of the rocks, which results
in some weird rock-carving and potholes. Beyond
the river, on the south side of the glen, we look
into the heart of the wild fastnesses of the Ben Nevis
group of mountains, grim corries and precipices, where
few human feet have ever trod. Nevertheless, it was
through one of these gullies, in the snows of winter,
that Montrose led his men to the head of Glen Nevis,
on his way to the battle of Inverlochy. On the moorland, between the river and the mountain, is the farm
of Corriechoille, where lived one of the most famous, if
not *the* most famous, stock-breeders in Scotland during
the early part of last century. John Cameron was
his name, but he was always called "Corriechoille,"
or "Corry." He died in 1856, having been a real
Lochaber "worthy," and reigned cattle-king of the north.

Passing the little settlement of Inverroy we come to
the village of Roy Bridge, where the mountain waters
of the River Roy come rushing down a deep, rocky
channel through Glen Roy, to join the River Spean,
and at this confluence the Roy loses its identity. A
rough country road, splendid for tramping, climbs
along the hill-side into Glen Roy. Near the entrance
of the glen the road leads through a rich woodland of
oak, birch and bracken, and emerges at the little
crofting settlement of Bohuntine.

During the seventeenth century there lived in this
clachan a real rogue, called Iain Odhar, who regarded
murder as merely part of his work. His services in any
despicable deed were for hire if the fee was suitable.
Though living in the heart of MacDonald country he
was really a Campbell, but lived on good terms with
his near-by neighbours. Iain is said to have been
asked to give a helping hand at the Keppoch Murder
(which will be described later), but refused to do so,

K

his answer being, "No, no; if I put my hands in your blood [MacDonald] to-day you will put your hands in my blood [Campbell] to-morrow."

Of Iain, there are many stories told in Brae Lochaber, but that of his last day in life is surely as grim as any. Iain had escaped the gallows, as evidence against him was always difficult to obtain, the local people being terrified into silence. Thus he died in bed, harbouring his vicious nature to the end. As he lay dying, he asked his wife to fetch one of his neighbours with whom he wished to speak. When his friend bent over to speak, Iain made a strike at him with a dirk which he had hidden in the bed. Only by a quick jump did his friend escape fatal injury. On asking Iain what he meant by this hostile action, the latter replied: "Since I have lived here, the River Roy has drowned twenty, whilst I have only killed nineteen, and I wished to be even with the river before I went."

Beyond Bohuntine Hill the glen becomes bare and lonely, the road zigzagging as it climbs high along the hill-side. At the summit of the road, a few miles into the glen, the famed "Parallel Roads" of Glen Roy become conspicuous on the hill-slopes on either side. They really extend the full length of the glen, but are more obvious here.

The origin of these "roads," which appear as three parallel horizontal lines on the hill-sides, was long a subject of discussion. They were called roads by the ancient Gaels, who believed that they had been constructed by Fingal and his warriors, the legendary heroes to whom the Gael usually ascribes features of nature resembling the handiwork of man. Dr. John MacCulloch, the famous pioneer in Highland geology, was the first person to recognize that these roads were formed as lake beaches. In 1817 he formed this theory, but offered no satisfactory explanation as to how the lake originated. Darwin, the famous naturalist, suggested that the roads were beaches, but *sea*-beaches formed during intervals in the depression of the land, and exposed by its subsequent uplift. Geological research has revealed these roads to be beaches, at different levels of a lake which formed in Glen Roy by the melting of a glacier which filled the glen during the last great Ice Age. The waters of the lake were prevented from escaping, not by a *moraine* of debris, but by a glacial dam formed by a lateral glacier from Glen Spean projecting across Glen Roy near Roy Bridge. The recession of this glacial dam caused the waters of the lake in Glen Roy to alter in level.

"These '[roads']' are ledges due to the material that has been washed down the hill-side being held up where it fell into the water. The roads disappear at the head of each glen where the water was too shallow for this process to form such extensive ledges." Similar gravel ledges, or beaches, formed around Loch Lochy and Loch Ness within forty years of their level being raised during the construction of the Caledonian Canal.

The "roads" are about thirty feet wide, curving round every hill-side and turning into every recess in the glen. They are clad with a coarse grass of a paler shade than the heather slopes of the hills, which makes them conspicuous. "When the ice front had receded entirely from Glen Roy but stood as a barrier across Glen Spean near Spean Bridge, it would have formed a much larger lake which extended up the Spean valley: its surface was at about 855 feet, the height of which was determined by the pass at the north-eastern end of Loch Laggan (now 848 feet), over which the water could discharge to the Spey. Hence the lowest road extended not only up Glen Roy, but on both sides of Glen Spean, where it may still be seen in many places." *

* Extracts from an article by Professor J. W. Gregory in *The Scots Magazine*, August 1929.

There is a story told about the head of Glen Roy
relating to the escape of the Earl of Mar from the battle
of Inverlochy in 1431.   When Donald Balloch defeated
the Government forces, under the Earls of Caithness
and Mar, at Inverlochy, Mar made his escape to his
own territory.   On the first evening of his trek home-
ward, Mar found himself in Glen Roy, weary, wounded
and famished, where two herd-women gave him a little
barley-meal, which the Earl mixed with water in the
heel of one of his shoes.   It tasted so good to a hungry
man that he composed a Gaelic verse which has been
translated thus:

> "Hunger is a cook right good,
>   Woe to him who sneers at food—
>   Barley crowdie in my shoe,
>   The sweetest food I ever knew."

As darkness descended, Mar came to the head of Glen
Roy, where the only sign of habitation was a few rude
huts.   Knocking at the door of one of them he asked
if he could have bed and bite for the night.   The
occupant was a poor crofter called Omeron Cameron,
but he made the wanderer welcome and actually
killed his only cow to provide a good meal of meat.
After supper Omeron spread the cow's skin on the floor
near the fire as a bed for the stranger.   Tradition says
that Omeron was not aware of the identity of his guest,
but even Highland hospitality might be strained at the
killing of an only cow by a poor crofter.   It seems
probable that Mar would pay for the cow, though not
necessarily revealing his identity.   However, when
Mar left next morning he told Omeron that if he ever
required help he was to take his wife and family to
Kildrumy Castle in the Mar country and ask for a
certain Sandy Stewart.   Donald Balloch's clansmen
soon learned that Omeron had sheltered the fugitive
Mar, and they set out to punish him, so when Omeron
learned of their purpose he fled with his wife and

family to Kildrumy Castle, where he asked for Sandy
Stewart. Ultimately, he was led into the presence of
the Earl of Mar, in whom he recognized the stranger
he had entertained. The Earl was as good as his
word, and gave Omeron a piece of land on which to
settle with his family.

Near the head of Glen Roy, at a place called Bruniachan, there is an old quarry which was famed among
the old Highlanders for the excellent quern stones
which it produced. They were known as "Lochaber
stones" and were highly prized by their owners.
These Lochaber stones have been found as far away as
the Outer Hebrides.

Retracing our footsteps to the mouth of Glen Roy
at Roy Bridge, we see a road leading down by the bank
of the River Roy towards the River Spean. This road
leads past Keppoch House, the ancient home of the
MacDonells of Keppoch.

The first Keppoch House, or castle, was built by the
sixth chief of the clan at the beginning of the sixteenth
century. It was situated a short distance from the
present house on a mound at the junction of the rivers
Roy and Spean, and was at that time surrounded by a
moat, which, from the course of the River Roy having
changed, is now dry. After the incident known as the
Keppoch Murder, Keppoch Castle (it would be called
a castle in those days) was pulled down by the clansmen
in horror at the deed committed within its walls, and
no stone of it now remains on the site. According to
tradition, the Keppoch family had a residence here
before the old castle was built. The second Keppoch
House was burned by the Government troops after
Culloden, and until the beginning of the present
century two plane-trees beside the house bore the mark
of the flames. The present Keppoch House was built
by the eighteenth chief about 1760.

The progenitor of the MacDonells of Keppoch was

Alastair Carrach, the fourth, and youngest, son of John, first Lord of the Isles, by his second wife. His father offered him lands in Skye but he preferred the forest lands of Lochaber, and made his home at Tor Castle, near Banavie. His name is usually spelled Carrach, meaning "mangy," even in the old and well-known Gaelic poem *The Owl*, of the sixteenth century, but a number of reliable authorities believe that it should be spelled *Carach*, meaning "cunning."

The unusual spelling of the name of this branch of the Clan MacDonald, namely MacDonell, has been the subject of much discussion. It appears to have been adopted when the Gaelic MacDomhnull became anglicized as MacDonald. The first record of its use is by Coll, the chief who fought at Killiecrankie with Dundee: the previous chiefs used the Gaelic spelling of the name. The clan badge of the MacDonells of Keppoch is that of the whole MacDonald confederation, namely the common heather.

I beg permission to digress at this point for a few moments regarding crests and clan badges. Within modern times a practice has arisen among Highlanders of wearing on the Highland bonnet a white-metal or silver crest, surrounded by a metal belt and buckle on which is inscribed a motto, instead of wearing the appropriate clan badge. The crest assumed is usually that of the chief of a clan or a gentleman of the clan name who has registered arms in the Lyon Register. This practice is, however, erroneous and undesirable. A crest is part of the coat of arms of the person who has registered it and who pays a royalty for permission to use it. According to modern usage, the metal belt and buckle surrounding the crest are indications that the wearer is a non-armigerous clansman, whereas the chief wears the crest and motto without the belt and buckle.

The more correct and appropriate emblem for a member of a clan or a clan sept to wear is his clan *badge*, such as the common heather (MacDonald), bell heather (MacDougall), oak (Cameron), bog-myrtle (Campbell), and so on. If the actual plant, or whatever the clan badge may be, is unobtainable, a metal replica should be worn, with a scroll attached bearing the clan war-cry in Gaelic, and not in Latin or English as frequently occurs on crests, though quite often the motto on a crest is not even the clan war-cry. It should be clearly understood that there is no such thing as a *clan* crest.*

In the heyday of the clan system the ordinary clansman could not afford a metal crest on his bonnet, even if his chief permitted him to wear it, and thus he wore his clan badge, in bloom when in season or a bare sprig when out of season, though many clan badges are evergreens. So also, though he well knew his war-cry in Gaelic, such as *Buaidh no bas* ("victory or death"), the same war-cry given as *Vincere vel mori* would be unintelligible to him.

All the illustrations in MacIan's standard work, *The Clans of the Scottish Highlands*, show the clansmen wearing their clan *badge* in their bonnet, and Stewart of Garth, in his well-known *Sketches of the Highlanders*, says: "The dress of the common people differed only [from that of chief and gentleman of the clan] in the deficiency of finer or brighter colours, and of silver ornaments, being otherwise essentially the same; a tuft of heather, pine, holly or oak, supplying the place of feathers in the bonnet." In the *State Trial of Lord Lovat*, after the Forty-five, we find a question asked, "Did they wear any mark of distinction in their hats?" and the answer, "Some of them had sprigs of Yew . . . by which they were known to be of that party" (Frasers). Again, in *The Red Hand*, by Neil Munro, we find the statement, "He wore the dull tartan of the

---

* A few clan societies have recorded armorial bearings during the present century for use on stationery, banners, etc.

Diarmids, and he had a spring of gall in his bonnett."
In Iain Lom's poem *The Death of Glengarry* we find the
lines :

> "When the proud heather-badge was set
> In all their bonnets blue."

The adoption of coats of arms and, consequently,
crests, by Highland chiefs was of comparatively late
date compared to their adoption by the feudal lords of
the Lowlands. Previous to that time, a clan chief
wore in his bonnet his clan *badge* and three eagle
feathers to denote his rank. Since the adoption of
coats of arms, a clan chief wears in his bonnet the crest
of his personal (not *clan*) coat of arms and also three
eagle feathers. Indeed the clan *badge* and clan war-
cry are much more distinctive and correct emblems
of a clan than the present-day clan tartans, as there is
considerable doubt that tartans were originally distinctive of clans. They were probably district tartans
worn by all residents within certain areas, irrespective
of name, though the dominant family of a district may
ultimately have claimed the district tartan as its own.

The custom of wearing the chief's crest, surrounded
by a metal belt and buckle, is now common practice in
Highland costume. Nevertheless, ordinary clansmen
of to-day who wish to retain the ancient customs of
the clans, as far as possible, will help in doing so by
wearing their clan *badge*, either the original or a metal
replica, instead of wearing a decorated form of a crest
adopted by an individual for personal use.*

To return to Keppoch. There is an interesting story
told of Alexander, tenth Chief of Keppoch, which
illustrates the mode of life of a clan chief at the beginning of the seventeenth century. The story is called
"The Chief's Candlesticks."

---

* In the Inverness Museum there is a fine and very rare specimen of
the old Highland Blue Bonnet of the 1745 period which shows distinctly
the double slit for insertion of the clan badge or the pin to hold it.

On one occasion, when sojourning in England, Keppoch was entertained at the mansion of an English baron who, on showing Keppoch over his house, drew his attention to some handsome silver candlesticks, wonderfully carved and of great value, and said to him:

> "Say now, MacDonald, in your home
> Beyond the mountain ranges lone,
> If aught like this you own?
> These stems are richly crusted o'er
> With strange device, from foreign shore,
> I'd give their value, yea, and more,
> Were I their equal shown."

Drawing himself up to his full height, Keppoch replied: "I will pay you three times their value if I cannot produce candlesticks in my own home which far surpass these ones, both in design and intrinsic value." Some time later the Englishman accepted Keppoch's invitation to visit his home in Lochaber, and did not forget the wager about the candlesticks. As they were ushered into the banqueting hall at Keppoch six stalwart Highlanders in their picturesque native garb preceded them, and ranged themselves around the hall holding flaming pine-torches.

> "The tartan draped in many a fold
> With warlike trophies decked the hold,
>   And here within the hall
> Six stalwart men the entrance line
> Whose flaming torch of resinous pine
>   In ruddy shadows fall." *

"These," said Keppoch, "are my priceless candlesticks, which all the wealth of England could never buy." Needless to say, the English baron admitted he had lost the bet.

The most notable event at Keppoch, however, was

* From the poem *The Chieftain's Candlesticks*, by Alice C. MacDonell of Keppoch.

the Keppoch Murder, which took place in September 1663, but is still often talked about when olden times are recalled in the district.

When Donald Glas II, eleventh Chief of Keppoch, who had fought under Montrose at Inverlochy, died, his eldest son Alexander was a minor, and during the period that Alexander and his brother Ranald were completing their education in Rome the clan was governed by their uncle, Alasdair Buidhe. Shortly after the two lads returned home to Keppoch, Alexander gave a banquet to celebrate his accession to the chiefship of the clan. Among the guests were a father and his six sons of a branch of the Keppoch MacDonells known as the *Sioll Dughaill*, who, secretly, coveted the chiefship, and were encouraged by some members of the clan. By previous arrangement, this family picked a quarrel during the festivities, and in the mêlée they murdered young Alexander and his brother, but, of course, announced that it had been an accident. Alasdair Buidhe, the uncle who had ruled during the absence abroad of the two young lads, was suspected for some time of complicity in the murder, but no proof was ever brought against him.

Iain Lom, the Keppoch bard, on learning what had happened, set out for Invergarry and begged the Chief of Glengarry to take revenge against the murderers of his kinsmen, but Glengarry refused to give Iain any help, as he was not sure that it had not been an accident.

Nothing daunted, Iain betook himself to Sir James MacDonald of Sleat, in Skye, to seek aid in avenging the murder. Their meeting is thus described:

"Where are you come from?" asked Sir James.

"From Laodicea," replied the bard.

"Are they cold or hot, now, in that place?" asked Sir James.

"Abel is cold," cried the bard, "and his blood is in vain crying for vengeance. Cain is hot and red-handed, and the hundreds around are lukewarm as the black goat's milk."

At first Sir James refused help, but Iain returned to Skye several times and used all his powers of persuasion, until, two years after the murder, Sir James obtained a State commission to avenge it. He sent fifty men to the mainland, where they were met and guided by Iain. They proceeded to the house of the murderers at Inverlair, which they found strongly barricaded. Resistance, however, did not last long. Their defences were soon broken down and they were slain in their own house, like their victims. Iain, in his vengeful mood, cut off their heads and had their bodies buried in a knoll opposite the present Inverlair House. Making a rope of heather he threaded it through the seven heads, and slinging his ghastly burden over his shoulder set out for Invergarry, to show his trophies to the chief who had refused him aid. When passing along the side of Loch Oich he washed the heads in a well close to the shore, which ever since has been named Tober-nan-Ceann ("well of the heads"), and over which Alastair, Chief of Glengarry, who lost his life when shipwrecked at Inverscaddle, erected a monument to commemorate this gruesome incident. After showing the heads to Glengarry, Iain sent them to Sir James MacDonald of Sleat as evidence that justice had been carried out. Later, he composed a mournful Gaelic lament in memory of the tragedy, entitled *Mort na Ceapaich* ("the death of Keppoch"). Iain carried out this act of revenge in loyalty to his chief, though his (Iain's) sister was married to the father of the murderers.

During the year 1818 a Dr. Smith, who was in practice in Fort William, and a few friends had the grave at Inverlair opened, and found seven headless skeletons, thus dispelling any doubts regarding the action of Iain Lom.

There is an old tradition in Lochaber that when any member of the Keppoch family dies a greyish-white bird appears at the scene of mourning. When the body of Alexander, the third son of Keppoch of Culloden, and who was known as the Maidsear Mor, was being borne from his home in Prince Edward's Island, Canada, this bird settled on the coffin and remained there until the coffin was lowered into the grave, when it flew straight up into the air until it was lost to sight. Locally, the bird is known as *Eun Glas na Ceapaich* ("the grey bird of Keppoch").

For many years there was a charm stone at Keppoch, which was used for curing illness. It was an oval of rock-crystal, about the size of a pigeon's egg, fixed in a bird's claw of silver and with a silver chain attached, by which it was suspended when being dipped in water drawn from a well near Keppoch, called Tobar Bhride ("St. Bride's Well"). A Gaelic rune, or incantation, was recited while the stone was being dipped. This charm stone is said to have been taken to Australia when the owner emigrated in 1854.

On the north side of the road at Roy Bridge there is a rounded whale-back-shaped hill called Mulroy, or Maol Ruadh, where, on the 4th of August 1688, the last clan battle in Scotland was fought and the last recorded use of bows and arrows as weapons by the Highlanders. The fight was between the MacDonells of Keppoch and the MacIntoshes. The MacDonells were in possession of Glen Spean and Glen Roy, but the MacIntoshes held an ancient charter from the Crown giving them right of possession of these lands. This right was conferred upon the MacIntoshes in 1443 as a punishment for Alastair Carrach fighting with Donald Balloch against the Government troops at Inverlochy.

The Chief of the MacIntoshes decided to assert his rights, and demanded of Coll of Keppoch (the famous

"Coll of the Cows," so named for his skill in cattle *creachs*) by what charter he held the district. Keppoch replied that he held his lands not by a sheepskin (parchment charter) but by the sword. Incensed at this reply, MacIntosh roused his clan and, obtaining the assistance of a party of Government troops, marched into the disputed country with a force of over one thousand men. On arrival he found Keppoch House empty, and learned that the MacDonells, with their kindred of Glengarry and Glencoe, were lying in a hollow at the back of Mulroy. He decided to climb the hill during the night to gain the summit before giving battle, but on nearing the summit, in the grey of the morning, found that the MacDonells were already there. As the pipe tune commemorating the event puts it, "*MacDonald took the Brae on Them.*" A fierce fight developed on the slopes of Mulroy. One of the Government soldiers on the MacIntosh side, named Donald MacBane, when describing the battle later, said: "The MacDonells came down the hill upon us, without either shoe, stocking, or bonnet on their heads: they gave a shout and then the fire began on both sides and continued a hot dispute for an hour."

Tradition says that the MacIntoshes fought with great bravery, but the deciding factor in the fight was a half-crazed cowherd, whom Keppoch had not summoned to the fight but who came of his own accord, armed only with a hefty wooden club. During the fight he was struck by a bullet, and became so incensed with pain that he rushed in a frenzy among the Mac-Intoshes, mowing them down like corn; this action so encouraged the MacDonells that they fought with renewed vigour and thoroughly routed the Mac-Intoshes. They sought to capture the standard-bearer of the MacIntoshes, but he escaped by jumping across the River Roy at a place still called "MacIntosh's Leap."

During the absence abroad on military service of Richard, nineteenth Chief of Keppoch, Keppoch House was let to MacDonald of Glencoe, who died there. The grant of his lands which Richard's father had obtained from the Crown, by the assistance of the Duke of Gordon, expired while Richard was abroad and, as he did not take the necessary steps to keep hold on it, the Keppoch estate passed into the possession of MacIntosh of MacIntosh, whose family had laid claim to these lands for centuries. Thus the MacIntoshes gained by the pen what they could not gain by the sword.

Richard was succeeded as chief by his nephew Angus, who spent his married life at Keppoch House, but, by the irony of fate, he had to rent it from the MacIntoshes, the ancient enemies of his clan. Angus died in 1855 and was succeeded by his son Donald, who spent much of his life abroad, and in his absence Keppoch House passed from the family. Donald died in February 1889, the last Chief of Keppoch.

From Roy Bridge the road leads in and out among woodlands of oak and larch, though there has been much tree-felling here recently. In a mile or so, we come close to the deep, rocky ravine which the swirls and eddies of the Spean torrent have worn into fantastic shapes. At Monessie there is, or rather was, a fine waterfall, where the river plunges through a heather- and hazel-fringed gorge and over a high ledge in delirious ferment into a deep, churning pool below. Since the construction of the Lochaber Hydro-Electric Power Scheme the waters of the Spean have been dammed, and thus east of Roy Bridge, where the River Roy joins it, the Spean is only seen to advantage when the hill burns are in spate, and there is an overflow from the dams at Loch Treig and Loch Laggan. At all other times the waters of this part of the river are sadly depleted.

Beyond Glenspean Lodge, on the left, at Achluach-rach, a rough track winds up the hill-side with con-spicuous cairns on either side. One of these cairns was raised to commemorate Ewan MacDonell, who distinguished himself during the Indian Mutiny and whose home was at Insch, near Keppoch House. Another of these cairns was raised to the memory of his son Alastair. The third cairn was erected in November 1891 to the memory of D. P. MacDonald, son of "Long John" of Ben Nevis Whisky Distillery.

This hill-track leads through a green hollow to the graveyard of Kil-a-Choireil ("Church of St. Cyril") on the summit of a rounded hill. Here lie many of the eminent warriors of Keppoch, including that worthy son of the clan, Iain Lom, the bard, who died in 1709. A vertical stone, carved with cross, harp and floral design, stands over what is usually regarded as his grave, on the south side of the little chapel in the graveyard. The circular "glory" of the cross is inscribed, "Ian Lom Bard na Ceapaich." The stone was erected by Dr. Fraser MacIntosh of Drummond, and on it there is an inscription in Gaelic, which has been translated by Dr. Alexander Stewart — *Nether Lochaber*—as :

> "Here in Dun-Aingeal, in the Braes of Lochaber,
> The Bard of Keppoch is very sound asleep :
> His name was John MacDonald, John the Bare—
> John the *Bare* and *Biting* ! but by some called
> John the Stammerer."

In an article in the *Celtic Monthly* of June 1901, however, Dr. Keith Norman MacDonald states: "The Priests of the glen are buried on 'Tom Aingeal,' the top of the place [Kil-a-Choireil], as also Iain Lom —bare John—the famous poet and politician; and the grave at the door of the church (where the late Fraser MacIntosh erected a monument to Iain Lom) is the grave of Domhnull MacFhiunlaidh—the old bard of

Loch Treig." This statement is corroborated by Miss Alice C. MacDonell of Keppoch in the *Celtic Monthly* of November 1903.

Iain was descended from Donald, one of the sons of the fourth Chief of Keppoch, and possessed unusual powers of sarcasm, cutting satire and caustic wit, of which he made full use. It is he who is supposed to be the speaker in Professor Aytoun's poem, *The Legend of Montrose*:

> "'Twas I that led the Highland host
> Through wild Lochaber's snows,
> What time the plaided clans came down
> To battle with Montrose."

There is an interesting story told of an event which occurred many years ago in Kil-a-Choireil. In olden days, the travelling packman was a welcome visitor to the clachans throughout the Highlands, as, in addition to his wares, he carried the latest news before the days of newspapers in the Highlands. One of these packmen took ill and died at Roy Bridge, and the good folk there buried him in Kil-a-Choireil. Shortly afterwards, a terrible commotion was heard at night-time in the graveyard, and the neighbouring crofters could get no sleep with the disturbance. Ultimately, it was found that the packman who had been buried was a Protestant, and this was a Roman Catholic burial-ground. A deputation waited upon the local Protestant minister, and asked him to have the pack-man's body removed to some other burial-ground, or there would be no peace at Kil-a-Choireil. The people said that the spirits were trying to remove him but he would not go. "Isn't he the hero?" said the minister. "If he had twenty of his kind with him, he would clear everyone else out of the graveyard. I am not going to remove him." The matter reached a climax one stormy night, when every spirit in the graveyard

THE VILLAGE OF CORPACH AND LOCH EIL

[To face page 160

PRINCE CHARLIE'S MONUMENT, GLENFINNAN

seemed to be kicking up a shindy. One old man, who could stand it no longer, went to see the local priest and asked him if he could do anything to quieten the spirits. The priest and the old man went to Kil-a-Choireil, and at a little stream near it the priest took off one of his shoes and made some holy water in it, with which he consecrated the ground. From that moment the tumult ceased, and it was never afterwards renewed.

From Achluachrach the road leads on through Glen Spean, past Murlaggan, Tulloch and Inverlair, where we have reached the north-eastern fringe of Lochaber, and approach the bounds of Badenoch.

L

CHAPTER VII

BY THE SHORES OF LOCH EIL

OPPOSITE Fort William the waters of Loch Linnhe turn abruptly towards the west, and become known as Loch Eil, stretching for about ten miles between the Lochaber Hills on the north and the Ardgour Hills on the south, thus separating the county of Inverness from that of Argyll. There is no definite demarcation line between the two lochs. Geographical publications usually indicate Loch Eil as commencing at the Narrows at Annat, but the local inhabitants regard the two lochs as being divided by an imaginary line striking northwards from the north-easterly point of Ardgour, called the Rudha Dearg ("the red point"), to the opposite shore, that is, from the point where the waters of Loch Linnhe turn westward from their northerly course. The waters opposite Corpach are always regarded, locally, as part of Loch Eil.

To explore the district around Loch Eil, from Fort William, we follow the main road from the town to the Lochy Bridge, but on crossing the bridge turn southward by the river bank, instead of continuing westward to Banavie. This secluded road winds close to the river, fringed by the fresh foliage of sycamore, hazel and hawthorn, through the little settlement of Lochyside. The houses are of modern roughcast and slate, perhaps more sanitary, but much less picturesque, than the little thatch cottages that nestled among the trees until the building boom after the Kaiser's war.

This little settlement originated by the squatting here of some of the crofters who had been evicted from

Glen Dessary and Loch Arkaig-side by the trustees of the Lochiel estate at the beginning of the nineteenth century. Lochiel of that time had become involved in financial difficulties and as he was a minor when he inherited the estate he placed it in the hands of trustees, whose manager was Sir Ewan Cameron of Fassifern. Lochiel resided in London and only paid occasional visits to Lochaber. On one of these visits he found the squatters at Lochy-side. He asked their reason for being there as he saw that they occupied only temporary shacks. When told that they had been evicted from their homes, and were awaiting an emigrant ship (one lot of crofters had already left on the first ship), he told them to settle permanently at Lochy-side as he had been unaware of the evictions. By dint of much hard work these settlers and their descendants wrested some ground from the margin of the large peat moss known as the Blar Mor, or Corpach Moss, and converted it into arable land. Interesting evidence on this subject was given by direct descendants of the original settlers at a public enquiry held recently regarding the proposed acquisition by the Inverness County Council of land in this vicinity for a housing scheme.

About a mile beyond the Lochy Bridge the road bends abruptly towards the west, away from the river, and leads across Corpach Moss past Caol farm to the Caledonian Canal. It was a short distance to the right of this part of the road that the last remnant existed of Loch Aber, from which the district derives its name.

Soon we come to the canal bank opposite the little settlement of Tomonie, or *tom moine*, meaning "the little hill above the peat moss." Though the little swamp between Tomonie and the canal at the present time is not a peat moss, the name would be appropriate before the canal was built, as Corpach Moss would then stretch right into the base of the high ground here.

Behind Tomonie there is a little hill called Tom a' Chrochaidh, meaning "the hill of hanging." Hills of this name in the Highlands usually denote the place where clan chiefs had capital punishment carried out.

Down on our left is the curved shore-line of Loch Eil called Breun Camas ("the turbulent bay"), where the tides of Loch Linnhe and Loch Eil, especially during stormy weather, churn and chop, casting large quantities of loose sea-wrack on to the shingle beach.

Following the bank of the canal for about half a mile we come to the pretty little village of Corpach, set on the hill-side overlooking the waters of Loch Eil where they mingle with those of Loch Linnhe. As we approach the village, by the canal bank, the Free Church appears clearly a short distance on our right, in which many celebrated Highland ministers have preached. Though commodious for a Highland church, it was often filled to overflowing when the religious stalwarts of last century held Communion services here. At the time of the Disruption a site was refused in any part of the Lochiel estate for the building of a church to house the Free Church secessionists from the Parish Church. At first they held worship in Kilmallie graveyard, seated on the tombstones of their forefathers, but they were even evicted from this site and had to worship in a canvas tent set up on the shore of Loch Eil between high-water and low-water marks, where they were free from eviction. Naturally, they required to arrange their services according to the tides. When, ultimately, a site was grudgingly granted to build the Free Church, which still stands, the ground given was a morass where, it is said, the people used to drive the wild horses when they wished to catch them. Considerable drainage was necessary before the building could be commenced.

According to old chronicles, the name Corpach has

not always been applied to the site of the present village of this name. Until the middle of the eighteenth century, at least, Corpach appears to have been a wide stretch of ground skirting the curve of Loch Eil from about the site of the present railway station up to, and including, Tomonie, and extending eastward to the River Lochy, including Caol and Lochy-side. Hence the reason for the moorland being called Corpach Moss. It was composed of scattered crofts rather than a village. The clustering of the houses into the present situation of Corpach was originally caused by the local people seeking employment at the construction of the Caledonian Canal. West of this area were the settlements of Kilmallie and Annat, quite distinct from Corpach. In a grant of lands, in Lochaber, by John of Islay, Lord of the Isles, to Murdoch MacLean of Lochbuie, in 1461, mention is made of "Corpych," "Kilmailzie," and "Anat," and again, similar mention is made in a charter by Alexander, Lord of the Isles, in 1492.

History seems to be repeating itself, as there is now a village at Annat, distinct from Corpach, and the Inverness County Council intend developing the area of Caol, from the canal to the River Lochy.

The name Corpach is believed to have originated from the shore-fields skirting Breun Camas, and is said to be derived from the Gaelic words *corp* ("a body") and *ach*, a suffix meaning "place of"—hence, "the place of bodies." Another suggested derivation of the name giving almost the same meaning is *corp teach*, meaning a mortuary. Corpach was so named because in ancient times when the body of an eminent personage was being borne from the north for burial in Iona it was rested near Breun Camas until the winds were favourable for the sea-voyage to the sacred isle. During stormy weather, in winter, it was sometimes necessary to inter the body here until weather conditions became suitable. This route is reputed to have been the one followed by the Norsemen (during the time of the Norse possession of the Hebrides) when bearing the body of a king or prince from Norway for burial in the sacred soil of Iona. They are said to have landed at Inverness and carried the body down the Great Glen to Corpach, where they embarked for Iona. By doing so they avoided the risk of losing the royal corpse if their galley encountered wild weather on the long and stormy route round Cape Wrath.

At Corpach is the western entrance to the Caledonian Canal, which in its day was regarded as a great feat of engineering.

After the suppression of the Rising of 1745, the trustees of the estates forfeited by the clan chiefs who had been "out" with Prince Charlie were anxious to introduce some commercial undertakings into the Highlands. They wished to divert the energy of the clansmen from fighting to some useful pursuit. The construction of a trans-Scotland ship canal was one suggestion for this purpose, and, in addition, they thought it might serve strategic purposes in case of national emergency.

In the year 1773 James Watt, the famous engineer, was commissioned by the Trustees of the Forfeited Estates to make a survey for a canal through the Great Glen from Loch Linnhe to the Moray Firth. It really meant the joining of the three lochs in the glen—Loch Lochy, Loch Oich and Loch Ness—and forming an exit to the sea at both ends of the glen. The result of this survey was that Watt regarded the construction of a canal to be practicable and, basing his estimate on a canal ten feet deep, he calculated that it would cost £164,000. His designs, however, were thought to be too ambitious and expensive and no action was taken on his report.

In 1793 a scheme for the same project was prepared

by Rennie, who, in doing so, consulted with Watt; but once again nothing was done.

Though the canal was proposed, originally, to encourage the fishing industry and facilitate coastal trade by enabling ships to pass safely from east to west and vice versa, different factors led ultimately to its construction. These were, to prevent British ships from being molested by French privateers off the north of Scotland during the Napoleonic wars and to arrest the great flow of emigration which had set in owing to considerable areas of the Highlands being converted into large stock farms, thus dispossessing large numbers of tenants. The Government realized that the Highlands were one of the principal recruiting centres for the army.

After Rennie's scheme nothing further was done regarding the canal project until 1801, when Thomas Telford, "the Colossus of roads," was asked to report to the Lords Commissioners of His Majesty's Treasury on the construction of a canal through the Great Glen to be of sufficient size to enable a frigate of thirty-two guns passing throughout its entire length. Telford submitted his report in 1802, providing for a canal having a depth throughout of twenty feet and a width of one hundred and ten feet at the surface and fifty feet at the bottom. He estimated that the construction would cost £350,000 and could be carried out in seven years.

An Act of Parliament, which received the Royal Assent on 27th July 1803, authorized the undertaking. On the passing of the Act, Telford and William Jessop, who had become Telford's partner, proceeded with final surveys and raised the estimate of construction to £474,000, exclusive of land purchased and compensation.

Construction of the canal was commenced at both ends in 1804, but as it advanced various factors caused the cost to mount rapidly. Owing to the Napoleonic wars the price of materials increased greatly, so also did workmen's wages. The demands of the Navy caused the price of oak to rise so much that most of the lock-gates in the canal had to be constructed of cast-iron sheathed with pine, though a few gates were made of oak. The construction of the eight locks forming Neptune's Staircase at Banavie cost £50,000. Difficulties also arose in connection with the purchase of land, as some of the Highland lairds saw visions of their despotic power passing from them if the Highlands were opened to commerce and did all they could to hinder Telford. There were other lairds, however, who did all they could to help him. Fortunately, Telford was a man gifted with a dauntless spirit and he triumphed over many obstacles, some of them material and some of them human. At the western end the freestone had to be taken from the Cumbraes, rubble from the north shore of Loch Eil, six miles from Corpach, granite from Ballachulish and limestone from Lismore.

During the construction of the canal a small brewery was established at Corpach, "that the workmen may be induced to relinquish the pernicious habit of whisky drinking."

The official opening of the canal took place on the 24th of October 1822, amid much celebration, though the work was incomplete, the general depth in the cutting being only about twelve feet. The cost up to this date amounted to £645,000.

By May 1827 the total expenditure on the canal amounted to £973,000, and a great deal more labour was necessary to complete the work satisfactorily. Between the years 1843 and 1847 extensive reconstruction and repairs were carried out at a cost of £228,000, the depth of the canal being increased to seventeen feet, which has never been increased to the original project of twenty feet. The canal was reopened for traffic on 1st May 1847, having cost in all £1,201,000. It can accommodate vessels of one hundred and sixty feet length, thirty-eight feet breadth and fifteen feet draught.

At the outset of the construction of the canal the resident engineer in charge of the Western Section was a young man named John Telford, but, apparently, no relation of the senior engineer, Thomas Telford. He died in 1807, at the age of thirty-six, and is buried in the old part of Kilmallie graveyard, where his grave is marked by a large tabular tombstone.

It is worthy of note that Coinneach Odhar, the Brahan seer, at the beginning of the seventeenth century, prophesied the canal thus: "Strange as it may seem to you this day, the time will come, and it is not far off, when full rigged ships will be seen sailing eastwards and westwards by Muirton and Tomnahurich."

The tall, ungainly building which still exists on the east side of the sea-lock at Corpach housed the workshops and the twenty-horse-power pump used for keeping the channel dry during the construction of the sea-lock and basin. It is still called the "engine-house" locally, though the pump has long since disappeared, and is now used for workshops and stores.

The canal was a great boon until it became too small to accommodate the ever-growing size of ships. Nowadays it is only used by small coasters, lighters, yachts and fishing vessels. Previous to the Kaiser's war several hundred brown-sailed fishing boats passed through the canal annually, from east to west and vice versa, during the fishing seasons, adding a picturesque touch to the scenery. For some time after the introduction of steam-drifters these vessels also utilized the canal in large numbers, but during recent years the fishing fleet passing this way has diminished greatly

owing to depression in the fishing industry, and also
for the reason that many of the modern steam-drifters
do not hesitate to sail round Cape Wrath to the fishing
grounds.

Out in Loch Eil, opposite Corpach, are four pretty
little green islands—the Tree Island, the Lily Island,
the Broom Island and the Rudha Dearg Island.
Above their clean gravel beaches they are richly clad
with long grasses, and on two of them grow bushes of
golden broom. During spring and summer they are
ablaze with wild hyacinths and narcissi, the former
growing so thickly as to appear like a vivid blue haze.
In the long grasses of these islands, and on the higher
reaches of their gravel shore, innumerable sea-birds
nest during early summer—seagull, tern, wild duck,
oyster-catcher, and many others. So numerous are
their nests, and so closely do they and the eggs resemble
their surroundings, that one has to be very careful to
avoid treading on them. The din which this feathered
colony creates when a visitor lands on their island home
is almost deafening. In the deeper waters around these
islands there is good fishing of cod, flounder, whiting
and saithe, or *piocaich* as they call them in the Gaelic.

On the Tree Island, or *Eilean nan Craobh*, the Lochiel
chiefs had a family residence during the sixteenth and
seventeenth centuries. In *MacFarlane's Geographical
Collections* it is stated: "In this Lough [Loch Eil],
there is little Illands and the Laird and his Superiours
of the countrey doeth dwell in one of them, haveing
but timber houses builded thereintill."

The widow of Iain Dubh (brother of Ewan, fourteenth
chief, and Donald, fifteenth chief) lived in this island
home with her infant son, Alan. This child became
sixteenth chief in infancy, on the death of his uncle, who
did not leave any issue. When Alan grew to manhood
he resided a good deal on this island and there are
several charters in existence signed by him on "Island

of Loch Eil." He was the direct progenitor of the present head of the house of Lochiel.

Alan's mother was a MacIntosh, who hated her son's clan with a bitter hatred, and, in addition, she had a fierce temper. On one occasion, during Alan's infancy, the Camerons annihilated a company of Mac-Intoshes at the head of Loch Eil, who had come on a raiding expedition. At that time, during the minority of the chief, the leader of the Camerons in battle was a young man nicknamed Taillear Dubh na Tuaighe ("the black tailor of the axe"), and it was his duty to convey tidings of the fight to the youthful Lochiel's mother, on the Tree Island at Corpach. He was well aware of the reception he was likely to receive, as he had experienced the widow's fierce temper, and he knew about the hefty stick which hung behind the door and which she could wield like a drummer. Nevertheless, armed with his trusty Lochaber axe, he set out immediately, and on reaching Corpach sailed over to the island. Knocking at the door, he begged admittance to deliver news of the fight. The young chief's mother invited him into the house, telling him to leave his axe outside; but he was not taking any risks, and replied: "Where I am myself, there also will be my axe." When he told her the result of the fight, and added: "Cats' skins were going cheap to-day" (the cat is the emblem of the MacIntoshes), she flew into a tantrum, and lifting her infant son, the young chief, she threw him on to the fire, vowing curses on all the Cameron Clan. As she made a rush for her stick, An Taillear Dubh intercepted her, and, raising his axe, threatened to brain her if she did not rescue the child immediately and promise to take good care of him. From the wild look in his eyes she knew he meant what he said, so she could do naught but obey him. Ulti-mately, the child was taken from her by the clansmen and given to foster-parents.

This famous Taillear Dubh na Tuaighe was a natural
son of Ewan, fourteenth Chief of Lochiel, by a
daughter of MacDougall of Lorn, and was born when
Ewan was quite young. Before his fighting career he
was called Donull MacEoghann Bhig, but received the
nickname *Tailleur Dubh* because he was brought up by
a foster-mother who was married to a tailor at Lundavra. Later, his skill in wielding a Lochaber axe
earned for him the *Tuaighe* part of his nickname.
Many stirring tales are related in Lochaber about the
terrible havoc he wrought with his celebrated axe in
clan fights. Indeed, he became so famous that his
effigy, with his axe, is incorporated in the Lochiel
coat of arms.

There is a second tradition regarding the origin of
the name Corpach, in which the islands in Loch Eil
form the subject. Away back on the fringes of history,
when dense forests covered the greater part of Scotland,
wolves were so plentiful that no mainland grave was
safe from their depredations. Therefore, wherever
possible, islands were utilized as graveyards. It is said
that the people of Lochaber brought the remains of
their dead relatives to Corpach, where they rested
awhile to solemnize the funeral after the custom of the
time. After that they hired boats to ferry the body
and mourners over to one of the islands in Loch Eil,
and interred the body there. It may be that both
traditions regarding the name Corpach are correct,
though these sunny little islands give no indication
now of the solemn purpose they are alleged to have
served.

About the year 1470 a fierce battle was fought at
Corpach between the MacLeans and the Camerons.
The former had been given the Cameron lands by
Alexander, Lord of the Isles, after his release from
Tantallon Castle, as punishment for the Camerons
fighting against Donald Balloch. The Camerons were

led in the battle at Corpach by their chief, Ailean nan Creach, eldest son of Donald Dubh, and completely routed the MacLean forces. Thus these lands returned to their rightful owners.

During the sixteenth century, in the heyday of feud and foray, a blacksmith at Corpach became famous throughout the Highlands for the excellent swords he forged. He supplied them to many Highland chiefs and eminent clansmen. In those days, a smith skilled in the art of forging weapons and armour was a man of importance, and ranked as third officer in the chief's household.

During the month of March 1746, when the Jacobites were prosecuting the siege of Fort William, a warship bombarded Corpach on two occasions.

To the west of the village the Parish Church of Kilmallie stands on a green eminence above the road. Beside it is the parish burial-ground and the conspicuous, tall obelisk raised to the memory of Colonel John Cameron of Fassifern, who was killed at Quatre Bras, the engagement two days before Waterloo.

Kilmallie is almost unbelievable in size for a parish. It is sixty miles in length and some thirty miles at its broadest part, lying partly in Inverness-shire and partly in Argyll. But Kilmallie Parish Church at Corpach does not mean that it is the only church in this vast territory. There are churches of the various denominations in different parts of the parish, but the church of Corpach (not, of course, the present building) is regarded as the earliest church in the parish.

Among the ministers of Kilmallie Parish Church, perhaps the most notable was Dr. Archibald Clerk, who came in 1844, the year following the Disruption, when the minister of the church had left. Dr. Clerk was one of the finest Gaelic scholars that Scotland has produced and was one of those chosen to retranslate the Scriptures into Gaelic in conformity with the Revised English

Version in 1881. He also produced a splendid translation of MacPherson's *Poems of Ossian*, fully annotated.
His wife was a daughter of Dr. Norman MacLeod—
Carraid nan Gaidheal—the celebrated minister of St.
Columba's Church, Glasgow, to whom he served as
assistant for some time. A stained-glass window in
Kilmallie church commemorates Dr. Clerk, who died in
the manse here on 7th February 1887, and was buried
in this churchyard. Dr. Clerk was succeeded as minister
of Kilmallie by the Rev. R. B. Crawford, who had also
been an assistant at St. Columba's Church, Glasgow.
It is worthy of note that the committee which selected
Mr. Crawford was presided over by Dr. Stewart of
Appin, better known as *Nether Lochaber*, the writer. Dr.
Clerk's term of office lasted from 1844 to 1887 and Mr.
Crawford's period lasted from 1887 till his death in
1931, so that Kilmallie Parish Church had only two
ministers in eighty-seven years, which speaks well for
the climate and conditions.

The records of the church go back to 1296, when
"Richard Fossard," parson to the Church of Kilmalyn,
swore fealty to King Edward I. In a confirmation by
King Robert III of certain lands in this district to
"Reginal de Insulis," there occurs "terra de Kilmald."
In 1685, a confirmation by King James VII of the
Marquisate of Huntly to George, Duke of Gordon,
included the patronage of "the church at Kilmalzie,"
and a yearly fair to be held there on the 18th August
called Mary Fair. The old spellings of Kilmallie
vary: Kilmalduff (1304), Kilmalzhe (1492), Kilmalye
(1493), Kilmalyhe (1495), Kilmailzie (1695). In the
Origines Parochiales Scotiae we read: "The church seems
to have stood originally on a hill above the town of
Kilmallie, which lay on the north shore of Locheil
opposite an island called Island Locheil. In the
seventeenth century it stood within the town of Kilmallie. It now stands at Corpach, to the eastward of

Kilmallie on the right bank of the Lochy, which is said to have been one of those stations at which the bodies of the dead rested for a time on their way to Iona. The second of these was the church traditionally believed to have been built by Gilli-dow-mak-chravolich ('the black child, son of the bones'), the original from which Sir Walter Scott has drawn his 'Hermit Monk,' Brian, in *The Lady of the Lake*."

Of this "black child, son of the bones," and his church at Kilmallie, the following strange tale is related in *MacFarlane's Geographical Collections*: "There is bot two myles from Inverloghie the church of Kilmalee in Lochyeld. In ancient tymes there was ane church builded upon ane hill, which was above this church which doeth now stand in this toune; and ancient men doeth say that there was a battell foughten on ane litle hill not the tenth part of a myle from this church, be certaine men which they did not know what they were and long time thereafter certain herds of that toune [Kilmallie], and of the next toune, called Unnatt, both wenches and youthes, did on a tyme conveen with others on that hill; and the day being somewhat cold, did gather the bones of the dead men that were slayne long tyme before in that place, and did make a fire to warm them. At last they did all remove from the fire, except one maid or wench, which was very cold, and she did remaine there for a space. She being quyetlie her alone, without aine other companie, took up her cloaths above her knees, or thereby to warm her; a wind did come and cast the ashes upon her, and she was conceived of ane man-chyld. Several tymes thereafter she was verie sick, and at last she was nowne to be with chyld. And then her parents did ask her the matter heiroff, which the wench could not weel answer which way to satisfie them. At last she resolved them with ane answer. As fortune fell upon her concerning this marvellous miracle, the child being borne his name was called *Gille dow Maghre-vollich*,* that is to say, the *Black Child, Son of the Bones*. So called, his grandfather sent him to school, and so he was a good schollar, and godlie. He did builde this church which doeth now stand in Lochyeld, called Kilmalie."

The little hill where "there was a battell foughten," and the "wenches and youthes did on a tyme conveen," is the wooded hillock of Cnoc nam Faobh ("hill of the spoils"), nowadays usually called "the bungalow hill," owing to the commodious bungalow on it which has been a familiar landmark for about fifty years. It is a short distance to the west of Kilmallie church.

The building of the next church of Kilmallie is attributed to the wild Cameron chief, Ailean nan Creach, who built it as part of his penance for the reiving life he had led. As mentioned in Chapter V, it would be more correctly attributed to Alan's son, Ewan. In his *Memoir of Colonel John Cameron of Fassifern*, Dr. Clerk says that the ivy-clad walls within the old part of the graveyard is "a ruinous aisle of the old church." I asked the Rev. R. B. Crawford, the parish minister, whose church I attended for years, if he knew of any remains of Alan's church. He said that he had made inquiries on this point himself, and the only information he had been able to locate was that the stones of the ruin of the church attributed to Ailean nan Creach were believed to have been utilized when building the wall round the old part of the graveyard. The unroofed ivy-clad ruin, mentioned by Dr. Clerk, forms the enclosure which is the ancient burial-place of the Lochiel family, and is about nineteen feet north to south and about sixteen feet east to west (internal). The walls are about ten feet high, the one facing south being two feet thick and the remaining three walls two feet eight inches thick.

* Should be Gille dubh mac na'n cnaimh.

PRINCE CHARLIE'S MONUMENT IN ITS ORIGINAL STATE
(With building attached and no statue on the summit of the tower)
From Keltie's *History of the Scottish Highlands*

[*To face page* 176

LOCH BEORAID

There is a deeply splayed window-opening, three feet six inches by two feet three inches, facing north, and an arched doorway, eight feet high by three feet six inches broad, facing south. There appears to be a sealed-up window in the west wall, the upper eighteen inches being sealed only on the outside, thus forming a recess, which may have been used for urns. The building seems rather small, even for an old Highland church, yet rather large for the annexe of such a building. It appears to have been roofed originally, otherwise there would be no necessity for windows.

Here, among his kindred, lies the famous Sir Ewan Cameron of Lochiel, probably the most famous chief of his line, and the last Lochiel to die in Lochaber until the present chief's father, who died on 30th November 1905. This recent chief was buried first in St. Andrew's Churchyard, Fort William, but, later, his body was removed and reburied in the new burial-ground at the foot of Loch Arkaig.

Beside Sir Ewan lies Colonel John Cameron of Fassifern, the hero of Quatre Bras, and his relative, Major-General Sir Alexander Cameron of Inverailort, who served with distinction in Holland, Egypt, Corunna, the Peninsula, Quatre Bras and Waterloo, and who died in Lochaber in 1850.

Set in the west wall of the Lochiel enclosure is a slate tablet bearing the inscription, "Colonel John Cameron of Fassifern K.T.S. 1815," and on the ground beneath it there is a recumbent tombstone bearing the inscription, "Colonel John Cameron of the 92nd Regt. who fell at Quatrebrâs, 1815." Alongside this grave stand two upright tombstones, one inscribed, "Erected by Mary Anne MacLachlan in memory of her father Dugal MacLachlan who died at Callart 20th March 1799," and the other bearing the inscription, "In memory of Alexander Cumming, late of Grishornish, Skye, who died 19th April 1863." These MacLachlans

M

were of Corounan, and were intermarried with the Cummings of Achdalieu, who held hereditary right of burial in the Lochiel enclosure conferred on them by Sir Ewan Cameron of Lochiel. Quite a number of the Cummings are believed to be buried here. The MacLachlans of Corounan were a cadet branch of Lochiel, to whom they were hereditary standard-bearers, so they may have had a right of their own for burial here.

The above Alexander Cumming was a son of Mary Anne MacLachlan, mentioned on the other tombstone, and it was he who, getting into financial difficulties, found it necessary to dispose of his ancestral lands of Achdalieu. His wife is buried with him in the Lochiel enclosure.

In the old part of the graveyard, surrounding the Lochiel burial-place, lie many worthy sons and daughters of Lochaber, including Mary MacKellar, the Loch Eil-side poetess and novelist, who was buried here in 1890. Over the grave of this sweet singer of Loch Eil rises a conspicuous Celtic cross, with a harp engraved in the base. Peacefully they sleep in this little God's Acre, in the shadow of Ben Nevis, by the quiet shores of Loch Eil, where the eerie hoot of the owl or the hoarse *cra-a-ak* of the heron or *Coraghriach* are the only sounds to disturb the stillness of a summer evening.

This little graveyard used to lie in the shelter of magnificent beeches and elms, which, year after year, shed their leaves over the tombs beneath. In their lofty branches the rooks congregated in large numbers during the nesting season, cawing to one another as they swayed in the tree-tops. During 1936 the County Council caused these trees to be cut down, because some of them appeared to be damaging the walls of the graveyard, and it was thought that the fallen leaves were making the place untidy. Nevertheless, it is a pity that some of the trees were not spared, as there was no sign of decay, and their removal has certainly lessened the solemnity of the atmosphere and dispelled the twilight shade they cast so appropriately.

The Rev. John Walker, D.D., who was Professor of Natural History in the University of Edinburgh towards the end of the eighteenth century, records in his book, *The Economical History of the Highlands and Islands*, a celebrated ash-tree which stood in the churchyard of Kilmallie close to the burn which flows past the graveyard. This ash was long supposed to be the biggest tree in Great Britain. It was held in reverence by Lochiel and his clansmen, which probably hastened its destruction, for in 1746 it was felled to the ground by Government troops when ravaging Lochaber. Examined in October 1764, its circumference could then be traced accurately, and its diameter was found to be twenty-one feet. Its circumference at the ground, taken before two reliable witnesses, Mr. Henry Butler of Faskally, and Mr. Cameron, Collector of Customs at Fort William, was fifty-eight feet. When Dr. Walker revisited the site, in 1771, he found that all vestiges of the tree were obliterated.

On a little green eminence in the foreground of the church and graveyard stands the most conspicuous memorial in the district, namely the tall, tapering obelisk, about sixty feet high, erected in 1816, at a cost of £1,400, by the officers of the Gordon Highlanders, to the memory of Colonel John Cameron of Fassifern. This brave son of Lochaber was mortally wounded while leading his regiment, the Gordon Highlanders, in the famous charge at Quatre Bras, on 16th June 1815, when they drove back the French with heavy losses. He was forty-two years of age when killed. On 30th September 1815 the Prince Regent, on behalf of the King, created Ewan Cameron of Fassifern a baronet to commemorate the services of his gallant son.

In April, after Waterloo, Colonel Cameron's body was borne on a warship to Corpach, where, in his native soil, it was laid to rest amid the mourning of his fellow-officers, Highland chiefs, and clansmen. It is said that more than three thousand mourners followed the remains to their last resting-place in Kilmallie church-yard, and that it was the greatest occasion ever witnessed at Corpach.

The epitaph inscribed on the base of the obelisk is said to have been composed by Sir Walter Scott:

"Sacred to the memory of Colonel John Cameron, eldest son of Ewan Cameron of Fassifern, Bart., whose mortal remains, transported from the field of glory where he died, rest here with those of his forefathers. During twenty years of active military service, with a spirit which knew no fear and shunned no danger, he accompanied or led in marches, sieges and battles, the 92nd Regiment of Scottish Highlanders, always to honour, and almost always to victory, and at length, in the forty-second year of his age, upon the memorable 16th June 1815, was slain in command of that corps, while actively contributing to achieve the decisive victory of Waterloo, which gave peace to Europe. Thus closing his military career with the long and eventful struggle, in which his services had been so often distinguished, he died, lamented by that unrivalled General, to whose long train of success he had so often contributed; by his country from which he had repeatedly received marks of the highest consideration; and by his Sovereign who graced his surviving family with those marks of honour which could not follow, to this place, him whom they were designed to commemorate. *Reader, call not his fate untimely, who, thus honoured and lamented, closed a life of fame by a death of glory.*"

Scott has also enshrined the memory of Colonel Cameron in his *Dance of Death*:

"Where, through battle's rout and reel,
Storm of shot and hedge of steel,
Led the grandson of Lochiel,
    Valiant Fassifern.
Through steel and shot he leads no more,
Low laid 'mid friends' and foemen's gore,
But long his native lake's wild shore
And Sunart rough and high Ardgour,
    And Morven long shall tell,

> And proud Ben Nevis hear with awe,
> How, upon bloody Quatre-Bras,
> Brave Cameron heard the wild hurrah
>   Of conquest as he fell."

Colonel Cameron is also the subject of Professor Blackie's poem, *The Lay of the Brave Cameron*, the last verse of which runs :

> "And now he sleeps (for they bore him home
>   When the war was done across the foam)
> Beneath the shadow of Nevis Ben,
> With his sires, the pride of the Cameron men.
> Three thousand Highlandmen stood around,
> As they laid him to rest in his native ground.
> The Cameron brave, whose eye never quailed,
> Whose heart never sank and whose hand never failed,
>   Where a Cameron man was wanted."

A short distance beyond Kilmallie church, and on the right-hand side of the road, rises the thickly wooded Cnoc nam Faobh, already mentioned in connection with the building of the first church, and down to the left, near the shore, is the old water-wheel mill where the grain from the surrounding district used to be ground. At several points on the shore, near to the mill, a row of decayed and seaweed-covered wooden posts run out into the loch. These were used in connection with the salmon-curing industry which was carried on here for several years towards the middle of last century. Close to the mill there is a large vault cut into a high earth bank, with only the roof showing above ground, where the salmon were stored.

Passing the farm-house of Annat on the right-hand side of the road, with its spacious fields of crops and sheep-grazing hills in the background, we come to the Annat Burn. Somewhere near here, probably by the hazel- and oak-clad valley of this burn, Prince Charlie and his army struck up from the shores of Loch Eil into Glen Laragain ("glen of the pass") on their

march northwards to Moy at the outset of the campaign of the Forty-five.   This route would bring them
back on to the main road at Sheangain, where the
branch road leads down to Tor Castle.   In order to
save the hill-climbing, the baggage party, consisting
of two hundred Camerons, went in advance through
Corpach and then up the Great Glen, but it was
thought best for the main body of the army not to
expose themselves to Fort William, as they would do
if they passed through Corpach.

The evidence relating to the route of the Prince's
army from Fassifern to Moy is somewhat conflicting,
but the route through Glen Laragain is most likely
to be correct.   When editing the *Memorials of John
Murray of Broughton* (the Prince's secretary), Robert
Fitzroy Bell states in a footnote on page 172 that the
Prince came to Moy by Glen Gloy (Glen Loy).   In
this statement he is followed by Drummond-Norie,
the well-known Jacobite writer, who says: "Here
[Fassifern, about four miles west of Annat] Charles
spent the night, the heavy baggage going forward to
Moy under a guard of two hundred Camerons by the
road which follows the northern shore of Loch Eil by
Kilmallie and Corpach.   A strong escort was considered necessary, as when passing through Corpach
the convoy would come into sight of the garrison of
Fort William."   Drummond - Norie further states:
"Upon leaving Fassifern, the Prince, by the advice of
his officers, instead of following the route taken by the
baggage, made a detour with the remainder of his army
by turning off to the left through Glen Suiliog and
Glen Loy."   If one reads Murray's diary carefully,
however, one finds that the Prince and his army
marched to Fassifern, "and the day following, after
making a short halt *in sight of Fort William*,* continued
his route and encamped all that night at a place called

* The italics are mine.

Moie." These words, "in sight of Fort William," mean that the Prince and his army reached Annat at least before striking through the hills, as Fort William could not be seen sooner. Murray, being the Prince's secretary, is not likely to have mentioned seeing Fort William on this occasion if he did not do so. In *The Lyon in Mourning*, the Glen Laragain route is apparent from the statement that the Prince and his army "marched to Moy, crossing a hill to avoid a ship of war lying off Fort William." Blaikie, on his map supplement to his *Itinerary of Prince Charles Edward Stuart*, also indicates the Glen Laragain route. O'Sullivan, in his manuscript, says: "From thence [Fassifern] he went to Mouy, about twelve miles, and was oblidged to cross a cursed montaigne, where the horses cou'd hardly passe, to avoid going within Cannon shot of Forte William." By the Glen Laragain route he would deviate from the main low-level road, or track, for only about four miles, whereas by Glen Suileag he would require to climb to a higher altitude than in Glen Laragain and diverge from the main route for about twelve miles.

Near to the Annat Burn was the site of the proposed carbide factory of the Caledonian Water Power Scheme which was rejected by Parliament in 1938. Undertakings of this kind must, undoubtedly, mar rural scenery and *atmosphere*, but facts must be faced, and the introduction or revival of some industries is necessary to prevent the further serious depopulation of the Highlands. Agriculture, stock-breeding, forestry, fishing and quarrying (such as slate, granite and marble) are industries much more suited to the Highland temperament and Highland scenery than engineering works, and there is ample scope for their development and extension in the Highlands. The Western Highlands, with their greater rainfall than the east, are more suited to pastoral than agricultural development. As national necessity demands that Great Britain should produce more foodstuffs in order to make herself more self-supporting, these truly Highland industries should be encouraged to the fullest extent, utilizing every suitable acre of land and placing fishing on a scientifically controlled basis, as an incentive to Highlanders to remain on their native soil.

Up in Glen Laragain (usually called "the glen" by Corpach inhabitants), which Prince Charlie traversed, there is a sedgy lochan, fringed with water-lilies during summer, from which the Sheangain Burn flows eastwards. Among the long, green goose-grass of the loch and burn fresh-water mussels are occasionally found, some of which contain small pearls, but diligent search is necessary for any hope of success.

A short distance west of Annat Burn we come to the shore of Loch Eil, where it widens out from the Narrows and presents an uninterrupted view of its full length of about ten miles. On the north side and on the south side of the loch are high but gently sloping heather-clad hills rising from shingle shores. The scene is a peaceful one, yet in the distance the hazy summits of the high hills around Glenfinnan warn us of the rugged scenery beyond Loch Eil, suggesting the mystery of a land that remains unexplored. By the loch-side the road leads through sylvan scenery of birch, oak and verdant grass, with the calm waters of the loch reflecting the surrounding hills as if in a mirror, while the brown seaweed fringing the shore sways in the gentle movement of the tide. One of the clearings in the wood by the road-side, before reaching Achdalieu, is pointed out by old Lochaber inhabitants as the place where the wizard confronted Lochiel. The latter was on his way to meet Prince Charlie at Arisaig, when the wizard accosted him and warned him of the tragedy awaiting the Rising as described by Thomas Campbell

in his poem, *Lochiel's Warning*.   Lochiel, scoffing at the
advice proffered, said:

> "Draw, dotard, around thy old wavering sight
> This mantle to cover the phantoms of fright."

But the wizard replied:

> "Lochiel, Lochiel! beware of the day;
> For, dark and despairing, my sight I may seal,
> But man cannot cover what God would reveal,
> 'Tis the sunset of life gives me mystical lore
> And coming events cast their shadows before."

This event, however, is generally believed to have
originated in Campbell's imagination, as there is no
historical record of it.   Nevertheless, some of the old
folk in Lochaber will tell you that it did occur, and at
the spot by Loch Eil-side.   Drummond-Norie says
that though Campbell's story relates to the Forty-five
it was based upon the warning which, tradition says,
Gormsuil, the Lochaber witch, uttered to Sir Ewan
Cameron of Lochiel against meeting the Earl of Atholl
unattended when proceeding to Lochan a' Claidheamh
("loch of the sword") on the Moor of Rannoch to
discuss certain boundaries of their clan territories.

Up to the end of the eighteenth century there was
no road of any kind between Fort William and Mallaig,
merely a footpath through heather, bog and rock.   In
1800 the construction of a road from Fort William to
Arisaig was commenced by Telford, but it made very
slow progress and was not finished until 1804, Arisaig
being decided upon as the point of embarkation for
Skye.   It was a very rough road and remained so
until Hitler's war, when military exigencies caused its
surface to be laid with tar macadam and a few other
improvements made, but still it has some nasty bends
and gradients.

At Achdalieu, which consists of a few scattered

houses and a shooting lodge built by Lochiel in 1885, we reach the scene of a well-known incident in Highland history which happened in 1654. It has been related often, but a description of Lochaber would not be complete without it.

When Cromwell's soldiers were stationed in Fort William they were ordered to destroy much of the forest which clad the surrounding district, as it offered good lurking-places for the rebellious Highlanders. It has been said that at one time it was possible to walk for the greater part of a bright sunny day in the Lochaber forest without seeing the sun, owing to the density of the trees. At any rate, the continued felling of the trees roused the anger of Lochiel (the famous Ewan who, later, was knighted) and his clansmen, and they harried the Government troops wherever they found them at their work of destruction.

On the occasion of our story, Lochiel and a number of his armed clansmen happened to be in Corpach when they received news that redcoats had landed from two sloops of war at Achdalieu, and were busy destroying the woods. Setting off immediately, Lochiel and his men crept through the dense woods till quite close to the soldiers, then with wild war-cries they dashed among them with broadswords, dirks and Lochaber axes. Though greatly outnumbered—there were one hundred and forty English soldiers and wood-cutters and only thirty-eight clansmen—the Camerons fought fiercely, and the suddenness of their attack had taken the English soldiers by complete surprise, so that they became panic-stricken, and most of them who were not killed jumped into their boats and pushed off into Loch Eil. During the fight, Lochiel became engaged in a hand-to-hand combat with a powerful English officer, who was well skilled in swordsmanship. Lochiel was only twenty-five years old at this time but, though not tall, was very sturdily built. The superior fencing of the Englishman enabled him to knock Lochiel's sword out of his hand, but the latter immediately grasped the Englishman around the waist and prevented him using his own sword. For some time they wrestled and swayed, till finally they fell to the ground with the Englishman on top, who, exerting his full strength, pinned Lochiel to the ground and reached for his sword in order to finish him off, but Lochiel, summoning all his strength for a final effort—

> "Like wolf that dashes through the toil,
> Like adder darting from her coil,
> Like mountain cat that guards her young,
> Full at his foeman's throat he sprung,"

and, burying his teeth into the flesh, tore the throat out of the Englishman. Lochiel said afterwards that it was the sweetest bite he had ever tasted.

The sequel to this incident occurred some years later, when peace had settled in the Highlands. Lochiel, while on a visit to London, had occasion to visit a barber for a shave. Hearing his accent the barber said: "You are from the North, sir." "Yes," replied Lochiel, "do you know anyone there?" "No," said the barber, "and I do not wish to; they are savages there. Would you believe it, sir, one of them tore the throat out of my father with his teeth, and I only wish I had the fellow's throat as near to this razor as I have yours just now." Naturally, Lochiel did not waste any time getting out of that barber's shop.

This combat between Lochiel and the Englishman at Achdalieu formed the model for Sir Walter Scott's description of the fight between Roderick Dhu and Fitzjames in *The Lady of the Lake*. The fight at Achdalieu began on the moor between the site of the present Achdalieu Lodge and the plantation to the west of it above the road. The English were attempting to retreat to their ships and the Highlanders followed them to the part of the sea-shore that lies between the two streams there.

Just before the commencement of the fight at Achdalieu a man named Cumming arrived with a letter for Sir Ewan from the Chief of the MacKenzies. This letter dealt with a secret visit to the Chief of the MacLeods in Skye of the exiled King Charles II, and treachery intended by MacLeod. Cumming was a trusted retainer of MacLeod but dare not return as he had agreed with MacKenzie to expose MacLeod's treachery and had already conveyed a warning to the King from MacKenzie and cleared out of Skye before discovery. MacKenzie wished to consult Lochiel on the matter and asked Cumming to convey a message to him. Knowing that Cumming's action would mean his death if he returned to Skye, he told him that Lochiel would aid him for what he was doing. Lochiel had no time to read the letter before the fight, but handed Cumming an axe and told him to fight bravely and he would be rewarded. Cumming fought so valiantly for Lochiel, and slew so many of Cromwell's men, that when the fight was over, and Lochiel had read the letter, he said to Cumming that as a reward for his valuable services for both his King and Lochiel he would give him and his descendants the lands of Achdalieu at a nominal rent. Later, the intimate and confidential friendship which developed between Cumming, Lochiel and Cameron of Fassifern earned for Cumming the privilege of burial in the Lochiel enclosure at Kilmallie for he and his descendants.

The axe which Cumming received from Lochiel, and with which he wrought such havoc among the redcoats, was preserved by his descendants as a treasured heirloom until the death of Alexander Cumming, the last laird of Achdalieu, in 1863. At the sale of that laird's effects it was purchased by Mr. Livingstone, schoolmaster at Fort William. From

Mr. Livingstone it passed into the possession of the present owner's father. It is now owned by Mr. J. S. Taylor Cameron, Edinburgh, whose family claim descent from An Taillear Dubh na Tuaighe ("the black tailor of the axe"), the famous Cameron warrior and another noted wielder of a Lochaber axe. By the courtesy of Mr. Taylor Cameron I have the privilege of reproducing a photograph in this book of the famous Cumming axe. It is twenty-six inches in length and the head, from the cutting edge to the point of the spike, is eight inches, with a rope loop for slipping over the wrist. This axe is of special interest, as it may represent the true Lochaber axe, and is a much more handy weapon than the halberd type with an unwieldy shaft about six feet long usually portrayed. In the *Celtic Monthly* for July 1895 there is a sketch showing Alastair Carrach's men (a Lochaber clan) at the battle of Inverlochy, drawn by Miss Josephine MacDonell of Keppoch, an authority on Lochaber lore. In her sketch Miss MacDonell shows the archers with a short-shafted axe thrust into their belts, evidently the Lochaber axe similar to the axe of Cumming. Mary MacKellar, in an article on Taillear Dubh na Tuaighe in the *Celtic Magazine*, vol. viii, April 1883, says that the Taylors of Strathheachaig, in Cowal, had An Taillear Dubh na Tuaighe as progenitor, and on one of the old family tombstones the axe is carved; not the long-shafted type, "but the old deadly-looking weapon, having a short handle with a rope attached." Thus we have evidence that the two most famous wielders of the Lochaber axe used the short-shafted type and not the long halberd type.

Though most historians state that the Lochaber axe was not used in the Fifteen or the Forty-five, the manuscript of O'Sullivan (*1745 and After*, by A. and H. Tayler), one of the principal advisers of Prince Charlie, says that, on approaching Edinburgh, "Armes and ammunition was delivered to those yt had 'um not, at least what armes we had were deliver'd, Lochaber axes and other instruments of war."

About a mile beyond Achdalieu the road bends back from the loch at the entrance to Glen Suileag, where, in a grove of sycamore and chestnut, stands white-walled Fassifern House.

When Prince Charlie landed in Scotland, in 1745, Lochiel's brother, John Cameron, resided in Fassifern, and when Lochiel was on his way to meet the Prince at Arisaig, with the intention of advising him to abandon his attempt at a rising at that particular time, he called upon his brother. Lochiel, like most other Highland chiefs, was against the proposed rising, because the Prince had brought neither men, money, nor arms to assist in the campaign. On learning the nature of Lochiel's errand, Fassifern advised him strongly to return to Achnacarry and send his message to the Prince in writing. "No," said Lochiel, "although my reasons admit of no reply, I ought at least to wait upon His Royal Highness." "Brother," said Fassifern, "I know you better than you know yourself; if this Prince once sets his eyes upon you, he will make you do whatever he pleases." But Lochiel was adamant and proceeded to Arisaig. History proves how true were Fassifern's words.

At the outset of his campaign Prince Charlie and his army of clansmen spent their third night on the march at Fassifern, but the host was not there to receive them. Fassifern would have nothing to do with the Rising and had left the district before the arrival of the Prince and his army. Consequently, Fassifern House was one of the few houses spared from the flames by the red-coats after Culloden. The room in which the Prince slept at Fassifern is still shown to visitors, but Blaikie, writing in 1897, says: "Fassifern still stands, but two years ago the rooms occupied by the Prince were considerably altered." The bedroom window is the upper-floor front window at the left (when facing the house) of the central portion of the building. The actual bed on which the Prince slept at Fassifern is now in Callart House, Onich, having been taken there by Sir Duncan Cameron of Fassifern when he purchased Callart estate from his cousin, Cameron of Callart, about 1789.

Though Fassifern took no part in the Rising, he was arrested in May 1753 on a charge of having corresponded with attainted persons, and committed to Edinburgh Castle, but two months later he was liberated on bail. Shortly afterwards he was arrested suddenly and charged with forging a claim to the forfeited estate of Lochiel. When he was committed to Edinburgh Castle for the second time his intimate friend and neighbour, Iain Cumming of Achdalieu, was in Edinburgh on business. Cumming learned that Fassifern had been arrested by redcoats and that Government officials were on their way to search Fassifern House for incriminating documents. He was the only person whom Fassifern trusted with knowing where he kept the box containing his private papers in Fassifern House, so Cumming set off immediately to forestall the Government officials. Knowing all the short-cuts, he managed to reach Fassifern House ahead of them and secured the box of private papers, which he buried in a wood. Very soon the officials arrived and searched the house minutely, but failed to find any incriminating documents.

After a long period of imprisonment, and much indignity, Fassifern was brought up for trial at Edinburgh. He was acquitted on the charge of forgery, but on the count of having been in communication with the late Lochiel * and other attainted chiefs he was

* He seems to have received 5,700 *louis d'or* of the Loch Arkaig treasure from Cluny for Lochiel's family.

found guilty, and sentenced to ten years' banishment from Scotland, the Government at that time being in a mood of revenge. During his exile he resided in Alnwick, in England. After his sentence had been completed he returned to Fassifern, where he died. The friendly action of Cumming in hastening to Fassifern House and hiding the private papers is believed to have saved Fassifern from a much more severe sentence.

It was at Fassifern that Colonel John Cameron, of Quatre Bras fame, was brought up. He was a grandson of John of Fassifern of the Forty-five. When Colonel Cameron's body was brought home to Lochaber for burial at Kilmallie, a year after Quatre Bras, the funeral feast was held in the house of his friend and neighbour, Alexander Cumming of Achdalieu, who, later, had to dispose of his ancestral lands. Alexander Cumming's wife, Jessie Cameron, was a cousin of Colonel Cameron, and at the time of the funeral Colonel Cameron's stepmother was in delicate health.

Leaving Fassifern, we continue by the loch-side to Corribeg, which consists of only a few crofters' houses. This settlement was the childhood home of Mary MacKellar, who, though mainly self-taught, was an accomplished writer both in prose and in poetry, in Gaelic and in English. She was a contributor to many magazines and newspapers, and to her was entrusted the translation into Gaelic of the second series of Queen Victoria's *Leaves from our Journals in the Highlands*. Her verse was collected and published in 1880 under the title, *Poems and Songs, Gaelic and English*.

Beyond Corribeg—where, incidentally, at Lochielside, the stationmaster is a stationmistress!—we pass through another little settlement called Kinlocheil, where Prince Charlie and his men rested on their first and second nights after leaving Glenfinnan. It was here that the Prince learned that the Government had offered a reward of £30,000 for his capture. He

THE HILLS AROUND LOCH AILORT

[*To face page* 192

EIGG AND RUM, FROM ARISAIG

immediately retorted by offering a reward of a similar sum to the person "who shall seize and secure till our further orders the person of the Elector of Hanover." It may seem surprising that the Jacobite army had not travelled further on their first day's march than Kinlocheil, which is only about six miles from Glenfinnan, but they experienced considerable difficulty in dragging their cannons through the boggy ground on the way. There was no road at that time. Kinlocheil is close to the head of Loch Eil, but the actual extremity is at Drumasallie, where the hill-waters of the Fionnlighe and Dubhlighe wind through a grassy plain and sandy shore to mingle with the brackish water of the loch. This little settlement derives its name from a hill overlooking it on the north, called Druim na Saille. Here, we are in a veritable oasis of peace, far from the turmoil of city life, but, be it mentioned, it is a favourite haunt of that bane of a calm summer evening — voracious midges. Their merciless attacks are sufficient to have inspired the Highland Fling, as Drumasallie midges are the real MacKay.

At the head of Loch Eil we enter a wide green strath of moorland which leads westward for about five miles, and forms the isthmus between Loch Eil and Loch Sheil.

Rounding the head of Loch Eil we enter the district of Ardgour, and pass from Inverness-shire into Argyllshire. Travelling eastward by the south shore of the loch there is a fine view of the high hills of Lochiel's country. Beinn an' t Sheachda rises above Corribeg to over two thousand feet, while east of Glen Suileag stretches the long high ridge of Druim Fada, casting clear reflections in the quiet waters of the loch. Should you be roving here in springtime you are likely to see long wreaths of smoke trailing along the hill-sides, and smell the pungent fragrance of burning heather. This work is carried out systematically to ensure fresh, green

N

buds appearing later on the heather, as these form the principal food of the grouse. All burning must be completed by the 16th of April, when the birds (officially) commence nesting. If you want a really thrilling blaze, however, with flame, smoke, crackling and fragrance, any Highland boy will tell you that nothing beats a large clump of dry, withered whin fanned by a strong breeze, though whin-burning, be it mentioned, is unofficial and, perhaps, illegal.

There is a peaceful seclusion on the south side of Loch Eil which relates to its history as well as to its scenery. The district of Ardgour is so scantily populated, and always has been, that few historic incidents are recorded of it. Stretching from Loch Eil southwards to Loch Sunart, and from Loch Linnhe westward to Loch Shiel, it is one of the least-explored regions of Scotland. Into the fastnesses of its hinterland few strangers have ever penetrated, and one will search in vain for a detailed description of its lonely glens and mountains. Even the fringe of Ardgour is seldom explored. Its only roads are those which skirt its shores, and habitation is conspicuous by its absence. Regions further north are much more explored, as Ardgour has no main road leading to it or passing through it. The tramper who pines for the real lonely places of nature should rove in this region, which has at least one claim to distinction in Scotland—it is one of the places which Prince Charlie and Mary Queen of Scots did *not* visit.

The Ardgour road by the south shore of Loch Eil leads through the little crofting settlements of Garvan, Duisky, Blaich and Achafubil, where, snuggling at the foot of the hill-slopes, are picturesque little white-washed thatched cottages. All along the loch-side is a fairy retreat, silent, secluded, well sheltered, and glowing with colour. It is varied with rich woodlands, pasture-land near the shore, and heather hill-sides where rabbits and pheasants abound. To view the

long fields of varied-hued crops stretching back from
the shore to the snug little cottages, where thin columns
of smoke rise vertically into the still air; to hear the
creak of the oars in the thole-pins of some fisher out in
the calm waters of the loch; or the *cra-a-a-k* of the
heron as it rises leisurely from the water's edge, is balm
to the pensive mind.

At Achafubil, opposite Corpach, and onwards round
the Rudha Dearg, the road leads through a rich
woodland of oak, ash, hazel and rowan and a dense
undergrowth of ferns and bracken rising from a thick
mossy turf. Up among the branches pretty little brown
squirrels scamper about, while through the interlacing
foliage long sunbeams come streaming down, casting
brilliant spotlights in the cool twilight of the woodland
glade. Little streams tinkle along their verdure-
hidden courses, and numerous rabbits gambol around
the mossy mounds. Thigh - deep in the bracken, a
young deer may be seen standing alert or bounding to
cover.

From the Rudha Dearg, the reddish-gravel shore is
backed by heather - clad rocks, and curves round
abruptly towards the south to form the sheltered little
Camas-nan-Gall, backed by a densely wooded hill-side.
In this little bay the Marquis of Argyll stood on the
deck of his galley and watched the rout of his clansmen
by the forces of Montrose at Inverlochy on that fateful
day of 1645.

Having now completed our circuit of Loch Eil, we
can return to Fort William by the ferry-boat, which
sails from a little gravel beach washed by the clear
waters of Loch Linnhe, beneath the whitewashed
cottage of the ferryman.

CHAPTER VIII

WESTWARD FROM GLENFINNAN

AT the present day the western boundary of Lochaber, though somewhat vague, is usually regarded as stretching from the head of Loch Arkaig to the head of Loch Shiel at Glenfinnan. The region west of this boundary to the shores of the Atlantic, which comprises the districts of Arisaig and Morar, is, however, so closely related to Lochaber in history, and in present-day social affairs, that a description of the one region does not seem complete without a description of the other. In any case, in olden times the districts of Arisaig and Morar were regarded as being within the bounds of Lochaber.

The approach to Glenfinnan, by road, from the head of Loch Eil, leads through a wide strath of flat moorland devoid of habitation, between lonely ranges of hills. Towards its western end we enter sylvan scenery, as we follow the waters of the River Callop winding their sinuous course between reedy banks overhung with birch and rowan. Just before reaching the plain at the head of Loch Shiel the road passes through a little gap in a screen of hillocks, which seems to act as a gateway between the picturesque but mild scenery around Loch Eil and the rugged grandeur westward. What an impressive scene presents itself as we emerge from this natural portal. Cupped in the hollow of high and rugged mountain ranges, the dark waters of Loch Shiel stretch away into the hazy distance in a region where Nature seems for ever brooding.

At Glenfinnan we are passing from the land of Clan

Cameron into the land of the MacDonalds of Clan-ranald. There is, alas, now no chief or ruling family in the district of this once-famous branch of the great Clan Donald, these lands having passed out of their possession many years ago.

The MacDonalds of Clanranald trace their ancestry from Reginald, or Ranald, one of the sons of John of Islay, First Lord of the Isles, and his wife Amie, or Aimée. The father of Amie was Roderick MacDonald, a faithful supporter of Bruce, and from whom he received the lands of Moidart, Arisaig, Morar and Knoydart, which comprise the region usually referred to as "the Rough Bounds," owing to their rugged nature. Amie inherited these districts from her father, and from her they descended to her son Ranald. She seems to have been ill-treated by her husband, John of Islay, and, after being forsaken by him, she retired to Moidart about 1350, and proceeded to build Castle Tirrim, which became the seat of the Clan-ranald chiefs, and remained so until burned in 1715 by the chief who was killed at Sheriffmuir. He had a presentiment that he would not return alive, and burned the castle as he set out, in order that it would not fall into enemy hands. His presentiment proved true, as he was one of the first killed in the battle.

During the eighteenth century the lands of Clan-ranald became very prosperous, but the folly and extravagance of Reginald George, eighteenth chief, during his youth, brought them to ruin at the beginning of the nineteenth century, after having been in the possession of his ancestors for five hundred years. When he inherited the chiefship, Reginald George, who was a grandson of the chief who fought for Prince Charlie, gave every promise of being a success, as he was a very likeable and talented young man, and the income from his estate for some years averaged from £20,000 to £25,000 per annum; but in the gay society of London he was led into bad company and gradually squandered all his ancestral possessions. He died in 1873, having lived for more than thirty years after all was gone, regretting the sad mess he had made of his inheritance. The only remnants of the estate left in the possession of his descendants were the little barren island of Risga in Loch Moidart, and the ruined Castle Tirrim, but even these were, later, relinquished, so that now the clan is both chiefless and landless in its native region. The ruins of Castle Tirrim are now the property of the Ancient Monuments Commission.

Many stirring events have happened in the land of Clanranald, but none of them to equal the scene which was enacted at Glenfinnan in 1745 when Prince Charlie raised his standard amid the wild cheers and war - cries of his kilted clansmen. Surely no more appropriate spot could have been chosen for this stirring event. What Scotsman, worthy of the name, can hear Glenfinnan mentioned without picturing with his mind's eye this thrilling episode in his country's history.

Standing conspicuously in the centre of the marshy plain at the head of Loch Shiel is the tall, gaunt stone column, surmounted by a statue of the Prince in Highland costume, erected on the spot where the standard was raised. It was built in 1814. Previous to that time a cairn of stones marked the spot. Though now universally known as "Prince Charlie's Monument," this column was not raised directly to the memory of the Prince, but to the memory of the ancestors of its builder, who had fought in the Forty-five. Set into the boundary wall surrounding the monument are three large metal tablets with an inscription on each —one in Latin, one in Gaelic and one in English. A similar inscription to that in English is engraved on a marble tablet above the doorway in the monument. The English inscription reads: "On this spot Prince

Charles Edward Stuart first raised his Standard on the XIX day of August MDCCXLV when he made his daring and romantic attempt to recover a throne lost by the imprudence of his ancestors. This column was erected by Alexander MacDonald, Esquire, of Glenaladale, to commemorate the generous zeal, and the inviolable fidelity of his forefathers, and to the rest of those who fought and bled in that arduous and unfortunate enterprise.

"This pillar is now alas! also become the monument of its amiable and accomplished founder who, before it was finished, died in Edinburgh on the IV day of January MDCCCXV at the early age of XXVIII years."

An English translation of the Gaelic inscription is not quite the same as the English inscription, though it expresses similar sentiments. A modern literary Gael translates the Gaelic inscription thus:

"Thou traveller, should it be your desire to express adoration of the great tales of the days that are gone, come near and make your obeisance. This is the spot where Prince Charlie unfurled his banner, when that young eagle spread his wings in the elation of his soul to win back the kingdom which his fathers had lost, and when he flung himself, without help or friend, on the worthy bosoms of the mettlesome Chiefs and the valiant heroes, who chose to rise on his behalf without considering it any disgrace, to restore his right or to lose their own lives.

"As a remembrance of their loyalty, their faithfulness, and their hardships in each desperate peril which followed, this monument was raised by the noble and valiant youth, Alexander MacDonald, Chieftain of Glenaladale, the prime head of hospitality, who died in Edinburgh in the year 1815 at the dawn of his worthy career."

The monument originally formed part of a shooting

box, but the adjoining buildings were demolished after standing for several years. The Rev. Archibald Clerk, of Kilmallie, writing in the *New Statistical Account of Scotland*, in 1838, says: "At Glenfinnan, a tower with apartments attached was erected by the late amiable and much lamented Alexander MacDonald of Glenaladale, in commemoration of the event which took place here in 1745. The inscription, which he did not live to see placed, was written by Dr. Donald MacLean (of Ardnamurchan), highly approved by the late Sir Walter Scott and translated into Latin by the late celebrated Dr. Gregory, of Edinburgh. The relative and successor of Glenaladale, Angus MacDonald, Esq., has of late improved this monument, having removed the buildings annexed, so that the tower stands singly on the plain, and erected on the summit a statue of the Prince." Dr. John MacCulloch, the geologist, writing in 1824, describes the appearance of the whole memorial building as resembling "a cake house . . . and with a tower—tower is a profanation of such a word, since the whole building resembles a carpenter's mallet with the handle uppermost." In the first (1834) edition of G. and P. Anderson's *Guide to the Highlands and Islands of Scotland* it is stated, on p. 302: "At the head of the latter lake [Loch Shiel] is a small square embattled building of two stories, with a round narrow tower, which no traveller can behold with indifference. It was erected by the late Mr. MacDonald of Glenaladale on the identical spot where upon the 18th August, 1745, Prince Charles Edward first unfurled his standard. . . . The building has, we understand, been recently altered and the tower alone left which is intended to be surmounted by a statue."

These three references leave no doubt that "Prince Charlie's Monument" of to-day was originally part of a larger building, and there is visible evidence on this subject in a plate facing page 552, vol. i, of Keltie's

History of the Scottish Highlands. This plate shows distinctly the building and tower attached, with no statue on the summit of the tower. It seems surprising that, after exhaustive enquiries, I have been unable to find anyone of the present generation who is aware of the original state of the monument, not even the National Trust for Scotland who now own it.

There is a stone staircase inside the monument, leading to the top, but owing to the damage caused to the statue of the Prince by vandal visitors the doorway was sealed at the beginning of the present century. One rascal broke off and purloined the stone feather in the Prince's bonnet, while the relief figures on the inscription tablets were badly chipped by perverted souvenir-hunters.

On the 20th of August 1938 Sir Walter Blount, proprietor of the Glenfinnan estates, officially handed over custody of the monument to the National Trust for Scotland. It is heartening for Scotsmen to know that it is now a national possession and that it will be kept in a good state of preservation. It was a happy coincidence that custody of the monument was accepted by the Duke of Atholl, as president of the National Trust, as it was a direct ancestor of his who unfurled Prince Charlie's Standard on this spot in 1745.

Since accepting custody of the monument, the National Trust has completed considerable repairs on it. The harling has been removed from the tower and the stonework pointed. The doorway to the stair inside the monument has been unsealed and access to it is granted in payment of a small charge. The missing feather on the bonnet of the Prince's statue has been replaced and the plaques on the boundary wall have been cleaned and the missing relief heads of the Highlanders and their axes on these plaques have also been replaced.

This monument at the head of Loch Shiel is something more than a memorial to the warriors of the Forty-five. It is a shrine of the spirit of adventure, and must always appeal in this sense to everyone who has heard the Red Gods call, but adventure need not mean war—peace hath her heroes and victories no less renowned than war.

For the participants and their dependants there was much wretchedness in the Forty-five and its aftermath, but of romance there was none—"'Tis distance lends enchantment to the view." Whatever we may think of the campaign, however, we must admit that, though the kernel was rough, through the mellowing years it has become surrounded by some fine fruit of song and story. Like other exploits of the Highland clans, it has added human interest of a thrilling nature to scenery which is itself inspiring. The recounting of these clan stories is a link with the past which supplies a healthy relaxation of thought in this age of mechanism.

On the 18th of August 1745 Prince Charlie and about fifty of Clanranald's clansmen sailed up Loch Shiel from Dalilea to Glenaladale in three boats. At Glenaladale they spent the night, being met there by the laird, Alexander MacDonald, and the veteran Jacobite, Gordon of Glenbucket, who had with him a prisoner in the person of Captain Switenham, who had been captured by the MacDonells of Keppoch, while on his way from Ruthven barracks, in Badenoch, to Fort William. On the following morning the Prince and his bodyguard continued their journey up to the head of Loch Shiel at Glenfinnan, having landed on the way for a meal at a spot on the loch-side which ever since has been called Torr a Phrionnsa ("the Prince's hillock").

Arriving at Glenfinnan about eleven A.M. on the 19th of August, the Prince was disappointed to find only a few of the local inhabitants there to greet him. He had expected to be welcomed by hundreds of clansmen. His attendants reminded him that, though this was the day arranged for the gathering, the day was yet young, and bade him have patience. Retiring into a little thatched hut at Slatach, the Prince anxiously awaited the arrival of the clans. Gradually, small numbers of men trickled towards the gathering place, including a number of Clanranald MacDonalds, but not sufficient to raise the Prince's hopes. About one P.M., however, the sound of the pipes came wafting from the northern hills, and soon appeared the Cameron clansmen, with Lochiel at their head, "all plaided and plumed in their tartan array," descending the slopes of Glenfinnan, in two columns of three men abreast, to the number of about seven hundred. Sir John Mac-Donald, one of the "Seven Men of Moidart" and a participant throughout the campaign, writes, in his account: "Never have I seen anything so quaintly pleasing as the march of this troop of Highlanders as they descended a steep mountain by a zigzag path." Shortage of weapons caused many of them to come unarmed, but the Fiery Cross, which they dared not disobey, had summoned them, armed or unarmed. The writer of the well-known song *The March of the Cameron Men* * would appear to have had this occasion in mind when she wrote:

> "I hear the pibroch sounding, sounding,
>   Deep o'er the mountain and glen,
>   While light springing footsteps are trampling the heath,
>   'Tis the march of the Cameron men.

> "Oh, proudly they walk, but each Cameron knows
>   He may tread on the heather no more,
>   But boldly he follows his chief to the field,
>   Where his laurels were gathered before."

---

* Miss Mary Maxwell Campbell, who wrote both the words and the music of the song, "after travelling from morning to night through Highland scenery with a member of the Lochiel family." She died in 1886, at the age of seventy-three years.

With them, the Camerons brought a few Government troop prisoners, who had been captured in the skirmish at High Bridge. Small additional contingents of Camerons arrived shortly afterwards, from Glen Dessary, Glen Pean, and Kinlocharkaig.

The Prince was now in high spirits and ordered the clansmen to be drawn up and the Standard raised. The Standard was a large banner of red silk with a white space in the centre and, after being blessed by Bishop Hugh MacDonald, was unfurled by the Marquis of Tullibardine. Though an old and invalid man, his spirit was bright and his heart was leal. Supported on either side by a clansman, he unloosed in the mountain breeze the banner that was to rouse the Highlands as they had never been roused before. Naturally, this event raised a storm of cheers and thrilling pipe music. It was followed by a short and stirring speech by the Prince.

Shortly after the raising of the Standard three hundred MacDonells from Keppoch arrived, also a number of MacLeods, who came, though their chief refused to have anything to do with the Rising. By the evening of the 19th the clansmen gathered at Glenfinnan amounted to about one thousand two hundred. Remaining here for two days, to allow a full muster, this Highland army, led by the Prince, set forth eastward, on the first stage of its campaign for victory or death in the Stuart cause.

Prince Charlie and his father are sometimes referred to, especially by *Sasunnaich*, as "The Pretenders"— "The Young Pretender" and "The Old Pretender"— in a rather slighting manner, but the word "pretender" when first applied to them was an English corruption of the French word *prétendant*, meaning "claimant."

The bicentenary of the raising of the Standard at Glenfinnan was celebrated on a beautiful summer day on Saturday, 18th August 1945 (the actual date of the bicentenary, the 19th, being a Sunday), when a large concourse of people gathered around the monument. Pipers played, speeches were delivered and Gaelic songs were sung in memory of that eventful occasion.

Up on the hill-side, to the north, and overlooking the head of Loch Shiel, is the pretty little Roman Catholic chapel, from the doorway of which there is a magnificent view of the surrounding scenery, resplendent in sunshine or sombre amid swirling mists. Within the chapel there is a little brass tablet set into the wall, bearing the inscription "Charles Edward Stuart, R.I.P."—a simple, yet eloquent, tribute of a loyal heart.

Close to the little chapel, a huge bronze bell rests on two rough stone pillars. It is said that, upon delivery, the bell was found to be too large and too heavy for hoisting to the belfry, so it was erected on its low framework near the chapel, and is rung in that position.

Northward, from the head of Loch Shiel, Glenfinnan strikes into the heart of the high hills. Spanning its entrance is an imposing concrete viaduct carrying the railway from one side of the glen to the other, consisting of twenty-one spans of fifty feet width and an extreme height of one hundred feet. The building of this viaduct was commenced in July 1897, and completed about two years later. Fortunately, it was built with due regard to the magnificent scenery around, and is really a commendable piece of engineering.

The extension of the West Highland Railway from Fort William to Mallaig, a distance of about forty-two miles, was commenced in January 1897, and opened to traffic on the 1st of April 1901. It is unique among British railways, in respect that for practically the whole distance west of Loch Eil it was blasted out of solid rock. Though it was built as economically as possible, it has many tunnels and concrete viaducts. Each mile of this railway cost about £13,500, exclusive of the sum of £40,000 paid for the ground on which the permanent way was laid. In so backward a state was the country-side when it was constructed, that even on the level ground alongside Loch Eil the road was so very crude that the contractors found it necessary to transport materials and plant by boats from Fort William, beaching them along the shores of the loch. The original scheme, as presented to Parliament, provided for a branch line to Roshven, in Moidart, at the south side of the entrance to Loch Ailort, but this part of the programme was not carried out.

From its low level at the head of Loch Shiel the road rises up a steep incline, where there used to be some fine larch, fir, spruce and pine, but they have all been felled recently.

Passing the little chapel and a few scattered houses, we enter a rugged defile where masses of bare rock on the hill-sides protrude through the heathery turf, and an occasional mountain-ash clings tenaciously in its struggle for existence. Rising to nearly two thousand feet, Fraoch Beinn sweeps upwards on the north, while on the south the slopes of Beinn Odhar Mor rise to nearly three thousand feet, the skirts of both mountains being thickly strewn with bare boulders. About two miles into this glen the road commences to dip down a long and sinuous course to Loch Eilt. Cradled between high, steep-sided mountains, this narrow stretch of water, about three miles long, has a very picturesque setting, and a distinguishing feature of small heather-clad islets from which rise clumps of tall Scots pine.

From the foot of Loch Eilt a lonely track leads northward over the hills for about six miles to Loch Morar. It is little better than a sheep-track through heather, bog and rocks, and in many parts there is no

track at all. Of habitation there is none. About
half-way over this route, and just about its summit, we
look down from a height of about one thousand feet
into Loch Beoraid, a lonely, narrow stretch of water,
about the same length as Loch Eilt, winding along a
deep hollow between two ranges of high hills. In all
directions is rugged solitude, the scene being really a
thrilling one, especially if the mists are creeping up
the mountain-sides and spots of sunlight are glancing
on rocky eminences. The photograph of Loch Beoraid
facing page 177 must be one of the very few, if not the
only, photograph of this loch published, as few people
ever visit it. Those who do go near it are mainly inhabitants of the sparsely populated surrounding district,
who are not in the habit of carrying a camera.

A short distance beyond the summit of the track, in a
little gully, clad with birch and ash, there is a hollow
in the rocks, called Prince Charlie's Cave, but it is
hardly worthy of the name of cave. This cave is
described in Blaikie's *Itinerary* and shown on his map
of the Prince's wanderings as "MacEachine's Refuge,"
as it was here that MacEachine, son-in-law of Borrodale,
sheltered the Prince after his wanderings in the outer
isles.

Clambering down a steep hill-side of deep heather,
bog-myrtle, marshy ground and rock, we reach the
Meoble river winding through a deep glen, about
three miles long, from Loch Beoraid to Loch Morar.
Through the glen we tramp along a country road, past
the three or four houses which constitute Meoble, to
the lonely shores of Loch Morar. The road has been
constructed for the use of the tenants of Meoble Lodge,
who reach this region by private motor-boat on Loch
Morar.

Loch Morar is famed as being the deepest loch, fresh
or salt water, in Europe, its deepest part lying directly
opposite the mouth of the Meoble river and about

half-way across the loch. In this vicinity there are about four acres where the depth is over one thousand feet. In April 1887 Sir John Murray, using a hempen-rope sounding line, recorded a depth of one thousand and fifty feet, but during the complete survey of the loch in 1902, when a wire-rope sounding line was used, the greatest depth found was one thousand and seventeen feet. One must go west of St. Kilda and Ireland to find a depth of over one thousand feet in the Atlantic Ocean. Though of such great depth, the surface of Loch Morar is only about thirty feet above sea-level, and only a narrow barrier, or threshold, about a quarter of a mile broad, separates its western end from the sea.

As there is no ferry across Loch Morar we must retrace our footsteps to the main road by Loch Eilt, and continue our journey westward, following the course of the River Ailort, through rugged mountain scenery, to where it flows into the head of the long, winding sea-inlet called Loch Ailort. High hills cup this loch in a sheltered hollow, where the brown sea-wrack sways in the shallows around its quiet shores. At Lochailort Inn the road into Moidart branches off around the head of the loch and follows its southern shore. It is a rough and lonely bridle track, where you may meet the postman mounted on his long-tailed white pony, the only suitable means of conveyance.

Beyond Lochailort, the road to the west winds over the inner end of the high-ridged peninsula of Ardnish to the head of Loch nan Uamh ("loch of the caves"), celebrated as being the loch into which the French brig, *La Du Teillay*, carried Prince Charlie to make his first landing on the mainland of Scotland, in 1745.

Turning inland for a short distance, by the bank of the Beasdale Burn, the road leads through a densely wooded region with a tangled thicket of undergrowth.

Fir, pine, hazel, oak, ash and rowan grow in profusion,
the dark green of the fir and pine causing them to
stand out conspicuously, especially when the landscape
is radiant in sunshine. From the mossy ground, tall
bracken and fern form an ideal haunt for rabbit,
weasel, adder, and young deer, while higher, on the
mountain slopes, roam the red deer, hill fox and wild
cat. Primroses star the mossy banks at the road-side
and the delicate wood-anemone finds shelter in the
hollows around the tree roots. In the dark days which
followed Culloden, bands of fugitives lurked among
these woods and solitudes, when the redcoats were
harrying this region.

Passing Beasdale railway station, where, like Lochielside, the stationmaster is a stationmistress, we wend our
way through rich woodlands for another mile or so,
until at a sharp bend in the road the white walls of
Borrodale House appear through the trees. This comfortable homestead is one of the most famous, if not
the most famous, houses connected with the Forty-five.
It was here that Prince Charlie resided when he first
set foot on the mainland of Scotland and it was here
that the whole campaign was mapped out. Soon after
Culloden, Borrodale House was burned by the notorious
Captain Ferguson, but the walls, window-openings and
much of the interior are still the same as they were
when Prince Charlie resided here. The green grassy
lawn in front of the house was, probably, also here in
Prince Charlie's time. The room where the Prince
slept and also the room where he interviewed the clan
chiefs and planned the Rising are still in existence, and
a portion of the wallpaper in the latter room, which
survived when the house was burned, has been framed
and preserved with varnish in its original position.
Miss M. E. M. Donaldson, in her book *Further Wanderings, Mainly in Argyll*, doubts the tradition regarding
this wallpaper, by asserting that in stripping super-

o

imposed wallpapers it could not be definitely known
which one existed in 1745. Apparently, she is unaware
that according to tradition no subsequent wallpaper
has ever been fixed on top of this portion since the
house was burned, therefore her doubts are based on
an erroneous supposition.

One can picture the busy scene here during the
Prince's residence, when the clan chiefs and their
retainers were constantly coming and going, and the
inhabitants of the surrounding district flocked in numbers to see their Prince. During this period the house
was guarded by one hundred MacDonald clansmen.

Borrodale House was the scene of the historic interview between Prince Charlie and Lochiel, when the
decision to proceed with or abandon the Rising hung
in the balance. It is generally agreed among historians
that if Lochiel had refused to support the Prince the
Rising would never have taken place. Lochiel had set
out from Achnacarry determined to refuse assistance
to the Prince at that time, as Charles had arrived with
neither men, arms, nor sufficient money to carry out
the campaign. Several books on the Forty-five state
that Lochiel went to interview the Prince immediately
he received the summons, but Hugh MacDonald,
brother of the Laird of Morar, told Bishop Forbes, the
compiler of *The Lyon in Mourning* (the standard work
on the Forty-five), that Lochiel did not reply in person
to the first summons from the Prince. MacDonald said
that Lochiel first sent his brother, Dr. Archibald
Cameron, to persuade the Prince to return to France,
but the Prince retorted by dispatching MacDonald of
Scotus to Achnacarry "to endeavour to persuade
Lochiel to do his duty." It was in answer to this
second summons, said MacDonald, that Lochiel went
in person to interview the Prince at Borrodale. This
statement of Hugh MacDonald is corroborated by
O'Sullivan in his narrative of the campaign. Dr.

Cameron interviewed the Prince on board *La Du Teillay*, as the Prince at that time had not taken up residence ashore.

On coming face to face with the Prince, Lochiel used all his arguments in his endeavour to persuade him to return to France until a more opportune time, but the Prince resisted all arguments. After considerable debate, without either side yielding, the Prince turned to Lochiel and said: "In a few days, with the few friends I have, I will raise the Royal Standard, and proclaim to the people of Britain that Charles Stuart is come over to claim the crown of his fathers—to win it or to perish in the attempt. Lochiel, who, my father has often told me, was our firmest friend, may stay at home, and learn from the newspapers the fate of his Prince." This appeal to his honour was too much for Lochiel, and he replied: "No, I will share the fate of my Prince, and so shall every man over whom nature or fortune has given me any power." Thus the die was cast and the seal set on the commencement of the Rising. Lochiel returned immediately to Achnacarry to raise his clan for service.

Following the path by the side of the little burn that flows past Borrodale House, we pass the modern mansion of Arisaig House, and come to the little bay with its grassy plain, and hemmed in by rocky woodlands, where Prince Charlie first set foot on the mainland of Scotland: he had landed, two days previously, on the lonely little Hebridean isle of Eriskay.

With the mind's eye we can picture the scene here on the 25th of July 1745, when *La Du Teillay* sailed up the Sound of Arisaig and Loch nan Uamh, and tacked round the little tree-clad Eilean nan Cabar, before dropping anchor in this little bay. On board she carried a youth who was to set the heather on fire with such a blaze that the sparks and smoke are not yet extinguished. On arrival, the captain spread the rumour ashore that they were liquor smugglers, but secretly arranged for a number of the head men of the surrounding district to come on board, where Prince Charlie interviewed them in a tent erected on the deck, in order to ascertain what chance his proposed campaign had of success. It soon became known locally that the Prince was on board, but the district was so isolated that the news did not reach the Government until some time later.

The first to answer the Prince's summons were the leading men of the Clanranald MacDonalds of the surrounding district. When they learned that he had arrived without either men or money, accompanied as he was by only half a dozen friends, they tried to persuade him to return until a more favourable opportunity, but the Prince refused to be balked of his purpose. The arguments and pleading of the Prince seemed to be in vain until, noticing an eager-looking Highlander walking the deck near him, who happened to be Ranald, younger brother of the Chief of Kinloch-moidart, the Prince turned to him and exclaimed dramatically, "Will you not help me?" Waving his bonnet in the air, Ranald replied: "I will! I will! Though not another man in the Highlands should draw a sword; I am ready to die for you." With tears in his eyes, the Prince thanked him heartily, and said he wished all Highlanders were like him. The honour of the hesitant chiefs was deeply touched by this incident and they forthwith promised their help to the Prince. Thus the Prince was heartened to do or die in his attempt. This incident between Prince Charlie and young Kinlochmoidart is described by Father Charles MacDonald in his valuable, and impartial, book, *Moidart, or Among the Clanranalds*, as "one of those sudden bursts of enthusiasm which, although creditable undoubtedly to the generous feelings of the actor, are not always complimentary to his common sense. The triumphant waving of Ranald's bonnet in the air was as good as a death warrant to many of his countrymen, and among them to his own brother."

Four days after the arrival of the Prince at Borrodale his ship proceeded into Loch Ailort, where his small stock of arms and stores were landed. Prince Charlie finally left the ship on the 4th of August to take up his residence in Borrodale House. Here he interviewed the chiefs and made arrangements for the campaign until the 11th of August, then he sailed across the Sound of Arisaig to Glenuig, in Moidart, landing there and proceeding to Kinlochmoidart. After spending a week at Kinlochmoidart he proceeded to Dalilea, where he embarked on Loch Shiel, on his way to Glenfinnan. At the time of Prince Charlie's landing, Borrodale farm belonged to Clanranald, but was tenanted by Angus MacDonald. It was not the residence of Clanranald himself, as is sometimes stated.

Among the bracken, on the face of the tree-clad hillock which rises behind the grassy plain at the bay, there is a small aperture forming the entrance to Prince Charlie's Cave, where he is said to have sheltered when a fugitive after Culloden, and when Borrodale House had been burned. The entrance to this cave is not easy to find among the bracken, but once inside it is quite commodious, and would provide good shelter for several men. The ground is of dry earth, which could be covered with bracken for beds. A fissure in the rock, near the inner end of the cave, forms a natural vent or chimney. Some writers assert, however, that the Prince spent his three days as a fugitive at Borrodale in a bothy in a neighbouring wood, and not in this cave.

The bay at Borrodale is bounded at its eastern end by a little promotory called Rudha ard Camasgaill ("the high promontory of the stormy bay"), on which there are the remains of a vitrified fort, almost covered with mossy turf, one of those relics dating back to twilight history.

Borrodale enters into the Forty-five more than any other place in the campaign. It was here that Prince Charlie first set foot on the mainland of Scotland, full of hope for his venture. After tragic Culloden, he sailed from Borrodale on the 26th April 1746, for the Long Island (the Outer Hebrides). A few days after he sailed, the two French ships carrying the "Prince's Treasure," or "Loch Arkaig Treasure," arrived at Borrodale and landed the gold. After his adventures on the Long Island and on Skye, the Prince returned to Borrodale, in July, when on his way to "Cluny's Cage." On 20th September he embarked finally from the little bay at Borrodale, where he first landed, to board the French frigate *L'Heureux*, which carried him to France, along with Lochiel, Lochgarry, John Roy Stuart and Dr. Archibald Cameron, after five months' skulking as a proscribed fugitive among the mountains and seas of western Scotland, despair in his heart at the tragic shattering of his hopes and ambitions.

Beyond Borrodale the road winds through woodlands and heather-clad clearings to the little village of Arisaig, nestling on the hill-side at the head of the sea-inlet called Loch nan Cilltean. Owing to the mild climate in this region all the year round there is a rich display of flowers everywhere. Almost every cottage is draped thickly with roses and other climbing plants, while fuchsia grows in almost unbelievable profusion. It is doubtful if there is any part of Scotland of equal area possessing such a variety of entrancing scenery as the district of Arisaig. This statement is really no exageration. Here we have coast scenery of rocky promontories, green isles and creamy sands; deep glens with rich woodlands and luxuriant undergrowth of fern, heather and bracken; wide, flat moorland and rugged hills; sylvan river scenes and rich meadows;

sub-tropical plant profusion and rocky pine-clad knolls. All within compass of a few miles and all unsullied by an age of machinery. Within a mile of Arisaig is the remarkable tropical garden of the late Mr. John A. Holms, of Bishopton, Renfrewshire, the famous collector of antiques. Before choosing the district in which he would establish his "Paradise," as he called his garden, he travelled for eight years throughout Britain recording temperature, rainfall and frost, and finally decided on Arisaig.

On the hill-side, to the west of the village, is the modern Roman Catholic chapel close to the ruins of the ancient place of worship. All the older inhabitants of this region are of the "old religion," as they call the Roman Catholic faith. When the wave of the Reformation swept northwards, it is said to have stopped abruptly at Loch Shiel and the River Shiel. To the north of this line the inhabitants all remained loyal to the Roman Catholic faith, and except for settlers from other parts they still remain so. In the year 1928 the Clan Donald societies erected a clock in the tower of Arisaig Chapel, to the memory of the celebrated Gaelic poet, Alasdair MacMhaigstir Alasdair, who ranks next to, or equal to, Duncan *Ban* MacIntyre as a Gaelic poet. He hailed from Dalilea, at the foot of Loch Shiel, in Moidart, but died in Arisaig, and was buried close to the chapel, owing to stormy weather preventing his body being borne to his ancestral burial-ground on Eilean Fionnan, in Loch Shiel. He is now believed to be the writer of a valuable and interesting account of personal experiences in the Forty-five campaign which is included in the *Lockhart Papers* but with no author's name attached.

A short distance beyond Arisaig Chapel, and at the summit of the road, a glorious seascape opens to view. From this elevated viewpoint we look down upon the surf-beaten shores of the Atlantic and, out to sea, we "behold the Hebrides." To the north-west the hazy-blue mountainous Isle of Skye rises from the sea, with the jagged Coolin Hills, or rather mountains, forming a conspicuous skyline. Due west appear the no less striking outlines of the isles of Rum and Eigg. The high peaks of Rum, often cloud-capped, and the long, level ridge and precipitous *Sguir* of Eigg are famed in geology as well as in scenery. They are remnants of the last great volcanic activity of Europe, and form part of a line of extinct volcanoes stretching from Antrim, in Ireland, to Iceland and east Greenland. These islands of Rum and Eigg, rising from the deep, present a very striking scene, which varies according to the kaleidoscopic conditions of the atmosphere in this region. When viewed through the pearly haze of a summer morning they possess a mystic, ethereal appearance. With a freshening wind from the north they rise with vivid effect in the crystal atmosphere, riding on an ultramarine sea of white-capped waves, under an azure sky. Their most dramatic appearance, however, is when seen rising in rich purple silhouette from a glittering sea, against the gold and crimson splendour of a sunset sky, just as the dark curtain of night begins to fall.

From the summit the road sweeps down to the sandy shore, and skirts it northwards through the scattered settlement of the Back of Keppoch, and along the margin of the Mointeach Mor ("the big peat-moss"), which stretches back to the steep slopes of Creag Mor and the hills of South Morar. From the summit of Creag Mor (1,152 feet) there is a remarkably extensive view, sweeping from Mull and Ardnamurchan in the south to the Outer Hebrides (and, of course, the Inner Hebrides), and northwards to Knoydart, while eastward lie the lonely hills and moors of Morar.

By beautiful little sandy bays, where the Atlantic surges spend themselves in lacy foam, and around hillocks of purple heather, with sea-birds wheeling overhead and the breeze scented with tangle and clover hay, we wend our way to the estuary of the River Morar, with its famed white sands. About half tide these sands are seen to advantage, when shimmering in sunshine and stretching far out to sea beneath the pale green waters. Down through their gleaming expanse flow the waters of the River Morar, a short but voluminous stream leading from Loch Morar to the sea. In its upper reaches it glides swiftly between grassy banks, but soon sweeps over a picturesque waterfall, overhung with oak and hazel, then, churning through a rocky bed, to the shore. Though of short course, this river yields many lusty salmon. Unfortunately, the River Morar and the falls will be obliterated by the Hydro-Electric scheme in course of construction here, as the dam is being built at the site of the falls.

The region we have been traversing, from Arisaig to Morar, forms the locus of many of the beautiful water-colour paintings of Mary Holden Bird, the well-known artist, who resides in Morar Lodge. Her delightful pictures of creamy sands, summer seas, rainbow shallows and sea-pools, glistening in the radiance of fleece-flecked azure skies, must have charmed countless people, though many of them may be unaware of the region depicted. The striking outlines of Rum and Eigg or the hills of Morar appear in many of her paintings. It is worthy of note that her husband, Mr. C. K. Bird, is *Fougasse*, the well-known cartoonist, and Art Editor of *Punch*.

A short walk eastward, by the river bank, from the main road, leads us to Loch Morar, which stretches east and west for about twelve miles between the hills of North Morar and those of South Morar. According to local tradition, the loch harbours a monster, which has been affectionately named Morag. In the

surrounding hills Prince Charlie spent much of his
fugitive wanderings, and one has only to rove in this
region to realize the privations he must have endured.
A rough track, but splendid for tramping, skirts the
northern shore of the loch eastward from Morar for
about eight miles to South Tarbet Bay. Here, it bends
northward away from the loch and over a narrow
isthmus to the head-waters of Loch Nevis at Kyles-
morar. A very isolated track continues eastward from
South Tarbet to the head of Loch Morar, and thence
through Glen Pean to the head of Loch Arkaig.

Towards the western end of the loch there are
several thickly wooded islands, which add to the
picturesque nature of its scenery and, like the rest of
Lochaber, they are not without human interest. On
one of them, called Eilean Ban, a house was built in
1705 for use as a preparatory school for young men
destined for the priesthood. For centuries, Morar was
the centre of the Roman Catholic life in the Highlands.
There is a Gaelic saying, "Great and blessed Morar
where no Protestant minister ever preached a sermon."

After Culloden, when the redcoats were scouring
the Highlands in search of fugitives, Simon Fraser,
Lord Lovat, the crafty man of the Rising, and Bishop
Hugh MacDonald, sought refuge in the island dwelling
of Loch Morar, which was at that time uninhabited.
The Bishop had been one of the earliest pupils in this
school. They felt themselves safe, as they had com-
mandeered all the boats in the neighbourhood and taken
them over to the island. From the beginning of May
until the 7th of June they stayed on this island guarded
by twenty armed clansmen. By some means, the
commanding officer of the Government troops at
Arisaig learned of their hiding-place and, obtaining
a lifeboat from the *Furnace*, a sloop which was cruising
in the vicinity, had it dragged across the narrow isthmus,
and sent an armed party over to the island to arrest the

fugitives. On seeing the naval boat approach, Lovat
and the Bishop fled in one of their own boats to the
south shore of the loch at Ceann Camas Ruadh, and
hid among the dense birch woods, which at that time
came down to the water's edge. Realizing that search
in these woodlands was useless, the armed party
returned to the island and confiscated all the Bishop's
correspondence and items of value which the fugitives
in their hurry had left behind. Finally, the soldiers
burned the house. Since that time no one has resided
on the island.

Lord Lovat and his friends proceeded to Meoble,
six or seven miles further up the loch, but owing to old
age and infirmity (he was over eighty and suffered
from asthma and gout) Lovat was unable to withstand
the hardships of a fugitive life. After a few days at
Meoble, he wrote to the military commander at
Arisaig offering to surrender. He was duly appre-
hended and taken on board the *Furnace* at Morar and
sailed round to Loch Moidart, where he was landed.
From Loch Moidart he was conveyed on a horse-litter
first to Fort William, then to Fort Augustus and finally
to London, where he was tried, found guilty and
executed on the block at Tower Hill for his participa-
tion in the Rising. Some writers state that Lord Lovat
was hiding in a hollow tree, near Loch Morar, when
the soldiers discovered him, but his more prosaic arrest
is according to local tradition, and is that given by
Father MacDonald in *Moidart, or Among the Clan-
ralds*. Bishop Hugh MacDonald, who accompanied
Lovat on Loch Morar, was the person who had blessed
Prince Charlie's standard when it was raised at Glenfinnan. He escaped to France after the capture of Lovat.

The report of Lovat's capture given in the *Scots
Magazine* for 1747 says: "It was concluded that Lord
Lovat's lameness must have rendered it utterly im-
practicable for him to travel in so rugged a country,

and that therefore he must probably be concealed in one or other of the numerous caves at the upper end of this lake [Loch Morar] where the boats had landed him. It was therefore deemed to make diligent search everywhere thereabout. This service was performed by Captain Ferguson and other officers and men with unwearied diligence for three days and nights; when, at length, Captain Campbell of Achachrosan found that unhappy Lord lying on two feather beds, not far from the side of the lake; to whom he surrendered and delivered up his arms and strong box. Hereupon his Lordship was put into one of our boats and rowed down the lake; at the lower end of which our sailors *made a run with him* (as they termed it) overland to the sea side, the pipers all the while playing the tune called *Lord Lovat's March* with which his Lordship pretended to be pleased: and finally they carried him on board of Captain Ferguson's ship."

When peace had settled in the Highlands, and the Forty-five was a thing of the past, the Clanranald family built a house at Buorblach, in 1768, on Morar Bay, to take the place of the seminary which had been burned on Eilean Ban. Here, young men destined for the priesthood were given preparatory instruction. Later on, most of them went to the Scots college in Paris or Rome to complete their education until they were ordained priests. Occasionally, however, students would commence and complete their course of instruction in the Scottish seminaries, and, to distinguish them from the Continental-trained men, they were called "heather priests." The training college at Buorblach was closed in 1779 and the teachers and students transferred to a new home at Samalaman, in Moidart. This college in Moidart was, in turn, disbanded in 1804, and its place taken by one on the Island of Lismore. Finally, the Lismore college was closed in 1831, its activities being merged

into the college at Blairs, in Kincardineshire. At the
present time there is a Roman Catholic chapel at the
western end of Loch Morar, in a peaceful and
picturesque setting among tall fir and spruce. The
whole region around Loch Morar abounds in rugged
natural beauty of a high order, but the Hydro-Electric
scheme at present in course of construction here will
no doubt dispel some of the rural charm of this district.
Let us hope it will mar it as little as possible.

Northward from Morar, the main road leads among
hillocks of fragrant bog-myrtle and heather, where the
grouse whir from covert to covert, and the bees,
butterflies and dragonflies flit around in the sunshine.
Eastward, the moorland of Morar stretches to the
distant mountains tinged with the haze like the bloom
on the blaeberry. Soon the road sweeps down by
the rocky shore into the little town of Mallaig, the
terminus of road and rail.

The best that can be said of Mallaig is that it is a
centre from which some of the finest scenery in the
Highlands and Islands of Scotland can be reached
conveniently. The Isle of Skye lies only a few miles
distant, across the Sound of Sleat. The town of
Mallaig itself, however, leaves much to be desired, both
in lay-out and architecture. In addition, being a
railway terminus and one of the principal herring ports
of the west coast and also a herring-curing station, its
atmosphere is badly tainted with train smoke and the
smell of herring. What a pity, because only the work
of man mars Mallaig. It is set in a beautiful situation
on a rocky coast with glorious surroundings. Sunsets
from this coastal region, with its island-studded horizon,
have to be seen to be believed; they are really wonder-
ful. If properly developed, Mallaig could become one
of the most delightful holiday resorts in Britain, with its
direct communication with the Western Isles and its
beautiful and romantic hinterland.

North of Mallaig, the coast-line curves round towards the east to form the southern shore of Loch Nevis ("loch of Heaven"), where the waters of the Atlantic wind far into the fastnesses of Morar and Knoydart. Cradled among the mountains of one of the most rugged regions of Scotland, where no highway, let alone railway, penetrates; where the mountain-slopes rise steeply from the shore, and habitation is conspicuous by its absence, Loch Nevis appeals strongly to those who like to commune with nature in the wild. When the western gales whip its deep waters into white-caps and the dark "scud" is sweeping across the sky; when mist wreaths are swirling along the mountain-sides and the sea-birds scream as they battle with the wind, then Loch Nevis presents an inspiring spectacle of grim grandeur.

BIBLIOGRAPHY

Loyal Lochaber, by W. Drummond-Norie.

Lochaber in War and Peace, by W. T. Kilgour.

Twenty Years on Ben Nevis, by W. T. Kilgour.

History of the Camerons, by Alexander MacKenzie.

The Clan Cameron, by John Cameron.

Memoirs of Sir Ewan Cameron of Lochiel. Published by the Maitland Club, 1842.

Memoir of Colonel John Cameron of Fassifern, by the Rev. A. Clerk, of Kilmallie.

Life of Dr. Archibald Cameron. Published in London, 1753.

MacDougalls, *Guide to Lochaber*, compiled by Mary Mac-Kellar. *Circa* 1888.

Lochaber and its Evangelical Traditions, by the Rev. John MacLeod.

The MacDonells of Keppoch, by Josephine M. MacDonell.

Moidart, or Among the Clanranalds, by the Rev. Charles MacDonald.

A History of the County of Inverness, by J. Cameron Lees.

Mountain, Moor and Loch. Anonymous.

Wanderings in the Western Highlands and Islands, by M. E. M. Donaldson.

Further Wanderings—Mainly in Argyll, by M. E. M. Donaldson.

The Massacre of Glencoe, by John Buchan.

Montrose, by John Buchan.

In the Tracks of Montrose, by I. F. Grant.

'Twixt Ben Nevis and Glencoe, by the Rev. Alexander Stewart.

Nether Lochaber, by the Rev. Alexander Stewart.

The Scottish Mountaineering Club Guides to—*The Central Highlands, Ben Nevis,* and *The Western Highlands.*

Wade in Scotland, by J. B. Salmond.

History of the Rebellion of 1745, by R. Chambers.

Itinerary of Prince Charles Edward Stuart, by W. B. Blaikie.

(NOTE.—Almost every book dealing with the Forty-five mentions Lochaber to some extent.)

The Transactions of the Gaelic Society of Inverness.

The Celtic Monthly.

The Celtic Magazine.

FICTION

The Flight of the Heron⎫
The Gleam in the North ⎬ A trilogy of Jacobite novels by
The Dark Mile⎭ D. K. Broster.

John Splendid, by Neil Munro.

In Far Lochaber, by William Black.

Children of the Dead End, by Patrick McGill. Gives a vivid account of navvy life during the construction of the Kinlochleven Aluminium Works.

INDEX

A

Abinger, Lord, 101, 102, 135
Achafubil, 194, 195
Achaladair, 23
Achandaul, 136
Achdalieu, 185, 186
  skirmish at, 186, 187
Achintee, 79
Achluachrach, 159
Achnacloich, 36
Achnasaul, 130
Achriach, 84, 85
Alan of the Forays, 110, 111, 173
Alasdair MacMhaigster Alasdair, 215
Allt a Mhuillin, 71
An Steall, 87
Annat, 162, 181
Aonach Dubh, 27, 28
Aonach Eagach, 28
Aonach Mor, 73
Appin Murder, 44, 45
Ardchattan, Priory of, 43
Ardgour, 18, 45, 48, 193, 195
Argyll, Duke of, 35
Argyll, Marquis of, 93, 195
Arisaig, 196, 214, 215
Auchinbreck, 97, 99, 101
Auchintore Beag, 54
Aytoun, Professor, 160

B

Back of Keppoch, 216
Badenoch, 18, 161
Bailey, Rev. James, 55
Balloch, Donald, 92, 148
Banavie, 18, 67, 107
Banquo, 17, 56, 112, 121
Banquo's Walk, 91, 115, 116
Barony of Lochiel, 19
Beasdale, 208, 209

Beinn a Crulaiste, 26
Beinn Fada, 27
Bell, Robert Fitzroy, 182
Ben Dorain, 20
Ben Nevis, 52, 66
  clear days on summit, 72
  derivation of name, 68
  geology, 73–76
  observatory, 70, 73
  races, 69, 70
Ben Nevis whisky distillery, 104
Ben Riabhach, 80
Bird, Mary Holden, 217
Black Child, Son of the Bones, 176
Black Parks, 88
Black Plague at Callart, 42
Blackie, Professor, 181
Blackmount, 18, 22, 37
Blaich, 194
Blairs College, 221
Blarmachfoldach, 40, 41
Blar Mor, 105, 163
Blar-nan-leinne, 143
Blount, Sir Walter, 201
Boece, Hector, 90
Bohuntine Hill, 146
Bone-setter, the Lochaber, 116
Borrodale, 132, 209, 210, 213, 214
Boulton, Sir Harold, 35
Brae Lochaber, 20, 135
Breadalbane, 18
  Earl of, 22, 23
  Marchioness of, 22
Breun Camas, 164
Bridge of Orchy, 20, 21
Broster, D. K., 126
Bruniachan, 149
Buachaille Etive, 22, 28
Buchan, John, 94, 95
Buorblach, 220
Burial-ground at Inverlochy, 89
Burt, Captain, 54
Byron, 64

P

C

Caillich, 133
Caithness, Earl of, 92, 93
Caledonian Canal, 104, 166, 169
Callart, 42, 43, 44, 191
   Mary of, 42, 43
Camas-nan-gall, 46, 51, 96, 195
Cameron, Dr. Archibald, 128,
   132, 133, 134, 210, 214
   Alan XII of Lochiel, 110
   Alexander Anthony, 140
   Alexander, the bone-setter, 116
   Campbell of Monzie, Mrs., 73
   Clan, 19, 20, 121, 122, 124
   Clunes, 125, 128, 130
   Donald, of Ballachulish, 42
   Donald, XXIV Chief, 61
   Donald, XXV Chief, 124
   Sir Duncan, of Fassifern, 42, 54
   Errachd, 61, 63, 65, 117
Cameron, Ewan, XIII Chief, 19
   Sir Ewan, of Lochiel, 97, 115,
     119, 120, 122, 124, 125, 129,
     177
   Glen Nevis, 78
   Jenny, of Glendessary, 131
   John, the bone-setter, 117, 137
   John (Colonel), of Fassifern,
     49, 54 177, 179, 192
   Miller, Dr. A., 95
   Omeron, 148, 149
   Sergeant Mor, 57
Cameron Highlanders, 61, 63, 64,
   65, 118
Cameron Square, 59, 60, 61
Campbell, Lord Archibald, 35, 36
   Colin of Glenure, 44
   Duncan, 18
   Glenlyon, 31
   Glenorchy, 120
   Governor of Fort William, 55
   Inverawe, 43
   Mary, Maxwell, 203
   Monzie, 42, 44, 57
   Thomas, 35, 184
Candlish, Dr., 108
Caol Farm, 163
Carn Mor Dearg, 69, 73, 74
Carrach, Alasdair, 92, 93, 113,
   114, 150

Castle Stalker, 34
Cat Field, 109, 110
Cat Pool, 109, 111
Cattle-stealing, 88
Caulfeild, Major, 40
Chancellor, The, 28
Charlemagne, 91
Chattan, Clan, 113, 122
Chief's Candlesticks, The, 152, 153
Cia-aig Falls, 128
Clachaig Inn, 29, 30
Clach an Turraman, 82
Clach nan Caimbeulach, 40
Clach Shomhairle, 79
Clan badges, 150, 151
Clerk, Dr. Archibald, 173, 176,
   200
Clunes, 119, 125
"Cluny's Cage," 214
Cnoc nam Faobh, 176, 181
Coinneach Odhar, 169
Coll Ciotach, Young, 99
Comyn, or Cumming, 91, 92, 114
Conaglen, 49
Cope, Sir John, 142
Corpach, derivation of name, 165,
   172
Corpach Mill, 181
Corran, 46, 47, 49
Corribeg, 192
Corriechoille, 137, 145
Corrour, 87
Coruanan, 49
Cow Hill, 79, 80
Craigs, The, 58, 62, 63, 65
Crannach Wood, 23
Crawford, Rev. R. B., 174, 176
Creag Mor, Arisaig, 216
Cromwell, 53
Cuilcheanna, 46
Culcairn's Brae, 126, 127
Culloden, 60, 80
Cumberland, Duke of, 81, 132
Cumming, Alexander, 177, 178
   at Achdalieu, 188, 191

D

Dalilea, 202, 215
Dalnabea, 137

"Dark Mile," 125, 126
Deirdre, 26, 84
"Devil's Staircase," 26, 35, 40
Diarmid Campbell of Inverawe, 43
Disruption, The, 62, 108, 164
Doire Darach, 21
Donaldson, M. E. M., 209
Druim Fada, 193
Druimliart, 22
Drumasallie, 193
Drummond-Norie, 94
Duisky, 194
Duke, Winifred, 53
Dun Dearduill, 84
Dun Dige, 80
Dundee, Viscount, 118

E

Eigg, 216
Eilean Ban, 218, 220
Eilean Munde, 35
Errachd, 65, 117
Erskine, Henry, 50
Eve of Waterloo, 64

F

"Famine Road," 41
Fassifern, 182, 190
Fingal, 26
Forbes, Bishop, 210
Ford car on Ben Nevis, 70
Fort Augustus, 52, 94
Fort William, 20, 21, 29, 31, 52, 58
"Forty-Five, The," 17
Fougasse, 217
Francis, Grant R., 134
Fraser MacIntosh of Drummond, 159
Furnace, The, 218

G

"Gardy Loo" Gully, 73
Gairlochy, 119, 140
Garvan, 194
Gear Aonach, 27

George IV, 50
Gillicattan Mor, 112
Glasgow Journal, 54
Glen Aray, 36
    Camgarry, 130, 131
    Coe, 20, 21, 23, 26, 27, 36, 37, 38, 56
    Dessary, 107, 131
    Etive, 26, 37
    Euar, 22
    Finnan, 18
    Garry, 31
    Gloy, 141, 142
    Laragain, 181, 183, 184
    Loy, 117, 118
    Mallie, 129
    Nevis, 39, 66, 77, 85, 86, 94
    Orchy, 26
    Pean, 131, 132
    Spean, 18
Glenaladale, 199, 202
Glenfinnan, 196, 198, 203, 205
Glenfintaig House, 141
Glengarry, Colonel MacDonell of, 49
Glenlochy Whisky Distillery 87
Glenlui, 18
Glenlyon, 31, 34
Glen Nevis House, 79, 80, 81
    burial-ground, 62, 79
    massacre, 83
    private "stills," 78
Gordon, General, 55
Gordonsburgh, 53, 54
Guide to Fort William, 91

H

Hamilton, Lieutenant-Colonel, 32
Heather-burning, 193
Henderson's Stone, 32, 33, 38
High Bridge, 40, 66, 137, 138, 143
Hill, Colonel, 58
Hillock of Evil Counsel, 82, 84
Hodgson, Victor, 60
Holinshed, 90
Holms, John A., 215
Huntly, Earl of, 92, 114
Hydro-electric schemes, 68, 87, 217

I

Iain Beag MacAindrea, 85
Iain Lom. See MacDonald
Inveraray Pipe Band, 36
Invercoe, 30
Inverlair, 83, 155, 161
Inverlochy, 53, 87, 90, 92, 93, 97, 103
  Castle, 54, 89, 135
Inveroran, 21
Inverscaddle, 49, 50

K

Kennedy, Dr., of Fort William, 60
Keppoch, charm stone, 156
  Coll of, 156, 157
  grey bird of, 156
  House, 149, 154, 155
  loss of lands, 158
  murder, 145, 149
Kil a Choireal, 159, 160, 161
Kilgour, W. T., 94
Killevaodain, 49
Kilmallie, Lochiel enclosure, 176, 177
  Parish Church, 173, 174, 175
King Achaius, 91
King Edward VII, 39
King George VI, 64
King James I, 92
Kingshouse, 23, 24, 36
Kinlocharkaig, 130
Kinlocheil, 193
Kinlochleven, 38, 39
Kinlochmoidart, 213
Kitson, Hon. Mrs., 38

L

La Du Teillay, 208, 211
Lagganmore, 99
L'Heureux, 214
Lamonts, 101
Lees, Dr. Cameron, 121
Letterfinlay, 122, 142
Loch Aber, 104, 163
  Arkaig, 18, 125, 127, 129
  Ba, 24
  Beoraid, 207

Loch Duich, 18
  Eil, 18, 47, 170
  Eilt, 206, 207
  Etive, 36
  Hourn, 131
  Laidon, 18
  Leven, 18, 26, 31, 41, 42
  Linnhe, 45, 162, 194, 195
  Lochy, 119, 125, 140
  Morar, 132, 207, 208, 217, 221
  Nevis, 131, 222
  Nan Uamh, 208, 211
  Quoich, 60
  Shiel, 47, 196, 198, 202
  Treig, 18, 35, 87
  Triochatan, 28, 29
Lochaber Axe, 189
Lochaber
  bounds, 17, 18
  derivation of name, 17, 106
  Gathering, 66
  Lordship of, 19, 114
  quern stones, 149
Lochan t'Suidhe, 71
Loch Arkaig Treasure, 132–134, 214
Lovat, Lord, 218, 219
Low Bridge, 141
Lower Falls of Nevis, 84
Lundavra, 40, 41
Lyon in Mourning, 81, 210

M

Mamore Deer Forest, 39, 77
March of the Cameron Men, 203
Marr, Earl of, 92, 148
Mary of Callart, 42, 43
Maryburgh, 53, 54, 56
Meall-an-t'-Suidhe, 67, 70, 73, 79, 80, 87
Meoble, 207, 219
Miller, Dr. A. Cameron, 95
Mitchell, Colonel, 136
Moidart, or among the Clanranalds, 212, 219
Monk, General, 53
Montrose, Marquis of, 40, 93, 94, 95, 98
"Montrose's Seat" (Glen Nevis), 95

Mort safe, 79
Morton, Earl of, 49
Moy House, 118, 119
Muccomer, 140
Mulholland, D., 70
Mulroy, 62, 156, 157
Murlaggan, 132, 161
Murray of Broughton, 118, 132, 182

MAC

Macaulay the historian, 124
MacBane, Donald, 62, 157
Macbeth, 17, 41
MacCulloch, Dr. John, 146
MacCullochs of Argyllshire, 101
MacDonald, Alastair, 99
    Clanranald, 197, 203, 212
    D. P., 159
    Flora, 50
    Glenaladale, 199, 200
    Glen Coe, 30
    Hugh, 204, 210
    Iain Lom, 94, 99, 100, 102, 154, 159
    James (Sir) of Sleat, 154
    Kinlochmoidart, 144
    "Long John," 104, 159
MacDonell of Glengarry, 49, 102
    of Keppoch, 20, 64, 134, 149
    of Keppah, Alice C., 160
    of Tirnadris, 138
MacDougall, Alan, 50
MacDougall of Reray, 99
MacDougalls, 19, 43
"MacEachine's Refuge," 207
MacFhiunlaidh, Domhnull, 159
MacGillonies of Strone, 122
MacGregor, Miss Edith, 78
MacGregors at Tirnadris, 144
MacIain of Glen Coe, 28, 31, 33
MacIain's Clans of the Scottish Highlands, 86
MacIntosh chiefs, 112, 113, 114
MacIntosh's Leap, 157
MacIntyre, Duncan Ban, 20
MacKay, General Hugh, 53
MacKellar, Mary, 178, 189, 192
MacKenzie, Ewan, 70

MacLachlan, Ewan, 49, 62
    Mary Anne, 177, 178
MacLean, Ewan, 48, 49
MacLeans of Ardgour, 47
MacLeod, Rev. John, 18
Macleod, Dr. Norman, 46, 174
MacLeod of Neuk, 133
MacMartins of Letterfinlay, 122, 141
MacMaster, Clan, 48
MacPhee, the outlaw, 60
MacPhees' burial isle, 129
MacPherson, Cluny, 130, 133
MacRae, Rev. Mr. of Kintail, 62
MacSorlies of Glen Nevis, 79, 122

N

Napoleon, 136
National Trust for Scotland, 37, 201
"Neptune's Staircase," 107
Nether Lochaber, 38, 39
Nether Lochaber (Rev. A. Stewart), 46, 81
Nevis Bridge, 66, 78, 87
"Nine Mile Bridge," 142
North British Aluminium Co., 39, 68

O

Odhar, Iain, 145
Ogilvie, Sir Thomas, 99
Old Red Sandstone Period, 25, 28, 73, 75
Omeron Cameron, 148, 149
Onich, 44, 45, 46
Osprey, 129
Ossian, 28
Ossian's Cave, 27
Ossian, Strath, 26
O'Sullivan, 210

P

"Parade, The," 61
"Parallel Roads" of Glen Roy, 146, 147
Pibroch of Donald Dubh, 93

"Pickle, the Spy," 134
Plague at Callart, 42
Pleistocene Ice Age, 75
Pococke, Bishop, 106
Pretenders, The, 204
Prince Charlie:
    and Jenny Cameron, 131
    and young Kinlochmoidart, 212
    arms landed at Loch Ailort, 213
    at Achnasaul (Loch Arkaig), 130
    at Annat, 181
    at Borrodale, 209, 210, 211, 214
    at Clunes, 125
    at Fassifern, 190
    at Glen Laragain, 184
    at Kinlocheil, 192
    at Moy, 118
    lands on Scotland, 211
    leaves Scotland, 214
    mirror portrait, 60
    raises his standard, 198, 204
    siege of Fort William, 56
    the land of, 17
    wandering by Loch Morar, 217,
        218
    wearing the kilt, 130
Prince Charlie's Cave (Achna-
    carry), 127
    (Borrodale), 213
    (Meoble), 207
Prince Charlie's Tree, 127, 128

R

Ramsay, Alan, 61
Rannoch Moor, 18, 20, 22, 24,
    25, 57, 73, 74
Reformation, The, 215
Risga, 198
River Arkaig, 126
    Callop, 196
    Coe, 28
    Cona, 28, 49
    Leven, 39
    Lochy, 87, 89, 104, 109
    Morar, 217
    Nevis, 66, 77, 79
    Orchy, 20, 21
    Scaddle, 49
Road by Loch Eil, 185

"Roaring Mill," 79
Romance of the White Rose, 134
Roshven, 206
"Rough Bounds," 18, 197
Roy Bridge, 94, 145
Rudha ard Camasgaill, 213
Rudha Dearg, 162, 195
Rum, 216

S

St. Andrew's Cross, 91
Saint Columba, 106
St. Munn's Island, 35
Salmond, J. B., 66
Samalaman, 220
Samuel's Cave, 86
Scarlett, Sir James, 101, 102, 135
"Scotland for Ever," 136
Scots Magazine, 219
Scott, Caroline, 82
Scott, Sir Walter, 50, 180, 187
Sgor a Mhaim, 80
Shairp, Principal, 131
Sheangain Burn, 116, 182
Signal Rock, 29
Skye, 216, 221
Slatach, 203
Smith, Sir Donald, 35, 36
Smyth, Frank S., 72
Spean Bridge, 67, 143
Spey, 18
Stair, Earl of, 31
Statistical Account of Scotland (Old),
    54, 91, 107
    (New), 200
Stevenson, R. L., 22
Stewart, Alexander (Rev.), 46, 81
    Donald, 34
    "James of the Glen," 44, 57
Stob Ban, 80
Strathcona, Lord, 35
Stratheden, Baroness, 102
Strath Ossian, 26
Strath Spey, 85
Stronaba, 141
Stronchreggan, 50
Strone, 116, 117
Stuart, Prince Charles Edward.
    See Prince Charlie

"Studdy, The," 27
Switenham, Captain, 202

T

Taillear Dubh na Tuaighe, 141, 171, 172
Tayler, A. and H., 189
Taylor Cameron, J. S., 189
Telford, John, 169
   Thomas, 107, 139, 185
"Three Sisters" of Glen Coe, 37
Threipland, Sir Thomas, 133
Tigh Gairm, 110, 111, 112
Tirnadris, 138, 143, 144
Tirrim, Castle, 197, 198
Tom-a-chrochaidh, 164
Tom-eas-an-t-slinnean, 79
Tom-na-faire, 88, 89, 98
Tomonie, 163
Tor Castle, 92, 109, 111, 112, 113, 116
Torlundy Castle, 102, 135
Torr-a-Phrionnsa, 202
Torr-na-bratach, 136
Treasure, Loch Arkaig, 132–134

Trislaig, 51
Tulla Water, 23

U

Uamh Shomhairle, 86
Upper Falls of Nevis, 87, 95

V

Victoria Park, 65, 66
Victoria, Queen, 129, 135

W

Wade, General, 40, 55, 63, 66, 88, 137
Walker, Rev. John, 179
Well of the Heads, 155
West Highland Museum, 58, 59
West Highland Railway, 57, 205
William of Orange, 30
Witch's Cauldron, 128
Wolf, last in Scotland, 123
Wragge, Clement, 70